Inhabiting the Cruciform God

Kenosis, Justification, and Theosis
in Paul's Narrative Soteriology

Michael J. Gorman

WILLIAM B. EERDMANS PUBLISHING COMPANY
GRAND RAPIDS, MICHIGAN / CAMBRIDGE, U.K.

Published 2009 by
Wm. B. Eerdmans Publishing Co.
2140 Oak Industrial Drive N.E., Grand Rapids, Michigan 49505 /
P.O. Box 163, Cambridge CB3 9PU U.K.
www.eerdmans.com

Printed in the United States of America

14 13 12 11 10 09   7 6 5 4 3 2 1

Library of Congress Cataloging-in-Publication Data

Gorman, Michael J., 1955-
Inhabiting the cruciform God: kenosis, justification, and theosis
in Paul's narrative soteriology / Michael J. Gorman.
p.   cm.
Includes bibliographical references.
ISBN 978-0-8028-6265-5 (pbk.: alk. paper)
1. Jesus Christ — Crucifixion — Biblical teaching.
2. Bible. N.T. Epistles of Paul — Theology.   I. Title.

BT453.G655 2009
234.092 — dc22
                                        2008043907

Unless otherwise noted, the Scripture quotations in this publication are from the New Revised Standard Version Bible, copyright © 1989 by the Division of Christian Education of the National Council of Churches of Christ in the U.S.A., and used by permission.

INHABITING THE CRUCIFORM GOD

With gratitude to
my family
and to Andy Johnson,
faithful friend and fellow-worker

CONTENTS

Contents

ABBREVIATIONS

AB	Anchor Bible
ABD	*Anchor Bible Dictionary*
ANTC	Abingdon New Testament Commentaries
BECNT	Baker Exegetical Commentary on the New Testament
BNTC	Black's New Testament Commentary
CBQ	*Catholic Biblical Quarterly*
ExpTim	*Expository Times*
HBT	*Horizons in Biblical Theology*
HTR	*Harvard Theological Review*
ICC	International Critical Commentary
IJST	*International Journal of Systematic Theology*
Int	*Interpretation*
JBL	*Journal of Biblical Literature*
JCTR	*Journal for Christian Theological Research*
JSNT	*Journal for the Study of the New Testament*
JSNTSup	Journal for the Study of the New Testament: Supplement Series
JSPSS	Journal for the Study of the Pseudepigrapha: Supplement Series
JTI	*Journal of Theological Interpretation*
JTS	*Journal of Theological Studies*
NTS	*New Testament Studies*
SBLDS	Society of Biblical Literature Dissertation Series
SNTSMS	Society for New Testament Studies Monograph Series
THNTC	Two Horizons New Testament Commentary
WBC	Word Biblical Commentary

L ike all books, this one is in important ways a collaborative effort. I am grateful to friends, colleagues, and critics who responded to early versions of the chapters in this book, even (perhaps especially) when they disagreed with one or another of its theses. These include fellow New Testament special-ists and theologians: Ben Blackwell, Kent Brower, Steve Fowl, Tim Geoffrion, Joel Green, Richard Hays, Suzanne Watts Henderson, Daniel Kirk, M. David Litwa, Steve McCormick, Mark Thiessen Nation, Chris Smith, Miroslav Volf, John Webster, Tom Wright, some anonymous reviewers, and above all (once again) Andy Johnson. Andy not only read and helped sharpen every chapter — at various stages of composition — but also shared some of his own yet-unpublished studies on subjects related to this book. He has been a constant companion and helpful, positive critic through the writing and rewriting of this book. The list of collaborators also includes my current and former stu-dents who served as sounding boards and research assistants: Bob Anderson, Kasimir Bujak, Jason Poling, and especially Lenore Turner. Lenore also proof-read everything twice and helped compile the indexes. Of course I hold none of these people responsible for any errors or weaknesses in this book, even as I am in debt to them for whatever contributions it may make.

I am also grateful to the *Journal of Theological Interpretation* and its edi-tor, Joel Green, for permission to reprint an adaptation of an article first published in that journal (chapter one),[1] and to Eerdmans for permission to

1. "'Although/Because He Was in the Form of God': The Theological Significance of Paul's Master Story (Phil 2:6-11)," *JTI* 1 (2007): 147-69.

reprint an adaptation of a chapter published in an earlier volume edited by Andy Johnson and Kent Brower (chapter three).[2] Finally, I wish to express my thanks once again to Eerdmans, and particularly to Jon Pott and John Simpson, for their interest in my work.

2. "'You Shall Be Cruciform, for I Am Cruciform': Paul's Trinitarian Reconstruction of Holiness," in *Holiness and Ecclesiology in the New Testament,* ed. Kent E. Brower and Andy Johnson (Grand Rapids: Eerdmans, 2007), pp. 148-66.

Inhabiting the Cruciform God

Paul and the Question of Theosis

I n his book *Paul: In Fresh Perspective*, N. T. Wright makes the following statement:

> As every serious reader of Paul has long recognized, though not so many have explored to the full, the cross of Jesus the Messiah stands at the heart of Paul's vision of the one true God.[1]

The logical corollary of this claim — a claim with which I heartily agree — is that an experience of the cross, a spirituality of the cross, is also an experience and a spirituality of God — and vice versa.

This book is thus the logical continuation of an earlier work on Paul, *Cruciformity: Paul's Narrative Spirituality of the Cross.*[2] Though the present book, *Inhabiting the Cruciform God,* is not the exploration "to the full" to which N. T. Wright refers, it does further develop some of the explicit and implicit themes in *Cruciformity,* with a focus on the central claim of its first chapter: that for Paul, God is cruciform.[3] If that is true, then *cruci*formity is really *theo*formity or, as the Christian tradition (especially in the East) has

---

1. N. T. Wright, *Paul: In Fresh Perspective* (Edinburgh: Clark/Minneapolis: Fortress, 2005), p. 96.

2. Michael J. Gorman, *Cruciformity: Paul's Narrative Spirituality of the Cross* (Grand Rapids: Eerdmans, 2001). The essentials of this monograph are also treated in a different format in *Apostle of the Crucified Lord: A Theological Introduction to Paul and His Letters* (Grand Rapids: Eerdmans, 2004).

3. *Cruciformity,* pp. 9-18.

sometimes called it, deification, divinization, or theosis.[4] It is conformity to Christ, or holiness, understood as participation in the very life of God — inhabiting the cruciform God. This conclusion is implicit in *Cruciformity,* but it is not fully developed there.

This new book unpacks the claim that cruciformity is theoformity, or theosis. It unfolds in four closely connected chapters. Chapter one examines Phil 2:6-11, which may be called Paul's master story, to show that Christ's kenosis (self-emptying) reveals the character of God, summoning us to cruciformity understood as theosis. Chapter two looks at several key texts in Paul, especially Gal 2:15-21 and Rom 6:1–7:6, demonstrating that justification is by co-crucifixion: it is participation in the covenantal and cruciform narrative identity of Christ, which is in turn the character of God; thus justification is itself theosis. This chapter is the book's longest, and the most heavily footnoted, because justification is such a central aspect of Paul's theology and spirituality, because justification is currently a matter of significant exegetical and theological debate, and because the proposal being made is bound to be controversial. It is the soul of the book.

Chapter three argues that for Paul holiness is redefined as participation in and conformity to the cruciform character of the triune God, Father, Son, and Spirit. Holiness is not a supplement to justification but the actualization of justification, and may be more appropriately termed theosis. And finally, chapter four maintains that nonviolence is one of the essential marks of participating in the life of the kenotic, cruciform God revealed in the cross and resurrection and narrated by Paul. Each chapter includes theological reflection on the contemporary meaning of Paul's message of kenosis, justification, and theosis. This reflection is not meant to be exhaustive, but it is integral to the book and to my aims as an interpreter of Paul.

Aspects of this thesis have appeared in the previously published books and essays noted here and in the acknowledgments. The argument also appears in a less technical, and less fully developed, way in my book *Reading Paul.*[5]

---

4. The transliteration of the Greek word *theōsis.* Theosis is not unknown in the Western Christian tradition — for instance, in Augustine — but it has never been prominent. See, e.g., J. A. McGuckin, "Deification," in *The Oxford Companion to Christian Thought,* ed. A. Hastings (Oxford: Oxford University Press, 2000). For a helpful overview of theosis written for Western Christians, see James R. Payton, Jr., *Light from the Christian East: An Introduction to the Orthodox Tradition* (Downers Grove: InterVarsity, 2007), pp. 132-54.

5. Michael J. Gorman, *Reading Paul* (Eugene: Cascade, 2008).

As a fundamental category for understanding Paul, "participation" — meaning participation in Christ, his crucifixion and resurrection, his story, and/or his present life — is now quite widely accepted.[6] Some, however, will agree that Paul has a robust "in Christ" spirituality and theology (what used to be called "Christ-mysticism") but will also insist that this is not to be confused with being in God or union with God. Even readers who are most sympathetic to an emphasis on participation may see the subtitle of this book and respond, "Kenosis is familiar to us, and justification we know, but what in the world is theosis?"

6. For a good introduction, see James D. G. Dunn, *The Theology of Paul the Apostle* (Grand Rapids: Eerdmans, 1998), pp. 390-441. The renewed interest in participation was triggered by E. P. Sanders, *Paul and Palestinian Judaism* (Philadelphia: Fortress, 1977). Of Sanders, Richard Hays would later write that "by focusing on participation in Christ as the central theme of Pauline soteriology, Sanders had put his finger on the heart of the matter" (Richard B. Hays, *The Faith of Jesus Christ: The Narrative Substructure of Gal 3:1–4:11*, 2nd ed. [Grand Rapids: Eerdmans, 2002], p. xxvi n. 12). Hays himself is among the most significant and influential proponents of the centrality of participation in Paul; for example, in his introduction to the second edition of *The Faith of Jesus Christ*, Hays has a section entitled "Participation in Christ as the Key to Pauline Soteriology" (pp. xxix-xxxiii). Daniel G. Powers stresses the corporate character of participation in *Salvation through Participation: An Examination of the Notion of the Believers' Corporate Unity with Christ in Early Christian Soteriology*, Contributions to Biblical Exegesis and Theology (Leuven: Peeters, 2001). For other recent treatments of participation, see, among others, Jouette M. Bassler, *Navigating Paul: An Introduction to Key Theological Concepts* (Louisville: Westminster John Knox, 2007), pp. 35-48; S. A. Cummins, "Divine Life and Corporate Christology: God, Messiah Jesus, and the Covenant Community in Paul," in *The Messiah in the Old and New Testaments*, ed. Stanley E. Porter (Grand Rapids: Eerdmans, 2007), pp. 190-209; and Robert C. Tannehill, "Participation in Christ," in *The Shape of the Gospel: New Testament Essays* (Eugene: Cascade, 2007), pp. 223-37. See as well the critical response to Dunn's understanding of Paul's doctrine of God by Francis Watson, "The Triune Divine Identity: Reflection on Pauline God Language, in Disagreement with J. D. G. Dunn," *JSNT* 80 (2000): 99-124. Watson writes persuasively that the "single divine action" of the death and resurrection of Christ and the gift of the Spirit is "brought to its *telos*" in "our own participation in the death that Jesus died to sin and the life he lives to God (cf. Rom. 6.10)" (p. 122) and that for Paul "the role of the Spirit is *to enable participation in the life that the crucified and risen Jesus shares with the God he addresses as 'Abba, Father'*" (pp. 121-22). For an attempt at a full-blown participationist interpretation of Paul's soteriology, or at least a foundation for such an interpretation, see Douglas A. Campbell, *The Quest for Paul's Gospel: A Suggested Strategy* (London/New York: Clark, 2005). Campbell has a concise summary of his thesis of "pneumatologically participatory martyrological eschatology" (PPME) on pp. 38-42 and pp. 56-62. For a theologian's initial consideration of participation as Paul's primary soteriological model, see David L. Stubbs, "The Shape of Soteriology and the *Pistis Christou* [Faith of Christ] Debate," *SJT* 61 (2008): 137-57.

Some years ago, Richard Hays saw that the study of Paul's soteriology needed to move in the direction of theosis, though he did not use that word. He wrote, "My own guess is that [E. P.] Sanders's insights [about participation in Paul] would be supported and clarified by careful study of participation motifs in patristic theology, particularly the thought of the Eastern Fathers."[7] Hays saw that his own approach to Paul, with its emphasis on narrative and on the confluence of God's faithfulness and Christ's faithfulness, raised questions about the relationship between God and Christ and therefore about the Trinity.[8] He rightly asserted that "[u]ltimately, *being united with Christ is salvific because to share his life is to share in the life of God.*"[9]

It is the burden of this book to make it clear that Paul's experience of Christ was precisely an experience of God *in se,* and that we must either invent or borrow theological language to express that as fully and appropriately as possible. For Paul, to be one with Christ is to be one with God; to be like Christ is to be like God; to be in Christ is to be in God. At the very least, this means that for Paul cruciformity — conformity to the crucified Christ — is really theoformity, or theosis. The argument of this book about these claims will also suggest that Paul's famous phrase "in Christ" is his shorthand for "in God/in Christ/in the Spirit." That is, his christocentricity is really an implicit Trinitarianism.[10]

Although the Eastern Christian tradition has spoken of "becoming God/god," it has also made it clear that theosis does not mean that people become little gods; nor does it mean apotheosis, the unChristian notion of the post-mortem promotion of certain humans (heroes, emperors, etc.) to

7. Hays, *The Faith of Jesus Christ,* 2nd ed., p. xxxii. In the same context (p. xxix), Hays also expressed his attraction to the Eastern theological interest in "recapitulation" (starting with Irenaeus), over against most Western atonement theories.

8. Hays, *The Faith of Jesus Christ,* 2nd ed., p. xxxiii.

9. Hays, *The Faith of Jesus Christ,* 2nd ed., p. xxxiii; emphasis added. For the narrative character of salvation and participation in Paul, see not only the entirety of Hays's *The Faith of Jesus Christ* but also his article "Christ Died for the Ungodly: Narrative Soteriology in Paul?" *HBT* 26 (2004): 48-69.

10. See especially the interesting phrase "in God the Father and the Lord Jesus Christ" in 1 Thess 1:1 (cf. 2 Thess 1:1) and the easy interchange of "in Christ" and "in the Spirit" found in Rom 8:1-11. Paul's Trinitarianism will be addressed most fully in this book in chapter three. See also Watson, "The Triune Divine Identity," and chapter four of my *Cruciformity,* "The Triune God of Cruciform Love" (pp. 63-74), as well as the literature mentioned there.

divinity. Rather, theosis means that humans become *like* God. The tradition of theosis in Christian theology after the New Testament begins with the famous dictum of Irenaeus, later developed by Athanasius: "God became what we are to make us what he is."[11] Theosis is about divine intention and action, human transformation, and the *telos* of human existence — union with God.[12]

The classic scriptural text for the doctrine of theosis is 2 Pet 1:4:

> Thus he has given us, through these things, his precious and very great promises, so that through them you may escape from the corruption that is in the world because of lust, and may become participants [other translations: "partakers"] of the divine nature [Greek *theias koinōnoi physeōs*].[13] (NRSV)

There is no precisely parallel text in the undisputed Pauline letters,[14] but, as we will see, there are texts that suggest transformation into the image or likeness of God, who is Christ. Our argument for theosis in Paul, and thus for the appropriateness of the term in discussing Pauline theology and spirituality, will be based on Paul's theology and experience of God, Christ, justification, and holiness.

Although Richard Hays's invitation to explore the Eastern tradition of participation has not yet evolved into a movement, there is a growing interest among Pauline scholars in using the word "theosis" to describe the

---

11. Irenaeus, *Against Heresies* 5.preface.1 says that the "Lord Jesus Christ . . . did, through his transcendent love, become what we are, that he might bring us to be even what he is himself"; cf. Athanasius, *Incarnation of the Word* 54. The same basic sentiment is expressed in several different ways in the two authors. As the quintessential patristic dictum of divine exchange, it is rooted in Pauline interchange formulas such as 2 Cor 5:21 and 8:9.

12. For two excellent introductions to theosis from biblical roots to contemporary expressions see Michael J. Christensen and Jeffery A. Wittung, eds., *Partakers of the Divine Nature: The History and Development of Deification in the Christian Traditions* (Grand Rapids: Baker, 2007); and Stephen Finlan and Vladimir Kharlamov, eds., *Theōsis: Deification in Christian Theology* (Eugene: Pickwick, 2006).

13. Or "come to share in the divine nature" (NAB); "may participate in the divine nature" (NIV). Translations with "partakers" include the older KJV and Rheims, as well as NASB and the NETBible.

14. But cf. Eph 3:19: "to know the love of Christ that surpasses knowledge, so that you may be filled with all the fullness of God." See also Col 1:15, 19; 2:9; and 3:10. Throughout this book, we will base our arguments on the seven undisputed Pauline letters, drawing occasional attention, especially in the notes, to texts from the disputed letters.

soteriological reality, or at least a significant aspect of that reality, to which Paul bears witness.[15] Stephen Finlan, for example, finds in Paul an overall three-stage process of conformation to Christ that is worthy of the name "theosis." It consists of (1) dying to sin, (2) moral transformation, and (3) eschatological transformation.[16] Finlan and others find certain passages to be especially reflective of what has been called theosis, including:

- Rom 8:29 — "For those whom he [God] foreknew he also predestined to be conformed to the image of his Son, in order that he might be the firstborn within a large family."
- 1 Cor 15:42-44, 49 — "42So it is with the resurrection of the dead. What is sown is perishable, what is raised is imperishable. 43It is sown in dishonor, it is raised in glory. It is sown in weakness, it is raised in power. 44It is sown a physical body, it is raised a spiritual body. If there is a physical body, there is also a spiritual body. . . . 49Just as we have borne the image of the man of dust, we will also bear the image of the man of heaven."
- 2 Cor 3:18 — "And all of us, with unveiled faces, seeing the glory of the Lord as though reflected in a mirror, are being transformed into the same image from one degree of glory to another; for this comes from the Lord, the Spirit."
- 2 Cor 5:17, 21 — "17So if anyone is in Christ, there is a new creation: everything old has passed away; see, everything has become new! . . . 21For

15. See Stephen Finlan, "Can We Speak of *Theosis* in Paul?" in Christensen and Wittung, eds., *Partakers of the Divine Nature*, pp. 68-80; and M. David Litwa, "2 Corinthians 3:18 and Its Implications for *Theosis*," *JTI* 2 (2008): 117-34. In addition, as I write, at least one Ph.D. student, Ben Blackwell in Durham, England, is preparing a dissertation on theosis in Paul in light of the Eastern Fathers, as Hays suggested. Litwa is particularly instructive in stressing that Paul's vision of theosis is not fusion with the divine as one might find in Hellenistic culture more widely (e.g., p. 128).

16. Finlan, "Can We Speak of *Theosis* in Paul?", especially p. 73 for the three stages. Finlan lays heavy emphasis on the eschatological phase and on what he calls the "anastiform" (resurrection-like, not just cruciform) character of theosis in Paul (pp. 74-75, 78). Finlan appears to believe that I disagree with him here by overemphasizing the cruciform dimension, but in fact I have repeatedly written, and will stress again in this book, that cruciformity is always participation in the life of the *resurrected* crucified Christ, and that participation in the resurrected crucified Christ is always a *cruciform* existence. Life in Christ, or theosis, is therefore always, paradoxically, both anastiform and cruciform, as Finlan says (p. 78).

our sake he made him to be sin who knew no sin, so that in him we might become the righteousness of God."

- Phil 3:10-11, 21 — "10I want to know Christ and the power of his resurrection and the sharing of his sufferings by becoming like him in his death, 11if somehow I may attain the resurrection from the dead. . . . 21He will transform the body of our humiliation that it may be conformed to the body of his glory, by the power that also enables him to make all things subject to himself."

David Litwa argues for theosis in Paul in a pioneering study of 2 Cor 3:18,[17] which Finlan calls "the most frankly theotic passage in Paul."[18] And Douglas Campbell, stressing the transformational character of participation in Christ, comes close to the language of theosis (without actually using it) when he describes Paul's into/in Christ language as "a metaphor for being or ontology, and its radical transformation," which makes people in Christ "fully relational beings . . . real, full persons" who "can relate to God and to each other as they ought to."[19] Indeed, the last phrase suggests a covenantal understanding of transformation/theosis, with which the argument of the present work will resonate strongly.

The purpose of this book is not to provide an extended description or defense of theosis. In the chapters that follow, however, we will explore some of the Pauline texts listed above, as well as other key passages in Paul's letters that may be less obviously "theotic," and argue for the following understanding of theosis in Paul:

> Theosis is transformative participation in the kenotic, cruciform character of God through Spirit-enabled conformity to the incarnate, crucified, and resurrected/glorified Christ.

As noted above, this understanding will be closely linked to Paul's understanding of justification and holiness.[20]

---

17. See Litwa, "2 Corinthians 3:18 and Its Implications for *Theosis.*"

18. Finlan, "Can We Speak of *Theosis* in Paul?" p. 75.

19. Campbell, *The Quest for Paul's Gospel,* p. 41. See also pp. 28 and 60. His "model is clearly committed to a radical transformation of the person, something only a creator can effect (anticipating this for creation as a whole)" (p. 60).

20. Two of my conversation partners, N. T. Wright and Douglas Campbell, completed manuscripts on topics directly related to the concerns of this book as this volume was going to press, so I was unable to interact significantly with them in writng even though their pub-

"Theosis" may not be the only word to describe the full soteriological process in Paul, but, this book contends, it is both appropriate and useful, especially in considering stages one and two of Finlan's three-stage process.[21] More importantly, *not* to use such a word would mean seriously misrepresenting what is perhaps at the core of Paul's theology: a narrative soteriology of Spirit-enabled full identification with and participation in the God revealed in Christ crucified, such that the gospel of God reconciling the world in Christ becomes also the story of God's justified, holy, Spirit-led people in the world.[22]

---

lishers generously provided advance copies. The two books (tentative titles) are N. T. Wright, *Justification in Pauline Perspective* (Downers Grove: InterVarsity) and Douglas A. Campbell, *The Deliverance of God: An Apocalyptic Rereading of Justification in Paul* (Grand Rapids: Eerdmans). I am particularly attracted to Wright's broad vision of Pauline theology and to Campbell's insistence on the centrality of participation and transformation to Pauline soteriology. Both are trying in their own ways to move beyond the conflict between old and new perspectives on Paul. However, I believe that Wright interprets justification too narrowly and that Campbell dismisses traditional interpretations too polemically and too completely.

21. This is not to say that the eschatological dimension of theosis is insignificant to Paul, but it will not be the focus of this book. Litwa ("2 Corinthians 3:18," especially pp. 128-33) defines Pauline theosis as moral transformation, sharing in the divine righteousness, and even "joyful obedience," linking the only two Pauline uses of the verb "transform" *(metamorphoō)* in 2 Cor 3:18 and Rom 12:2.

22. As further work on theosis in Paul is done by other scholars, there will no doubt be attention to themes that receive limited attention, at best, in this book, which should be seen as a first step in the direction of theosis, with a special focus on the relationship between theosis and justification. Among the themes that will deserve subsequent attention are adoption as God's children, life in the Spirit, the body of Christ, Adam typology, interchange/exchange, and the resurrection body and the nature of eternal life. As such work moves forward, it may well not only clarify our understanding of Paul, but also contribute to the reuniting of the fractured Christian church. The intersection of participation with justification, and both with theosis, is promising for the efforts at the reunion of Protestants and Catholics, and of Protestants and Catholics with the Orthodox. See also Stubbs, "The Shape of Soteriology," pp. 155-57. As a Methodist working in a Catholic seminary and its Ecumenical Institute of Theology among Catholic, Protestant, and Orthodox Christians, this gives me hope.

CHAPTER 1

"Although/Because He Was in the Form of God"

The Theological Significance of Paul's Master Story (Phil 2:6-11)

For many years, Phil 2:6-11, one of the most significant texts in all of Paul's letters, has been rightly mined for its testimony to early Christian worship and hymnody, its Pauline and/or pre-Pauline Christology, and its ethic, or lack thereof. One collection of studies even suggests it is "where Christology began."[1] Some interpreters, however, have concluded that this text also reveals something extraordinarily significant about Paul's theology proper, his doctrine of God. For instance, N. T. Wright concludes that the "real theological emphasis of the hymn . . . is not simply a new view of Jesus. It is a new understanding of God."[2] Richard Bauckham argues that this text asks whether "the cross of Jesus Christ actually can be included in the identity" of the exalted God of Israel, and answers that Christ's "humiliation belongs to the identity of God as truly as his exaltation does."[3] And John Dominic Crossan and Jonathan Reed wonder rhetorically, as they contrast the Philippians text with imperial ideology,

> Is kenosis not just about Christ, but about God . . . , not a passing exercise in ultimate obedience, but a permanent revelation about the nature of

---

1. Ralph P. Martin and Brian J. Dodd, eds., *Where Christology Began: Essays on Philippians 2* (Louisville: Westminster John Knox, 1998).

2. N. T. Wright, *The Climax of the Covenant* (Minneapolis: Fortress, 1993), p. 84.

3. Richard Bauckham, *God Crucified: Monotheism and Christology in the New Testament* (Grand Rapids: Eerdmans, 1998), p. 61.

9

God? . . . Does, then, a kenotic Son reveal a kenotic Father, a kenotic Christ image a kenotic God?[4]

In a careful analysis of the text to determine the validity of this theological interpretation, the question arises — answered affirmatively by a line of exegetes from C. F. D. Moule to N. T. Wright, Gerald Hawthorne, Markus Bockmuehl, and Stephen Fowl — whether the first words of the poem should be translated "*Because* he was in the form of God" rather than "*Although* he was in the form of God."[5] This chapter, consisting of an exegetical exploration followed by theological reflection, contends that Phil 2:6-11, as Paul's master story, is (in part) about the counterintuitive, essentially kenotic — or cruciform — character of God.[6] More specifically, we will argue that the Greek phrase *en morphē theou hyparchōn* in Phil 2:6 ("being in the form of God") has two levels of meaning, a surface structure and a deep structure (to borrow terms from transformational grammar), one concessive and one causative: "although he was in the form of God" and "because he was in the form of God." These two translations, which, as we will see, are really two sides of the same coin, correspond to two aspects of Paul's understanding of the identity of the one true God (or "divine identity") manifested in this text: its counterintuitive character ("although") and its cruciform character ("because").[7]

---

4. John Dominic Crossan and Jonathan Reed, *In Search of Paul: How Jesus's Apostle Opposed Rome's Empire with God's Kingdom* (San Francisco: HarperSanFrancisco, 2004), p. 290.

5. See the discussion and references in n. 74 below. The point of this chapter is not merely to affirm the work of these interpreters but to strengthen their interpretation with new linguistic arguments and to develop further the theological significance of this reading of the text, especially as the foundation for a new interpretation of Paul's soteriology.

6. The terms "kenotic" and "cruciform" will be understood throughout this chapter as inseparable and overlapping in meaning, though not quite synonymous (as will become evident below). As for the terms "story" and "narrative," space does not permit an extensive discussion of the terms or of the scholarly debate about the presence of story and narrative in Paul. I generally prefer to use the word "narrative" to refer to a specific textual manifestation of a larger, overarching "story." For the debate about Paul, see Bruce W. Longenecker, ed., *Narrative Dynamics in Paul: A Critical Assessment* (Louisville: Westminster John Knox, 2002).

7. In using the term "divine identity," I follow Bauckham, *God Crucified*, p. 7 n. 5: he refers to it "by analogy with human personal identity, understood not as a mere ontological subject without characteristics, but as including both character and personal story (the latter entailing relationships). These are the ways in which we commonly specify 'who someone is.'" We should add that a crucial part of narrative personal identity is the existence of patterns of similar acts/behaviors.

In addition, these arguments clearly have an impact on our understanding of the Christology present in the text. This chapter maintains that this Christology is essentially Chalcedonian in affirming that Christ embodied both true divinity and, as the antitype of Adam, true humanity, with both "natures" manifested in the story of incarnation and cross. The text also reveals clearly, if only implicitly, what it means for human beings in Christ to be conformed to his image and story.

The Text

Before proceeding to our close reading of Phil 2:6-11 with a focus on 2:6, we consider a translation and graphic arrangement of the text and its introduction (2:5).[8]

> 5Cultivate this mind-set [see 2:1-4] in your community, which is in fact a community in Christ Jesus, who,
> 6Although [x] *being* in the form of God,
> **did not [y] consider his** [or **this**[9]] **equality with God as something to be exploited for his own advantage,**
> 7but [z¹] **emptied himself,**
> *by taking* the form of a slave,[10]
> that is, *by being born* in the likeness of human beings.
> And *being found* in human form,
> 8he [z²] **humbled himself**
> *by becoming obedient*
> to death —
> even death on a cross.
> . . . .
> 9Therefore God has **highly exalted** him

8. My translation. For the rendering of 2:5 offered here, see Michael J. Gorman, *Cruciformity: Paul's Narrative Spirituality of the Cross* (Grand Rapids: Eerdmans, 2001), pp. 40-43.

9. Taking the article *to* to be anaphoric, referring back to Christ's being in the form of God mentioned in v. 6. Either "his equality" or "this equality" captures that sense; see the discussion below.

10. I take the first two participles in v. 7 and the one in v. 8 as indicating the means by which the actions described in the main verbs of self-emptying and self-humbling were expressed.

and **bestowed** on him the name [title] that is above every name [title],
10so that [in fulfillment of Isa 45:23] at Jesus' name [title][11]
every knee should **bend**,
  in heaven and
  on earth and
  under the earth,
11and every tongue **acclaim** that
Jesus Christ is Lord,
to the glory of God the Father.

N. T. Wright correctly asserts that the entire context of Philippians, especially 3:2-21, shows Paul "had the material and language of 2:5-11 in his bloodstream."[12] Less widely recognized is the evidence that this text permeates all his letters,[13] and so much so that 2:6-11 should be called not merely the centerpiece of Philippians but Paul's master story.[14]

There are at least four reasons to call Phil 2:6-11 Paul's master story:

1. its comprehensive scope in relation to the story of Israel, from protology to eschatology;[15]
2. its simultaneously creedal and counter-imperial character, rooted in the confession that "Jesus [— not Caesar —] is Lord";[16]

---

11. The genitive in this phrase ("the name *of Jesus*") should be read as a genitive of possession and understood to indicate the name/title Jesus has ("Jesus' title/name") — i.e., "Lord" — rather than as a genitive of apposition ("the name 'Jesus'").

12. Wright, *Climax*, p. 59. On the use of 2:6-11 throughout the letter, see the evidence in Michael J. Gorman, *Apostle of the Crucified Lord: A Theological Introduction to Paul and His Letters* (Grand Rapids: Eerdmans, 2004), pp. 419-22, and L. Gregory Bloomquist, *The Function of Suffering in Philippians*, JSNTSup 78 (Sheffield: JSOT, 1993), p. 165.

13. Karl Barth (*The Epistle to the Philippians*, trans. James W. Leith [Richmond: John Knox, 1962], p. 49) called 2:1-11 "a little compendium of Pauline testimony."

14. See Gorman, *Cruciformity*, pp. 88-92, 164-72, 278-80, 316-19, 357-58, *et passim*.

15. Some may object that this text is too narrow in its focus to be rightly described as Paul's master story. In particular, some may say that it does not relate the story of Christ to the story of Israel. However, if there is an echo of the Adam story, a reworking of the Isaianic servant hymns, and a direct citation of a text (Isa 45:23) anticipating a glorious future when God is recognized as the earth's rightful Lord, then this story of Christ is placed directly into the larger story of Israel and of Israel's God from protology to eschatology. See especially N. T. Wright's interpretation of this passage for the connections to Israel (*Climax*, pp. 56-98).

16. See, e.g., Richard A. Horsley, ed., *Paul and Empire: Religion and Power in Roman Imperial Society* (Harrisburg: Trinity, 1997).

3. its inclusion of a wide range of significant Christological narratives or patterns;[17] and

4. its generative power for Pauline theology and its ubiquity in the Pauline corpus.[18]

For all these reasons, I would suggest, Phil 2:6-11 is truly Paul's master story. If this claim is correct (or at least the reasons for the claim are correct), the significance of our text and our exegesis increases immensely.

We will now look carefully at this rich narrative.

Poetic Narrative and Intertextual Overlapping

One of the persistent questions in the study of Phil 2:6-11 has been the issue of the text's background(s) and sources. But as we approach Phil 2:6-11, we must never forget that it is a *poetic narrative*.[19] Like most poetry, this text is rich in metaphor and allusion, and it is probably more accurate for us to speak of intertextuality rather than sources or even "backgrounds." Although we must strive for appropriate historical and philological precision, we must also learn to live with semantic overlapping and ambiguity in this rich tapestry of intertextual threads. This poetic intertextuality means that there may be words, allusions, and echoes that stand in creative tension with one another.[20]

---

17. See Gorman, *Cruciformity*, pp. 88-92. The brief story in 2:6-11 contains several important narrative patterns, like subplots (including possession of status but renunciation of selfish exploitation, self-emptying, and humiliation-exaltation) that appear elsewhere in Paul. This usage is most evident in the echoes of the narrative pattern "although [x] not [y] but [z]" found in 2:6-8 that we will discuss below.

18. The story as a whole, plus its subplots, reverberates throughout Paul's letters. Although the text is neither explicitly soteriological nor explicitly ethical, it is clear from its reverberations in Philippians and elsewhere that Paul himself has mined it in the service of both soteriology and ethics. He regularly adopts and adapts the text's narrative patterns to display his (a) Christology/soteriology (and, as we will see, his theology proper), but also both his (b) apostolic self-understanding and his (c) ethic or spirituality as derivatives of that polyvalent Christological narrative. See the pages cited from Gorman, *Cruciformity*, in n. 14 above.

19. Stephen E. Fowl, *Philippians*, THNTC (Grand Rapids: Eerdmans, 2005), p. 89, says that the text "poetically narrates Christ's status and activity."

20. Similar points about interpretive method are made by James D. G. Dunn, "Christ, Adam, and Preexistence," in Martin and Dodd, *Where Christology Began*, pp. 74-83, here

This does not mean, however, that chaos reigns, or that the poetic narrative has no internal structure, consistency, plot, or logic. Quite the contrary: once we abandon the quest for absolute precision with respect to sources and lexicography, we can look to the poem itself to explain itself. Many of the debated words and phrases in this text are glossed within the poem (e.g., as many scholars have recognized, the clarification of main verbs by participles, which are italicized in the translation above). Moreover, the overall sense of the poem can be discerned by examining how Paul uses, and thereby interprets, the poem in its immediate context, elsewhere in Philippians, and throughout his extant letters.[21] Thus, although we should not treat this poetic text as an essay in systematic Christology, we can reasonably assume that the narrative made, and makes, theological sense.

We may identify at least five echoes of scriptural images, as well as allusions to at least three cultural realities, that inform the text and should inform our reading of it. The scriptural echoes include

1. preexistent Wisdom,[22]
2. the form and/or glory of God,
3. Adam,[23]
4. the Isaianic suffering servant,[24] and

---

pp. 75-76 (stressing the fluid character of allusions), and Moisés Silva, *Philippians,* 2nd ed., BECNT (Grand Rapids: Baker, 2005), p. 11 (stressing semantic ambiguity in the use of words).

21. For example, this usage confirms the growing consensus about one of the key philological and interpretive debates, namely, the meaning of *harpagmos* in v. 6.

22. Despite Dunn's hesitation ("Preexistence," p. 82 n. 41).

23. Dunn (*Christology in the Making,* 2nd ed. [Grand Rapids: Eerdmans, 1996], p. 120) says that "the hymn . . . describes in Adam language *the character of Christ's whole life.*" L. D. Hurst asserts that "virtually all" interpreters "on both sides of the question" about Christ's preexistence in the hymn acknowledge an Adam-Christ parallel ("Christ, Adam, and Preexistence Revisited," in Martin and Dodd, *Where Christology Began,* pp. 84-95, here p. 84), but he rightly stresses that the "view that once the Adam parallel is admitted it must dominate the hymn so completely that every detail must be paralleled by the experience of Adam is questionable" (p. 88).

24. Isaiah 40–55, especially the fourth servant hymn and 45:23. See Bauckham, *God Crucified,* pp. 51-53, 56-61. In his *The Function of Suffering,* Bloomquist argues persuasively that Philippians depicts Christ, Paul, Paul's coworkers, and the Philippians in terms of the Isaianic suffering servant who will be vindicated by God.

5. Israel's "eschatological monotheism" within the framework of Isaiah 40–55 more generally.[25]

Although there is still some opposition to the possibility of finding both preexistence (and thus incarnation) and Adam in the text, the work of N. T. Wright and others indicates that both can be heard here.[26] Even James Dunn, who earlier argued for Adam and against preexistence, admits this.[27] As for cultural echoes, we may identify three:

1. the reality and ideology of slavery,[28]
2. the Roman ideology and pursuit of honor,[29] and
3. the theology and practices of the imperial cult.[30]

It is difficult to weigh the significance of these various scriptural and cultural echoes and allusions, but for our purposes the three most important will be the Isaianic suffering servant within the context of Isaiah 40–55, Adam, and the imperial cult.[31]

---

25. The term is Bauckham's from his "The Worship of Jesus in Philippians 2:9-11," in Martin and Dodd, *Where Christology Began*, pp. 128-39; see also his *God Crucified*, pp. 47-51.

26. N. T. Wright argues correctly (*Climax*, pp. 59-61, 90-92) that the Adam Christology does not rule out allusions to the suffering servant or even preexistence and incarnation.

27. Dunn's later work on Philippians 2 explicitly leaves open the possibility of a thoroughgoing Adam-Christ parallelism that still allows for an affirmation of Christ's preexistence in the hymn. Dunn would characterize this interpretation of preexistence as part of an "extended metaphor" about Christ that is based in Adam's "prehistory," similar to early Christological affirmations indebted to the language of preexistent Wisdom ("Preexistence," pp. 78-79).

28. C. F. D. Moule, "Further Reflexions on Philippians 2:5-11," in *Apostolic History and the Gospel: Biblical and Historical Essays Presented to F. F. Bruce on His 60th Birthday,* ed. W. Ward Gasque and Ralph P. Martin (Grand Rapids: Eerdmans, 1970), pp. 264-76, here pp. 268-69.

29. See especially Joseph H. Hellerman, *Reconstructing Honor in Roman Philippi:* Carmen Christi *as* Cursus Pudorum, SNTSMS 132 (Cambridge: Cambridge University Press, 2005).

30. See, among many others, Crossan and Reed, *In Search of Paul*, pp. 235-42, 284-88. Peter Oakes, *Philippians: From People to Letter,* SNTSMS 110 (Cambridge: Cambridge University Press, 2001), pp. 129-74, emphasizes the echoes of imperial ideology especially in 2:9-11. Erik M. Heen ("Phil 2:6-11 and Resistance to Local Timocratic Rule: *Isa theō* and the Cult of the Emperor in the East," in *Paul and the Roman Imperial Order,* ed. Richard A. Horsley [Harrisburg: Trinity, 2004], pp. 125-53), argues that the text was an expression of resistance to the support of imperial ideology by the local elite.

31. For an emphasis on these three, see also Gorman, *Apostle*, pp. 434-35.

These overlapping echoes together suggest that the text portrays the preexistent Christ as the self-emptying "form of God" — in contrast to the self-exalting Adam and self-glorifying Roman emperors — who, by virtue of his self-humbling incarnation to the status of a slave and consequent death by crucifixion, is the fulfillment of the Isaianic servant of God and thus the one worthy of universal acknowledgment and worship as Lord.

The narrative is divided into two basic parts, humiliation (2:6-8) and exaltation (2:9-11), the division indicated by the "therefore" at the beginning of v. 9, together with the change of subject, or Actor, from Christ in vv. 6-8 to God and then all creatures in vv. 9-11.

Philippians 2:6-8

The Narrative Pattern of 2:6-8: "Although [x] Not [y] but [z]"

Phil 2:6-8 is about Christ's voluntary self-humbling. It sets forth his status, disposition, and activity.[32] That is, verses 6-8 assert Christ's equality with God and narrate, both positively and negatively, his disposition toward that equality and the action he takes regarding it. This is accomplished in the form of a narrative pattern we can describe as "although [x] not [y] but [z]," as noted in the translation above, meaning "although [status] not [selfishness] but [selflessness]." This narrative pattern, with its corresponding semantic and syntactic patterns, may be displayed as on page 17. The basic sense of the text, then, is that Christ existed as someone with a certain status (2:6a) who did not do one thing (indicated by the negated main verb in 2:6b) but did do something else — specifically two things, acts of self-humbling and self-emptying, denoted by the two main verbs of 2:7-8 ("emptied himself . . . humbled himself").

The narrative of 2:6-8 has been rightly described as one of "downward mobility."[33] Joseph Hellerman argues that it is a *"cursus pudorum,"* or downward-bound succession of ignominies, constructed in contrast to Rome's *cursus honorum,* the elite's upward-bound race for honors, imitated

---

32. The phrase "status and activity" and the term "disposition" are borrowed from Fowl, *Philippians,* pp. 89, 94.

33. See, e.g., A. Katherine Grieb, "The One Who Called You: Vocation and Leadership in the Pauline Literature," *Int* 59 (2005): 154-65, here p. 158.

Narrative, Semantic, and Syntactic Patterns in Phil 2:6-8

	2:6a	2:6b	2:7-8
Text	although [in the form of God]	did not [exploit equality with God]	but [emptied himself . . . humbled himself]
Narrative Pattern	although [x]	not [y]	but [z]
Semantic Pattern	although [status]	not [selfish act/ selfishness]	but [selfless acts/ selflessness]
Syntactic Pattern	[concessive participle]	negated [verb]	*alla* + [affirmed verbs]

in various ways throughout the provinces and colonies. According to Hellerman, Paul's depiction of Jesus' humiliation in three main verbs modified by participles corresponds to "three progressively degrading positions of social status in the Roman world . . . equality with God; . . . taking on of humanity and status of slave; . . . [and] public humiliation of death on a cross," the "utter degradation."[34]

Hellerman's analysis shows that what we have labeled "[z]" has, in fact, two successively lower parts (which we could label [z¹] and [z²]). The two analyses are complementary; his stresses the progressively downward movement itself, while ours stresses the reality of the downward movement as the antithesis of the alternative — selfish exploitation of status (i.e., what Christ *did* do over against what he did *not* do).[35] Hellerman's observations are extraordinarily important theologically. The *preexistent Christ's* self-emptying, self-lowering incarnation/enslavement finds a parallel action in the *human Jesus'* self-humbling, self-lowering obedience to the point of death by crucifixion. *The fundamental character of the actions taken by the "form of God" and the "form of a slave," by the preexistent one and the incarnate one, is the same: downward movement.* We will return to this below.

34. Hellerman, *Reconstructing Honor*, p. 130. On the literary structure and the importance of three levels of social status, see also p. 203 nn. 2, 5.

35. The accuracy and usefulness of the present literary analysis are confirmed by Paul's use of it elsewhere; as Hellerman (*Reconstructing Honor*, p. 204 n. 6, citing Oakes, *Philippians*, p. 197) says, only in Philippians is what we have called the "[z]" action spelled out in two stages.

Philippians 2:6: Christ's Preexistence and Equality with God

From earliest times in the study of Paul's letters, the first verse of the poem has been most often understood as a witness to Christ's preexistence and equality with God. This ancient understanding of Phil 2:6 has been most notably challenged in recent times by James Dunn. While debate of course still exists, even Dunn is willing to admit a metaphorical reference to preexistence.[36] Three major aspects of this difficult text point to its affirming Christ's preexistence and equality with God.

First, two different, plausible, and complementary interpretations of the phrase "in the form of God" argue for this view. (1) Markus Bockmuehl, followed by Stephen Fowl, argues that being in "the form of God" is a variation on a theme of Jewish mysticism and refers to "the visual characteristics of Christ's heavenly being."[37] Similar is the contention of Gerald Hawthorne and others that the reference is to Christ as God's glory.[38] (2) Furthermore, and from another angle, Crossan and Reed demonstrate, using a variety of ancient texts and images, that "the form of God" is about "normal" Roman theology, and that "the 'form of God' present in an Augustus or any divine emperor manifested itself . . . through the sequence of Piety, War, Victory, and Peace. It was simply normal divinity."[39] Kenosis and deity do not belong together.[40]

Whatever its precise (or polyvalent)[41] meaning, three things seem clear:

1. Christ actually possessed the status of being "in the form of God,"
2. "form of God" is in a relationship of antithetical parallelism to "form of a slave," and

---

36. See n. 27 above.

37. Markus Bockmuehl, *The Epistle to the Philippians*, BNTC (Peabody: Hendrickson, 1998), pp. 127-29 (here p. 129). Cf. Fowl, *Philippians*, pp. 90-94.

38. E.g., Gerald F. Hawthorne, "In the Form of God," in Martin and Dodd, *Where Christology Began*, pp. 96-110, here p. 101.

39. Crossan and Reed, *In Search of Paul*, p. 288.

40. Crossan and Reed, *In Search of Paul*, p. 284. Similarly, Wright says that 2:6 is the antithesis of "the standard picture of oriental despots, who understood their position as something to be used for their own advantage" (Wright, *Climax*, p. 83). "Oriental despots," of course, were often understood to be gods or godlike.

41. See the helpful discussion in Silva, *Philippians*, 2nd ed., pp. 101-2.

3. the phrase "form of God" "is related to and more fully clarified by the clause that immediately follows ['equality with God']."[42]

Second, then, Hawthorne, Moisés Silva, N. T. Wright, and others suggest that we should take "equality with God" *(to einai isa theọ)* as an explanation of the phrase "form of God" and should therefore translate it as *"this"* or even *"his* equality with God." This does indeed seem to be the force of the Greek article *to,* which functions in this articular infinitive phrase anaphorically to refer back to something already mentioned.[43] This connection of the two phrases is ratified by the work of Erik Heen, who shows that the "terminology *isa theọ* (godlike/equal) . . . has a long history in the Greek ruler cult and in the first century C.E. was applied to the Roman emperor."[44] Heen shows that after Augustus such language, at least in the East, was only to be applied to the emperor,[45] so that *isa theọ* language, like "form of God" language, "sets Christ over against the Roman emperor."[46]

Finally, there is the term *harpagmos.* There has of course been considerable debate about whether Christ already possessed or tried to grasp equality with God. Roy W. Hoover, seconded by Wright and many others (including the NRSV translators), seems to have settled that question with a slightly different but convincing answer. Hoover concluded that the idiomatic expression *ouch harpagmon hēgēsato ti* always "refers to something already present and at one's disposal [such that the issue is] not whether one possesses

---

42. Hawthorne, "Form of God," p. 101. Silva (*Philippians,* 2nd ed., pp. 100-101) says "form of God" and "equality with God" refer to the same reality; so also Fowl, *Philippians,* p. 94, and Bockmuehl, *Epistle,* p. 126. Some (e.g., Ralph P. Martin, *A Hymn of Christ: Philippians 2:5-11 in Recent Interpretation and in the Setting of Early Christian Worship* [Downers Grove: InterVarsity, 1997; orig. *Carmen Christi,* 1967], pp. 143-53) make a distinction, saying that in the form of God Christ did not strive for equality with God in lordship/rulership of the world but was given this status as the reward for obedience.

43. Wright (*Climax,* p. 83), for example, reads the "equality" phrase "epexegetically" as a reference back to "form of God" and therefore suggests that "the stronger translation 'this divine equality'" may be best. See also Bockmuehl (*Epistle,* p. 114; "this equality") and Silva (*Philippians,* 2nd ed., pp. 94, 103; "his equality"), as well as Hawthorne ("Form of God," p. 104). On the Greek definite article, see F. Blass and A. Debrunner, *A Greek Grammar of the New Testament and Other Early Christian Literature,* trans. and rev. R. W. Funk (Chicago: University of Chicago Press, 1961), p. 205, para. 399.

44. Heen, "Phil 2:6-11," p. 125.

45. Heen, "Phil 2:6-11," pp. 132-34.

46. Heen, "Phil 2:6-11," p. 137.

something, but whether or not one chooses to exploit something."[47] This means clearly that Christ already was, in fact, equal with God.[48]

Thus the language, syntax, and most plausible cultural and intertextual echoes in 2:6 point to a status Christ possessed, equality with God, but did not exploit for himself. The text does not explicitly specify the precise nature of this equality, or the way in which he could have selfishly exploited it. The text is most interested in Christ's disposition — "although [x] not [y]" — toward his equality with God, and the cultural context and echoes suggest that he did not pursue honor or divinity the "normal" way. It is this equality with God that is assumed as the story continues in vv. 7-8,[49] and examination of parallel Christological, apostolic, and hortatory (ethical) texts confirms this reading of the story.[50]

Philippians 2:6: "Although He Was in the Form of God . . ."

The first verb form that appears in Paul's master story is not a main verb but a participle, *hyparchōn* ("being"), the fourth Greek word in Phil 2:6. It is dependent on the main verb of the sentence, *hēgēsato*, a form of the verb "consider." Its translation is crucial to the exegesis of the poem.

There are three principal ways to translate *hyparchōn*. It can be rendered

- concessively: "though" or "although" he was in the form of God;
- causally: "because" or "since" he was in the form of God; or
- temporally, and more neutrally: "being" in the form of God, or "while" he was in the form of God.[51]

The vast majority of translators opt for "although," which appropriately stresses both the existing reality of the status of being in the form of God and the dramatic downward mobility and status reversal that ensues to the point of Christ's taking on the form of a slave. At this juncture we need only

47. Roy W. Hoover, "The Harpagmos Enigma: A Philological Solution," *HTR* 64 (1971): 95-119, here p. 118.

48. Hoover's interpretation "has been adopted as the correct understanding . . . by the majority of recent interpreters" (Hawthorne, "Form of God," p. 102).

49. See already Barth, *Philippians*, p. 62.

50. See Hurst, "Preexistence," p. 90, and further discussion below.

51. So Bockmuehl, *Epistle*, p. 114.

emphasize the absolute importance of this majority translation for understanding the narrative pattern noted above, with the interrelated elements [x], [y], and [z] that Paul puts forward here and throughout his letters. However, we will need to return to the translation of the participle after considering the text of vv. 7-8 and some of the parallels to 2:6-8 elsewhere in Paul.

Philippians 2:7-8: Parallels in the Narrative of the Preexistent and the Incarnate Christ

Phil 2:7-8 recounts Christ's two-step alternative to selfish exploitation of his equality with God, $[z^1]$ and $[z^2]$ in the "narrative pattern." The first step "down" is his voluntary incarnation (self-emptying), the second his voluntary humiliation (self-humbling) and obedience that led to death on a cross. Much could be said about these two verses. Of particular importance to note, however, is the similarity in the two acts narrated and expressed by the two main verbs, "emptied himself" and "humbled himself."

The phrase "emptied himself" in 2:7 should not be read as a reference to the divestiture of something (whether divinity itself or some divine attribute), or even as self-limitation regarding the use of divine attributes,[52] but "figuratively,"[53] as a robust metaphor for total self-abandonment and self-giving,[54] further explained by the attendant participial phrases "taking on the form of a slave" and "being born [found] in human likeness." That is, he "poured himself out,"[55] probably an echo of the suffering servant.[56] The lan-

---

52. So Ben Witherington, *Friendship and Finances in Philippi: The Letter of Paul to the Philippians* (Valley Forge: Trinity, 1994), pp. 66-67.

53. So, e.g., Silva, *Philippians*, 2nd ed., p. 114 and Gerald F. Hawthorne, *Philippians*, WBC (Waco: Word, 1983), p. 86 ("a poetic, hymnlike" expression).

54. This was recognized already in 1897 by M. R. Vincent: The phrase "emptied himself," says Vincent, is "a graphic expression of the completeness of his self-renunciation. It included all the details of humiliation which follow, and is defined by these. Further definition belongs to speculative theology" (*A Critical and Exegetical Commentary on the Epistles to the Philippians and Philemon*, ICC [New York: Scribner, 1897], p. 59).

55. So Hawthorne (*Philippians*, p. 86) and most recent commentators. That is, Christ gave himself completely, and in so doing he renounced all privilege (Bonnie B. Thurston and Judith M. Ryan, *Philippians and Philemon*, Sacra Pagina [Collegeville: Liturgical, 2003], p. 82 [hereafter cited as Thurston, *Philippians*]).

56. Silva rightly says that the various interpretations of "emptied himself" (see Mar-

guage of "the form of a slave" is clearly an antithesis to "the form of God" in 2:6. It is reminiscent not only of the suffering servant of Isaiah, but also of the plight of those in slavery, "the extreme in respect of deprivation of rights."[57] The parallel phrases "form of God" and "form of a slave" mean that to the extent that this one really took on the form of a slave, he also really was in the form of God — and vice versa.[58]

The divine one emptied himself by becoming a slave, becoming human. So, too, the human one humbled himself by becoming obedient to death. There is continuity of actor and of attitude, of disposition. Phil 2:7-8 narrates the similarity in selfless acts performed by the preexistent Christ and the incarnate Christ/human Jesus.

The Wider Context: "Although" Also Means "Because"

The "although [x] not [y] but [z]" pattern — the story line of "although [status] not [selfishness] but [selflessness]" — appears throughout the Pauline corpus, sometimes explicitly in complete form, sometimes more implicitly and/or abridged. This pattern provides a narrative structure in Philippians and elsewhere to a cruciform life in contrast to "normalcy."[59] We can see this pattern, critical for the exegesis of Philippians 2, in three types of texts: Christological texts, apostolic autobiographical texts, and hortatory (ethical) texts. In fact, two or three types sometimes occur in an interrelated cluster of texts, summarized in the Pauline dictum "Be imitators of me, as I am of Christ" (1 Cor 11:1). Space permits only a consideration of two apostolic autobiographical texts.[60] They will serve to demonstrate that the Pau-

---

tin, *Hymn*, pp. 169-94) all have plausibility because it "may well have evoked a larger network of associations (including Isa 53:12), and those would be part of the 'total' meaning" (p. 114).

57. Moule, "Further Reflexions," p. 268, who unnecessarily downplays the suffering servant allusion.

58. So also, e.g., Thurston, *Philippians*, p. 82.

59. See, e.g., 1 Thess 2:7; 1 Cor 9:12-23 (especially 9:19); 2 Cor 8:9; and my *Cruciformity*, pp. 88-91, 164-75, 181-99, 209-12, 230-61. "Normalcy" is from Crossan and Reed, *In Search of Paul*, pp. 242, 284, *et passim*.

60. Two key Christological texts that echo Phil 2:6-11 in form, syntax, and vocabulary are 2 Cor 8:9 and Rom 15:1-3. In each case, both Christ and believers perform a version of the story of "although [x] not [y] but [z]."

line narrative affirmation "although . . ." also means "because . . . ," whether used autobiographically or christologically.

The first text is 1 Thess 2:6-8. Here Paul depicts his behavior as "although [x] not [y] but [z]" when he says that "although we [x] might have thrown our weight around as apostles, we did not [y] seek honor from humans, but we [z] were gentle among you and were pleased to share with you, not only the gospel, but our own selves."[61] Similarly, in 1 Corinthians 9, Paul puts himself forward as an example of freedom expressing itself in love (i.e., refraining from eating meat offered to idols for the sake of the weaker believers; 1 Corinthians 8) when he tells the Corinthians that "although [x] as an apostle I was free, and I had the right to take a wife along with me and the right to be paid for my ministry, I did not [y] make use of any of these rights but rather [z] enslaved myself to all in multiple ways, including self-support and adaptability to different kinds of people" (1 Cor 9:1-23, paraphrased summary). Paul hopes the meat-eating Corinthians will act similarly toward the non-meat-eaters.

In these two texts, Paul claims that although [x] *as an apostle — by virtue of being in fact an apostle, and only by virtue of this "preexisting condition"* — he had certain apostolic rights and could have exercised power in certain ways, he freely chose not [y] to exercise those rights and powers but rather [z] to freely give and spend himself for the good of others (cf. 2 Cor 12:15). He thereby becomes an "imitator" of Christ crucified (1 Cor 11:1), a Christlike slave (cf. *emauton edoulōsa*, lit. "I have enslaved myself," in 1 Cor 9:19 with Phil 2:7, "emptied himself by taking the form of a slave," *heauton ekenōsen morphēn doulou labōn*).

When Paul describes himself as an imitator of Christ and calls others to be imitators of him and thus of Christ (1 Cor 11:1), he is speaking, not about an option, but about a nonnegotiable mandate in which one does not *deny* but rather *exercises* one's true identity as an apostle (and one's true apostolic freedom), or, more generally, one's identity (and true freedom) as a "Christian." *Imitatio Christi* (or, better, *conformatio Christi*) is nonnegotiable because those whose freedom is defined by being *in* Christ must be conformed *to* Christ, as Phil 2:5 suggests by linking 2:1-4 to 2:6-11. Thus when Paul or the Corinthian community performs the narrative "*although* [x] not [y] but [z]," this performance is also a matter of "*because* [x] not [y] but [z]." For instance, when Paul says he did not exercise his apostolic authority (1 Thess

---

61. My translation.

2:7) or rights (1 Cor 9:12-18), he is saying that he acted in this way (1) *although* he had certain rights by virtue of his status as an apostle, and (2) *in spite of* normal expectations of apostles, but also (3) *because* he is an apostle of the self-giving and loving crucified Lord. Thus in not throwing his weight around and in forgoing rights, Paul is acting *in* character, not *out of* character as an apostle.

For Paul, the possession of a right to act in a certain way has an inherent, built-in mandate to exercise truly the status that provides the right by sometimes refraining from the exercise of that right out of love for others. This is not to *deny* one's apostolic or general Christian identity (and associated rights), or to void it, or to put it aside, or to empty oneself of it, but to *exercise* it as an act of Christlike love. For Paul, love does not seek its own interest or edification but rather that of others (1 Cor 13:5; 1 Cor 8:1b), which is the core meaning of conformity to Christ. Apostolic or general Christian freedom and identity are revealed in the performance of "not [y] but [z]." Thus the "[x]" in the narrative pattern is preceded simultaneously, in effect, by both "although" and "because."

We see, then, that Paul believes that in his decisions not to use or exploit his apostolic power and rights, he does not *renounce* his apostleship or *divest himself* of his apostleship but in fact *exercises* true apostleship because he thereby acts in ways that are in conformity to Christ. That is to say, *as* an apostle — an ambassador (2 Cor 5:20) of the self-emptying, crucified Lord — Paul acts kenotically and cruciformly. Thus Paul's use of the narrative pattern "although [x] not [y] but [z]" to recount his own narrative identity as an apostle confirms the interpretation of Phil 2:6 offered above based on philology and grammar. That is, the "[x]" in the pattern represents a status that is *already possessed* and that can be either exploited for selfish gain or not. Moreover, the evidence of truly possessing such a status is in the refusal to exploit it selfishly and thus to use it in such a selfless way that its use *seems* to be a renunciation of the status but is *in fact* a different-from-normal manner of incarnating that status.

Looking at Paul's use of this "although [x] not [y] but [z]" pattern also confirms the suggestion that the "not [y] but [z]" dimension of the pattern is in fact constitutive of the "[x]" dimension of the pattern. That is to say, "not [y] but [z]" glosses, or explicates, "[x]." Paul's apostolic status ([x]) is most truly and fully exercised, not in throwing his weight around — coercively making use of his power to compel or order others to act in certain ways — or making use of his right to financial support ([y]), but in practicing self-

24

giving, Christlike, parental love (1 Thessalonians 2) or enslaving himself by working with his hands in self-support so as not to be a burden to others (1 Corinthians 9) ([z]).

So, too, to return to Philippians, Christ's status of being "in the form of God" (and thus possessing "equality with God") — his [x] — was most truly and fully exercised, not in exploiting that status for selfish advantage ([y]), but in the self-emptying and self-enslaving that manifested itself in incarnation and crucifixion ([z]). Moreover, the similarity in the christological and apostolic uses of this pattern leads us also to conclude, in light of the similar pattern used to describe appropriate behavior in Christ generally (e.g., Phil 2:1-4), that the true and full exercise of "mere Christianity" (as opposed to apostleship) also involves the practice of "not [y] but [z]."

In sum, Paul's use of the "although [x] not [y] but [z]" pattern elsewhere confirms that the pattern narrates an existing condition that is not exploited, and it suggests that the one who does "not [y] but [z]" acts in character for one who is [x]; that is, "although [x] not [y] but [z]" also means "because [x] not [y] but [z]." It is not just *although* Christ, Paul, and all believers possess a certain identity ([x]) that their story has a certain shape (not [y] but [z]); it is also *because* they possess that identity.

Philippians 2:6-8: The Counterintuitive Narrative Identity of Christ and of God

We may now come to the conclusion that the text of Phil 2:6-8 reveals the narrative identity of the Messiah Jesus as one who possessed equality with God ([x]), did not exploit it for selfish advantage ([y]), but, like a slave, emptied himself in incarnation and humbled himself obediently ([z]) such that the result was death — death on a cross. By examining the parallels to Paul's description of his own apostleship, we have seen that the "not [y] but [z]" dimension of this pattern actually reveals the full and true being of the "[x]" dimension of the pattern. That is, Christ's divinity, and thus divinity itself, is being narratively defined as kenotic and cruciform in character. The text "subverts and even lampoons how millions within the Roman Empire took it for granted that somebody with the 'form of God' should act."[62] Phil 2:6-8 narrates the counterintuitive kenotic and cruciform identity of God dis-

62. Crossan and Reed, *In Search of Paul*, p. 289.

played in Christ. That is, "Although he was in the form of God" really means "Because he was in the form of God."

This of course seems at least paradoxical, if not dubious. We must now return, therefore, to the sense of the participle *hyparchōn* in Phil 2:6. As noted in the initial discussion of 2:6 above, the voluntary, dramatic, and unexpected downward shift in status narrated in Phil 2:6-8 compels us to translate that participle, not merely temporally ("while he was" or "while being"), but concessively: "although he was." But before we can also solidify the argument of the preceding section that the participial phrase should also be translated "because he was," we must next wrestle with the question of how to account for the clearly concessive character of the narrative ("although [x]") that, on first read, would suggest that the "not [y] but [z]" dimension of the narrative indicates, not Christ's divinity, but his repudiation of divinity, or at least of divine prerogative. This has been, of course, one of the common interpretations of this text.

Having established the importance of recognizing both that Christ already possessed equality with God and that the participle *hyparchōn* is used concessively ("although"), we must now carefully consider the semantic sense of this concessive use of the participle in the construction "although [x] not [y] but [z]." What Crossan and Reed call "the normalcy of imperial divinity"[63] forms the basic assumption lying behind the concessive use of the participle in 2:6. Nevertheless, two fundamentally different senses about what is being conceded are possible. One implies that Christ's condescension was a *contravention* of his true identity, while the other implies that it was the *embodiment* of his true identity. Option one would be something like this:

> Although Messiah Jesus was in the form of God, a status that means the exercise of power, he acted *out of* character — in a shockingly ungodlike manner, contrary in fact to true (imperial) divinity — when he emptied and humbled himself.

In this reading, Christ, in effect, renounced his deity, or at least some aspect of it. He acted abnormally for one possessing equality with God. That is, the form of God that Christ had (and thus also essential divinity) is *in fact* one that would never condescend to the humiliation of incarnation and crucifixion. To do so would in fact be ungodlike.

---

63. Crossan and Reed, *In Search of Paul*, p. 284.

Option two would be something like the following:

Although Messiah Jesus was in the form of God, a status people assume means the exercise of power, he acted *in* character — in a shockingly ungodlike manner according to normal but misguided human perceptions of divinity, contrary to what we would expect but, in fact, in accord with true divinity — when he emptied and humbled himself.

In this reading, Christ *exercised* his deity. What is *out of* character for normal divinity in our misguided perception of the reality of the form of God is actually *in* character for *this* form of God. That is, although Christ was in the form of God, which leads us to certain expectations, he subverted and deconstructed those expectations when he emptied and humbled himself, which he did *because* he was the *true* form of God.

In other words, such a form of God (and thus also essential divinity) is *in normal human perception* one that would never condescend to incarnation and crucifixion. Normal human perception of deity is such that the story of Christ is counterintuitive, abnormal, and absurd as a story of God.[64]

That this is precisely Paul's point is confirmed by 1 Cor 1:18-25.[65] There Paul argues that Christ crucified is the counterintuitive reality of divine wisdom and power, that the cross is in fact *theophanic* — revelatory of God's essential attributes, known in the reality and the narrative of the crucified Messiah. Thus Paul is doing in Philippians 2 something very similar to what he does in 1 Corinthians 1: reconstructing the meaning of God's essential attributes and thus the meaning of divinity itself. Like the wisdom of God and the power of God, so also the very form of God is displayed for Paul on the cross by the one who was and is equal to God. The story of Christ in 2:6-8 show us that kenosis — specifically cruciform kenosis, or cruciformity — is the essential attribute of God while at the same time, paradoxically, being the expression of divine freedom (parallel to Paul and his apostleship/kenosis/freedom, according to 1 Thessalonians 2 and 1 Corinthians 9).[66]

---

64. C. F. D. Moule ("Further Reflexions," p. 264) believes that 2:6b-8 presents a story of the "essence of divinity" and thus translates 2:6a as follows: "who, although in the form of God (and therefore, by worldly reckoning, one who might have been expected to help himself to whatever he wanted). . . ."

65. The connection between Phil 2:6-11 and 1 Cor 1:18-25 is also made, independently, by Fowl, *Philippians*, p. 96. See further discussion of 1 Cor 1:18-25 in chapter three below.

66. If we are correct that 2:6-8 as a whole narrates a theophany, then Fowl rightly argues that Christ's self-emptying is not primarily about a one-time decision but a divine "dis-

God, we must now say, is essentially kenotic, and indeed essentially cruciform.[67] Kenosis, therefore, does not mean Christ's emptying himself of his divinity (or of anything else), but rather Christ's *exercising* his divinity, his equality with God.

Calvin, followed by Barth, claimed that "the *humilitas carnis* (humility of the flesh) covers the *divina majestas* (divine majesty) like a curtain."[68] Similarly, Gregory of Elvira said that Christ's majesty and divinity, though never lost, were "momentarily hidden," as the sun is briefly hidden by a cloud.[69] Many of the Fathers were very concerned to argue that Christ's self-emptying was not the termination of his deity, which is permanent. We must agree that the (metaphorical) self-emptying is not the end of Christ's divinity. But is it really the case that Christ's self-emptying or humility *hides* his divinity? Is it not rather Paul's point that the humility of incarnation and cross *reveals* the divine majesty, like a *transparent* curtain? "Look here to see true divinity," calls Paul.[70]

If this line of reasoning is correct, then we must translate the participle

---

position of self-emptying" that displays the form and glory of God to humans from incarnation to cross to exaltation (Fowl, *Philippians,* p. 96, with a footnote reference to Wright, *Climax,* p. 84). William C. Placher (*Narratives of a Vulnerable God: Christ, Theology, and Scripture* [Louisville: Westminster John Knox, 1994], p. 64) therefore also correctly refers to 2:6 as a narrative of "generosity" and "mutual deference" that "characterizes all the Persons of the triune God." And Bauckham (*God Crucified,* p. viii) is right to say that "[t]he inclusion of Jesus in the unique divine identity had implications not only for who Jesus is but also for who God is. . . . [N]ot only the pre-existent and the exalted Jesus but also the earthly, suffering, humiliated and crucified Jesus belongs to the unique identity of God."

67. By "cruciform" I do not mean that God is constrained in being or act by a particular (Roman) form of death, namely, crucifixion. Rather, I mean to say that because Paul's understanding of God's kenotic character is inseparable from the revelation of that character in Christ's cross, we must define this divine kenosis with content derived from Paul's narratives of the cross, especially voluntary rejection of power/privilege and humble self-giving.

68. Barth, *Philippians,* p. 63, in agreement with Calvin.

69. *On the Faith* 88-89, cited in Mark J. Edwards, *Galatians, Ephesians, Philippians,* Ancient Christian Commentary on Scripture, New Testament VIII (Downers Grove: InterVarsity, 1999), p. 242.

70. This is only to say that Christ's humility reveals rather than hides his divinity. It does not at all imply that this revelation is therefore easy to accept as such, for this form of revelation is completely unexpected. Nor does it conflict with the emphasis of J. Louis Martyn on the *apocalypsis* of God in Christ as divine invasion and rupture. See, e.g., his *Galatians,* AB 33A (New York: Doubleday, 1997), Comment 3, pp. 97-104.

hyparchōn in 2:6 as "because" in addition to "although" — "in addition to" because we should not relinquish the importance of what is conveyed semantically by the translation "although," and yet we should indeed conclude that at the deepest level the "although" of v. 6 is in fact a "because." Without accepting all the tenets of a particular linguistic theory,[71] I would suggest that it is helpful to distinguish between this text's surface structure ("although") and its deep structure ("because"). The participle *hyparchōn* in Phil 2:6 may also be translated causatively ("because") since "Because he was in the form of God" represents the deep structure of the text. Christ Jesus did what he did because that is what it means to be in the form of God. Cruciform kenosis is the counterintuitive "truth about God."[72] It is the constitutive characteristic of the divine identity that this narrative reveals. Phil 2:6-11 is therefore rightly called a "narrative of a vulnerable God" (to use Placher's apt phrase),[73] and it displays the cross as theophany.

We would be right, therefore, to join the line of interpreters that runs from Moule to Wright, Hawthorne, Bockmuehl, and Fowl and render Phil 2:6a as "precisely because" Christ Jesus was in the form of God and equal with God, he emptied himself. . . .[74]

Philippians 2:9-11

We have focused on the first half of the poem, but must now turn briefly to the second part. The imperial and cosmic overtones of 2:9-11 should not be

---

71. That is, transformational grammar, from which the terms to be used are borrowed.

72. A phrase from Stanley M. Hauerwas and William J. Willimon, *The Truth about God: The Ten Commandments in Christian Life* (Nashville: Abingdon, 1999).

73. Placher, *Narratives of a Vulnerable God: Christ, Theology, and Scripture*.

74. Moule writes of the "causative sense: precisely because" ("The Manhood of Jesus in the New Testament," in *Christ, Faith and History: Cambridge Studies in Christology*, ed. S. W. Sykes and J. P. Clayton [Cambridge: Cambridge University Press, 1972], pp. 95-110, here p. 97; see also his "Further Reflexions," pp. 264-65). Wright notes the influence of Moule (*Climax*, p. 83 n. 110) and concludes that "the one who was eternally 'equal with God' expressed that equality precisely in the sequence of events referred to in vv. 6-8" (*Climax*, p. 90; cf. pp. 83-84). Wright also says, "If my whole argument is correct, *the causative sense is clearly the one required*" (Wright, *Climax*, p. 83 n. 110, emphasis added). Cf. Bockmuehl, *Epistle*, pp. 133-34. Fowl (*Philippians*, p. 94; cf. pp. 94-97) interprets 2:6 to mean "precisely because." Barth had said that the text is about "what Christ, acting as God's Equal, is, does, and means" (*Philippians*, p. 61). See also Hawthorne, *Philippians*, p. 104.

missed.[75] Jesus is honored along with God the Father as integral to the divine identity.[76] Jesus shares in the reign of God over all creation, continuing the scriptural theme of God's rightful rule over the cosmos and challenging all others who might issue a claim to universal sovereignty or demand obeisance from human beings (or any other creatures). As we will see below, the character of Jesus' lordship continues to overturn normal expectations about the meaning of divinity and of divine power.

In considering 2:9-11, we must especially avoid the conclusion that God the Father is here portrayed as "promoting" Jesus by virtue of his self-emptying and self-humbling. Something quite different is happening. Verses 9-11 suggest that human beings will appropriately render a kind of homage to Jesus that is properly due only to God, as the quotation of Isa 45:23 makes clear. Thus the "therefore" of v. 9 does not signal that God has promoted Jesus to a new status, as if divinity (for a Jew) could be manufactured or gained by some act, however noble. Rather, it indicates that God has publicly vindicated and recognized Jesus' self-emptying and self-humbling as the display of true divinity that he already had, and that makes the worship of Jesus as Lord (i.e., YHWH, the God of Israel) perfectly appropriate.[77]

Jesus' exaltation is not the divine reward for his incarnation and death as God's suffering servant (as this text is normally interpreted), but divine recognition that his suffering-servant behavior is in fact truly "lordly," even

75. As Oakes points out, there is also a strong echo of imperial events: "raised to power on account of deeds, universal submission, universal acclamation as Lord" (*Philippians*, p. 174; cf. pp. 129-74).

76. Richard Bauckham has called Phil 2:9-11 "a christological version of Deutero-Isaianic eschatological monotheism" ("Worship of Jesus," p. 133), a fitting summary of the application of themes from Isaiah 45 and elsewhere to Jesus that occurs in these verses. In Christ's humiliation and exaltation, God's salvation, sovereignty, and sole deity are manifested and acknowledged. The worship of Jesus is appropriate because "Jesus himself is seen as belonging to the unique divine identity" (p. 136). "God's sole deity receives universal worship when *the crucified and exalted Jesus reveals the unique divine identity* to which he himself belongs" (p. 136, emphasis added).

77. Against promotion, see also Fowl, *Philippians*, p. 104. Larry J. Kreitzer says that we should not overload one word *(hyperypsōsen)* to conclude that Christ's new station is higher than his preexistent station ("'When He at Last Is First!': Philippians 2:9-11 and the Exaltation of the Lord," in Martin and Dodd, *Where Christology Began*, pp. 111-27, here p. 118). Thurston (*Philippians*, p. 84) insists correctly that the contrast of "super-exalted" is not with the original state but with the "absolute degradation." On the worship of Jesus and thus "rethinking God," see also N. T. Wright, *Paul: In Fresh Perspective* (Minneapolis: Fortress, 2005), pp. 83-107.

godly, behavior. C. F. D. Moule renders the beginning of 2:9 as follows: "And that is why (i.e. the fact that Jesus displayed the self-giving humility which is the essence of divinity is the reason why) God so greatly exalted him. . . ."[78]

There are also here intimations of the common early Christian theme of the Son's obedience to the Father (despite the absence of "Son" language, see the language of obedience in v. 8 and of Father in v. 11), a theme that elsewhere in the NT brings together language that affirms both Christ's divinity and his incarnated humanity (e.g., Hebrews, John). As in the theology of Hebrews (1:1-14; 5:1-10; 10:5-10), so also in Philippians 2: Jesus' obedience demonstrates that he is in fact God's Son, God's image and reflection and glory. The underlying logic seems to be that the principle of "like Father, like Son" means that inasmuch as Christ does the will of his Father, he does so because he is in the Father's likeness, even as he freely chooses to exercise obedience as the Son and human being that he is. But of course this underlying logic, in Paul's case, assumes that the servant-like, kenotic activities attributed to Christ in 2:6-8 are in fact divine in character, or to put it the other way around, that divinity has kenotic servanthood as its essential attribute.

In light of the various echoes of Isaiah 40–55 in Philippians 2, we are compelled to conclude that its author reads Isaiah 40–55 as a key theological source (and perhaps even as an integrated unit) with a radical message: that the suffering servant is one with the universal Lord, and the universal Lord is one with the suffering servant. It turns out that the God who is sovereign but also condescending in compassion (Isa 57:14-21) has been manifested in the career of the servant. Phil 2:6-11 asserts this while recognizing that the servant was raised and vindicated by someone other than himself (the fourth Isaianic hymn plainly stating this twice: 52:13; 53:12), such that at least a binitarian theology, or christological monotheism, is the necessary conclusion.[79] *The identifying characteristic of this Isaianic eternal and sovereign Lord is, henceforth, kenotic servanthood.*

The notion of kenotic servanthood also brings us back to the subject of echoes of Adam in Philippians 2. As the obedient suffering servant who behaves in the pattern "although [x] not [y] but [z]," Christ displays not only true divinity but also true humanity. Unlike Adam, he does not exploit his status as God's image-bearer or disobey God the Father. Rather, he acts in

---

78. Moule, "Further Reflexions," pp. 264-65.
79. See Bauckham, *God Crucified*, especially pp. 46-79.

obedience to the Father in a way that serves not himself but others, bringing about their redemption from sin.[80]

Finally, the exaltation raises also the question of the ongoing significance of the humiliation. The confession "Jesus is Lord" means, implicitly, that the crucified, servant Jesus, and no other Jesus, is Lord. There is continuity between his humiliated and his exalted status, just as there was continuity between his preexistent and his incarnate, humiliated status (revealed in the parallel phrases "emptied himself" and "humbled himself"). That is, Jesus' lordship, paradoxically, has the form of servanthood even in the present (which is why it is no surprise that Paul tells the Romans that Christ is praying for us [Rom 8:34]). That is why a community that lives "in Christ" (Phil 2:1-5) will be shaped like the story of Christ narrated in 2:6-8. Such a community does not simply remember and imitate a story; rather, it experiences the present activity of Father, Son, and Spirit mentioned in 2:1-13, which is formation into the eternal, unchanging image of the eternal Son of God (cf. Rom 8:29; 2 Cor 3:18), an image manifested in the story of 2:6-8.[81] This transformative work of the triune God in humans is what the Christian tradition, especially in the East, has called theosis, as noted in the introduction to this book.

Phil 2:9-11, then, narrates God's vindication of the story of Christ as the story of true humanity and true divinity. In this part of Paul's master story, we see how God's exaltation of the Son confirms the character of true divinity and calls humanity to become truly human by sharing in that divinity.

Theological Conclusions

Having explored Phil 2:6-11 in some depth, we may now draw some theological conclusions.

The Counterintuitive Kenotic Character of the God of the Cross

The counterintuitive God revealed in Christ is kenotic and cruciform, the Eternal vulnerable and self-giving One, the God of power-in-weakness.

---

80. Even though Philippians 2 is not explicitly soteriological, as a rereading of the servant hymns it is clearly implicitly soteriological within its larger canonical-literary context, just as it is clearly ethical within its literary context in Philippians and the Pauline corpus.

81. See also Crossan and Reed, *In Search of Paul*, p. 290.

Thus we may now paraphrase Ernst Käsemann, who said that the cross was the signature of the Risen One, and assert that the cross is the signature of the *Eternal* One.[82] Any other understandings of God are henceforth rendered either incomplete or obsolete or idolatrous.

Some may object to the notion of a cruciform God and argue that in the discussion of God's holiness, we cannot forget God's majesty and power. Here John Webster is helpful, because he rightly defines God's holiness, not as pure majesty, but as "majesty in relation."[83] Because God's majesty and God's relationality cannot be separated, we must understand God's majesty in light of God's revealed relationality. We do not simply hold the majesty and relationality of God in *tension;* with Paul, we must see them in *concert,* a unison revealed in the power of the cross. God is not a god of power *and* weakness but the God of power *in* weakness. As Webster also reminds us, we must always keep divine activity and divine attribute together: God's actions are self-revelatory, the expression of God's essence or character.[84] Thus if the cross is theophanic, God must be understood as essentially cruciform.[85] This is the corollary of Bauckham's thesis in his treatment of Paul in *God Crucified*. It was also clearly articulated by John Howard Yoder in reflecting on the particularity of incarnation and cross:

> An apostolic report can be forgotten or contested. A communal memory can grow dim or be reinterpreted or seem strange. That one event way back there is so specific and so local. Can we really go on celebrating it as the

82. The cross is "the signature of the one who is risen": Ernst Käsemann, "The Saving Significance of the Death of Jesus in Paul," in *Perspectives on Paul*, trans. Margaret Kohl (Philadelphia: Fortress, 1971; repr. Mifflintown: Sigler, 1996), pp. 32-59, here p. 56.

83. John Webster, *Holiness* (Grand Rapids: Eerdmans, 2003), p. 41. See further in chapter three below.

84. Cf. Webster, *Holiness*, pp. 39-40, and Colin Gunton, *Act and Being: Towards a Theology of the Divine Attributes* (Grand Rapids: Eerdmans, 2002). See also Francis Watson, "The Triune Divine Identity: Reflection on Pauline God Language, in Disagreement with J. D. G. Dunn," *JSNT* 80 (2000): 99-124. Watson (pp. 105-11) relies on the work of Hans Frei (see p. 105 n. 11), who argued that intentions that have become acts reveal and constitute a person's identity, to conclude that "[a]ction is the mode of divine being" (p. 106).

85. See also Gorman, *Cruciformity*, especially pp. 9-18, and Miroslav Volf, *Exclusion and Embrace: A Theological Exploration of Identity, Otherness, and Reconciliation* (Nashville: Abingdon, 1996), pp. 22-31 *et passim,* though (surprisingly) Volf does not deal with Philippians. For several reasons, I prefer the designation "cruciform God" to "crucified God." For one thing, it conveys the idea that God is habitually and essentially cruciform, rather than occasionally or particularly so. (See also *Cruciformity*, pp. 17-18 n. 26.)

hinge of history? It is to this that the authors or the poets behind the high points of the New Testament witness respond when they proclaim that what happened on the cross is a revelation of the shape of what God is, and of what God does, in the total drama of history. They affirm as a permanent pattern what in Jesus was a particular event. The eternal Word condescending to put himself at our mercy, the creative power behind the universe emptying itself, pouring out itself into the frail mold of humanity, has the same shape as Jesus. God has the same shape as Jesus, and he always has had. The cross is what creation is all about. What Jesus did was local, of course, because that is how serious and real our history is to God. But what the cross was locally is universally and always the divine nature.[86]

Here we must emphasize that the cross is not just one theophany among many; it is the *definitive* theophany, as we will consider again in later chapters. Unfortunately, however, the embedded theology of most Christians still revolves around a non-cruciform model of God's power, and a crucial corrective is needed. If we know God in the cross, then we should also know that God's majesty is one of power-in-weakness.[87]

The Idolatry of "Normal" Divinity

In light of this first theological conclusion, we must affirm that the "normal" "civil" god of power and might is an idol, and it must be named as such. This god is not the Lord God revealed in Jesus Christ and narrated in the theopolitics of Phil 2:6-11. The "normal" god of civil religion combines pa-

---

86. John Howard Yoder, *He Came Preaching Peace* (Eugene: Wipf and Stock, 1998), pp. 84-85. Yoder reinforces our claim that in self-emptying and self-giving, God in Christ does not contravene the divine identity but expresses it. For that reason, a suffering, cruciform God is not a God who has changed. I am not maintaining that God in Christ suffers simply to reveal his character as a "suffering God" and therefore simply to identify with those who are suffering. While this is certainly true (minus the word "simply"), in Christ God really undergoes suffering and death *in order finally to undo both suffering and death* in the vindicating resurrection of the crucified Christ, the first fruits of humanity's resurrection and a microcosm of the redemption of the entire cosmos from suffering and death. (My thanks to Andy Johnson for making this point in personal correspondence, May 2008.)

87. For the cross as epistemological criterion, see also J. Louis Martyn, "Epistemology at the Turn of the Ages" (originally published in 1967), in *Theological Issues in the Letters of Paul* (Nashville: Abingdon, 1997), pp. 89-110.

triotism and power; this is the god of many American leaders and of many Americans generally. (This god has, of course, had many other incarnations in human history.) Most especially idolatrous in light of our exegesis of Philippians 2 is the image of God (and/or of Christ) as military power incarnate, whether in the crusades or in Iraq or at Armageddon. As the Spanish historian-theologian Jaume Botey Vallès said about the political theology that underwrote the U.S. response to 9/11, including the invasion and occupation of Iraq, the god of George W. Bush (and, we might add, of many other presidents, prime ministers, and kings) is a god of military might.[88] That simply is not the God revealed by Jesus, Vallès rightly says. Neither is it the cruciform God of Paul. In other words, military power is not the power of the cross, and such misconstrued notions of divine power have nothing to do with the majesty or holiness of the triune God known in the weakness of the cross. The "civil" god, though perfectly "normal," is not only unholy; it is an idol.

A Cruciform, Kenotic Chalcedonian Definition

Traditionally, Phil 2:6-11 has been read as a text about Christ, but we have read it also as a text about God. It is of course about both, about Christ as God incarnate. The fully divine and fully human Christ of kenosis and cross is the definitive theophany. It is especially imperative that we see the *modus operandi* of both incarnation and cross as theophanic. The narrative identity of Christ reveals a similar disposition in his preexistent and his incarnate life: self-emptying and self-humbling.[89] This is theologically important because it demonstrates that for Paul true humanity and true divinity are analogous at the most fundamental level.

We therefore do not need to agree with Richard Bauckham's claim — in his otherwise superb book — that N. T. Wright's taking both a "divine incarnational and an Adam christological approach" to Phil 2:6-11 is an example of trying to have one's cake and eat it, too.[90] Again, quite the contrary is the case in light of the continuity of the preexistent and incarnate Son of

88. Jaume Botey Vallès, *El Dios de Bush* [*Bush's God*], Cuadernos Cristianisme i Justícia 126 (Barcelona: Centre d'Estudia Cristianisme i Justícia, 2004), especially pp. 19-25.

89. So also, e.g., Witherington, *Friendship and Finances*, p. 66.

90. Bauckham, *God Crucified*, p. 57 n. 7. For Wright's argument holding together representative Israel/humanity and incarnate divinity, see his *Climax*, pp. 56-98.

God. Christ was the antithesis of Adam because he truly and faithfully incarnated the image of God that Adam, by his disobedience, embodied unfaithfully and falsely. By being unlike Adam, Christ revealed his own true divinity as well as his true humanity. James Dunn goes so far as to say that "[e]ven if it were judged not to be an expression of Adam Christology, it [Phil 2:6-11] would still be a powerful way of saying that in Christ, his death and resurrection, God's original design for humanity finally achieved concrete shape and fulfillment." This, Dunn says, is a life of "serving and not grasping," and it is the basis of the appeal in 2:1-4.[91]

Kenosis is thus the *sine qua non* of both divinity and humanity, as revealed in the incarnation and cross of Christ, the one who was truly God and became truly human.[92] His preexistent and incarnate actions — [z^1] and [z^2] in our narrative analysis — had essentially the same character. As Chalcedonian and therefore anachronistic as this claim will sound to some, it seems to be the inevitable conclusion of the line of thought we have been pursuing; it is Chalcedon with a Pauline, cruciform twist.

True Humanity as Counter-Imperial Theoformity

To be fully human is to be Christlike and thus Godlike in this kenotic and cruciform sense. Cruciformity, it turns out, is really *theoformity*. That is, in more traditional Western theological language, *imitatio Christi* is really *imitatio Dei*. John Chrysostom, in the East, said as much in his homily on Phil 2:5-8: "For nothing so sustains the great and philosophic soul in the performance of good works as learning that through this one is becoming like God."[93] The (primarily) Eastern theological vocabulary for this process was,

---

91. Dunn, "Preexistence," p. 79.

92. Some may object, with an anonymous reviewer of an earlier form of this chapter, that the assertion about God's essential kenotic character limits God's freedom, making kenosis a divine necessity rather than a free act of love and grace. While I want to maintain with the Christian tradition (and Paul) that God in Christ acts in freedom and grace, I also want to maintain (with Paul, I think) the corollary, if paradoxical, conviction that if the cross is theophanic, kenosis must be something other than one of several options on the divine table.

93. *Homily on Philippians* 7.2.5-8, cited in Edwards, *Ancient Christian Commentary*, p. 236. Cyril of Alexandria, who was particularly fond of Philippians 2, emphasizes both the incarnation and the exaltation as the means of theosis: "For he humbled himself that he

and is, theosis. The emphasis is on transformation by union, or participation, more than imitation, and is more appropriate than the language of *imitatio,* as we will see in later chapters. From either perspective, however, the key point for now is that human beings, including Adam, are most like God when they act kenotically. In Christ's preexistent and incarnate kenosis we see truly what God is truly like, and we simultaneously see truly what Adam/humanity truly should have been, truly was not, and now truly can be in Christ. *Kenosis is theosis.* To be like Christ crucified is to be both most godly and most human. Christification is divinization, and divinization is humanization.[94]

Our text provides the basis for understanding this theoformity, or theosis, as a counter-imperial style of life. Fowl puts it this way:

> In worlds such as ours and Paul's where power is manifested in self-assertion, acquisition, and domination, Christ reveals that God's power, indeed the triune nature, is made known to the world in the act of self-emptying. Self-emptying is not so much a single act as the fundamental disposition of the eternal relationship of the Father, Son, and Spirit. The incarnation, life, death, and resurrection of Jesus become the decisive revelation to us of that "self-emptying" that eternally characterizes the triune life of God.[95]

The goal of the Christian community is to allow the life and Spirit of this God, rather than the imperial spirit of domination and acquisition, to flow in and through it — to participate in God.

---

might exalt that which was by nature lowly to his own high station; and wore the form of a servant, though he was by nature Lord and Son of God, that he might uplift that which was by nature enslaved, to the dignity of sonship, in conformity with his own likeness, and in his image" (*Commentary on John* 2.663). Cyril's point is well taken, but it is a faithful interpretation of Paul only to the extent that it includes Paul's paradoxical perspective that our exaltation to conformity with Christ's nature is a process, in this life, of becoming more servant-like and self-emptying. (I owe this reference to Cyril to Ben Blackwell.)

94. The term "Christification" is used by Panayiotis Nellas, *Deification in Christ: Orthodox Perspectives on the Nature of the Human Person,* trans. Norman Russell (Crestwood: St. Vladimir's Seminary Press, 1997). Though less common than theosis or its synonyms, divinization and deification, the term "Christification" is a reminder that for Christians theosis must always be understood christologically.

95. Fowl, *Philippians,* pp. 96-97.

Kenosis, Crucifixion, and the Missio Dei

Finally, we must note that our reading of Phil 2:6-11 suggests that kenosis and crucifixion are intimately expressive of the *missio Dei* in the world, because divine being and act are inseparable. The community that bears witness to this divine mission (Phil 2:12-18) does so through participation, by means of Spirit-enabled theoformity, in the reality of the life of the kenotic triune God that is described in Phil 2:1-4 and revealed in Paul's master story of the incarnate, crucified, and exalted Messiah (Phil 2:6-11) who effects the eschatological mission of God the Father. This is Paul's story of God's salvific mission in the world, and it challenges all other claims to universal salvation on offer, whether ancient or modern.[96] A people characterized by communal kenosis for the good of the world is both the means and the goal of God's saving activity here and now.

Conclusion

This chapter has explored aspects of the Christology, ethics, and especially theology (proper) of Phil 2:6-11, one of the most significant texts in the Pauline corpus, by focusing on the interpretation and significance of 2:6. We have shown that both the concessive ("although") and the causative ("because") interpretations of the participle *hyparchōn* ("being") in Phil 2:6 are correct and theologically significant, the former being the surface structure of the text, the latter its deep structure. The *surface* structure ("although . . .") is significant because it is part of a linguistic pattern that Paul exploits christologically and ethically throughout his letters: "although [x] not [y] but [z]." At the same time, because Paul says that Christ was in the form of God and that this equality with God was properly expressed through the kenosis of incarnation and crucifixion, we can say that the *deep* structure of the text is causative: "because. . . ." Thus Paul compels us to rethink God and to speak of a cruciform God or, in the words of Crossan and Reed, a "kenotic divinity."

The chapter has also argued that the incarnation and cross manifest, and the exaltation recognizes, both Christ's true divinity and his true hu-

---

96. See especially Sylvia C. Keesmaat, "Crucified Lord or Conquering Saviour: Whose Story of Salvation?" *HBT* 26 (2004): 69-93.

manity, all of which leads us in a Chalcedonian direction, though with a Pauline (cruciform) twist. The understanding of God in Paul that emerges from this interpretation was then linked to John Webster's notion of divine holiness as "majesty in relation," which, for Paul, means power in weakness. We then contrasted this counterintuitive view of God with popular notions of divinity that focus on power, especially military power, and offered it as the foundation of a counter-imperial lifestyle. To be truly human is to be Christlike, which is to be Godlike, which is to be kenotic and cruciform. Theosis is the process of transformation into the image of this God.

These constitute some key aspects of the theological significance of Paul's master story in Phil 2:6-11. They lead us to consider how one enters into this life of God to which Paul's master story bears witness. That is the subject of the next chapter.

CHAPTER 2

"Justified by Faith/Crucified with Christ"

Justification by Co-Crucifixion:
The Logic of Paul's Soteriology

In chapter one we considered Phil 2:6-11 and the character of God manifested in Christ's self-emptying incarnation and self-humbling death by crucifixion — a kenotic, cruciform God. We also briefly considered the nature of participation in the life of that God and introduced the notion of theosis. In this chapter we look especially at Gal 2:15-21 and Rom 6:1–7:6 and thus at the foundational Pauline experience of the God known in Christ's cross, an experience described by Paul both as justification and as death and resurrection with Christ. Our goal is to show the connection between justification, on the one hand, and co-crucifixion and co-resurrection on the other, arguing that for Paul justification is an experience of participating in Christ's resurrection life that is effected by co-crucifixion with him.

This is a much more robust, participatory, and costly understanding of justification than one often finds attributed to Paul. It does not, however, in any sense whatsoever reduce the need for, or meaning(s), of Christ's death as God's gracious salvific act on our behalf while we "still were sinners" (Rom 5:8) and were "dead through our trespasses" (Eph 2:5). Nor is justification by co-crucifixion a form of self-justification or justification by "works," for it is only by grace and the work of God's Spirit that co-crucifixion is possible. What justification by co-crucifixion will imply, however, and not surprisingly, is that a theological rift between justification and sanctification is impossible, because the same Spirit effects both initial and ongoing co-crucifixion with Christ among believers, a lifelong experience of cruciformity or, in light of chapter one, theoformity — theosis.

Introduction

The doctrine of justification is in crisis, or at least in flux.[1] For some, the debate has become an exercise in parallelomania (Samuel Sandmel's term), focusing only on detailed linguistic and comparative studies. For others, it has become an opportunity to question the orthodoxy of one or another of the world's leading biblical scholars or theologians.[2] For still others, it has become an occasion for retrenchment toward the divisions of the sixteenth century.

There have always been legitimate theological arguments about justification, as well as less noble but understandable interconfessional squabbles. But it may also be the case that there is another, more subtle (and thus more dangerous) theological reason for at least some aspects of the current situation regarding justification. To paraphrase Dietrich Bonhoeffer, parts of the Christian church have become enamored with cheap justification. Cheap justification is justification without justice, faith without love, declaration without transformation.

At the same time, however, many students of justification, particularly of Luther's view, have begun to re-think the doctrine.[3] Princeton theologian George Hunsinger has even said that "[f]aith as participation . . . is the very heartbeat of the Reformation" and is "the key to the doctrine of justification

---

1. Among many recent works on the topic, see especially the two volumes of *Justification and Variegated Nomism* (vol. 1, *The Complexities of Second Temple Judaism;* vol. 2, *The Paradoxes of Paul*), ed. Donald Carson, Peter T. O'Brien, and Mark A. Seifrid (Grand Rapids: Baker, 2001, 2004); Mark A. Husbands and Daniel J. Treier, eds., *Justification: What's at Stake in the Current Debates* (Downers Grove: InterVarsity, 2004); Bruce L. McCormack, ed., *Justification in Perspective: Historical Developments and Contemporary Challenges* (Grand Rapids: Baker, 2006); David E. Aune, ed., *Rereading Paul Together: Protestant and Catholic Perspectives on Justification* (Grand Rapids: Baker, 2006); Wayne C. Stumme, ed., *The Gospel of Justification in Christ: Where Does the Church Stand Today?* (Grand Rapids: Eerdmans, 2006); and Douglas A. Campbell, *The Deliverance of God: An Apocalyptic Rereading of Justification in Paul* (Grand Rapids: Eerdmans, 2009).

2. See, for example, N. T. Wright's lament: "My own name has been linked with proposals that have been variously dismissed, scorned, vilified, and anathematized" ("New Perspectives on Paul," in McCormack, ed., *Justification in Perspective*, pp. 243-64, here p. 243). He also describes himself as "regularly . . . carpet bombed" regarding his views on Paul more generally (p. 247).

3. On the rereading of Luther championed especially by the Finnish school see Tuomo Mannermaa, *Christ Present in Faith: Luther's View of Justification* (Minneapolis: Fortress, 2005; orig. 1989), and Carl E. Braaten and Robert W. Jenson, eds., *Union with Christ: The New Finnish Interpretation of Luther* (Grand Rapids: Eerdmans, 1998).

by faith alone."[4] This re-thinking of Luther and other Reformers has shifted the emphasis in Reformation soteriology from declaration and legal fiction to real participation and even "divinization" — a term found even in Luther.[5]

So too in the study of Paul: there is foment and re-thinking, especially about the relationship between faith and participation. In this chapter we will be contending, with Bonhoeffer, for costly justification in Paul. Or, to put it in more academic terms, for a "thick" rather than thin description of justification and of faith.[6]

It is commonplace in the study of Paul to find two basic soteriological models in his writings, the juridical (or judicial) model and the participationist model. (See, e.g., Bart Ehrman's popular text and Douglas Campbell's technical study.[7]) In fact, E. P. Sanders referred to "the relationship among the various soteriological terms" as "the problem of Pauline exegesis."[8] What this chapter will propose is a new model for Pauline soteriology, a new understanding of both justification and participation in

4. George Hunsinger, *"Fides Christo Formata:* Luther, Barth, and the Joint Declaration," in Stumme, ed., *The Gospel of Justification in Christ,* pp. 69-84, here p. 75. Although I agree with the general direction in which Hunsinger is moving, he makes a very unpauline (and rather polemical, anti-Catholic) division between faith and love (see especially p. 79).

5. See Hunsinger, *"Fides Christo Formata,"* pp. 73-77 ("divinization" on p. 77). On Luther, see also Bruce D. Marshall, "Justification as Declaration and Deification," *IJST* 4 (2002): 3-28.

6. Simon Gathercole is aware of this need when he (rightly or wrongly) characterizes N. T. Wright's definition of justification ("reckoned to be in covenant with God") as "minimal" and "minimalistic." See Gathercole's "The Doctrine of Justification in Paul and Beyond: Some Proposals," in McCormack, ed., *Justification in Perspective,* pp. 219-41, here pp. 228-29.

7. Bart Ehrman, *The New Testament: A Historical Introduction to the Early Christian Writings,* 3rd ed. (New York: Oxford University Press, 2004), pp. 353-57 (including a good graphic on p. 357), with special reference to Romans. Ehrman sees the two models (and thinks Paul saw them) as distinct but mutually complementary and compatible. Douglas A. Campbell (*The Quest for Paul's Gospel: A Suggested Strategy* [London/New York: Clark, 2005]) identifies three models, but they really amount to two, a juridical — justification by faith (abbreviated JF) — and a participationist — "pneumatologically participatory martyrological eschatology" (PPME). A third model, "salvation-historical" (SH), receives little attention from Campbell, who incorporates salvation-historical concerns into his version of the participationist model (PPME), Campbell also identifies a fourth possibility, not a model but an "approach," that he labels "anti-theological" (AT), referring to those who see Pauline soteriology as ad hoc, unsystematic, and/or confused.

8. E. P. Sanders, *Paul and Palestinian Judaism: A Comparison of Patterns of Religion* (Philadelphia: Fortress, 1977), p. 508.

Paul, though other scholars of Paul are also beginning to develop similar perspectives.[9]

In this model there will be echoes of Albert Schweitzer, E. P. Sanders, Richard Hays, and, more recently, Douglas Campbell. However, rather than privileging the juridical (justification-by-faith) model (thus many traditional readers), subsuming it under the participationist model (so, e.g., Schweitzer and Sanders[10]), rejecting it in favor of a participatory model (so, e.g., Douglas Campbell[11]), or even allowing the two models to stand in complementary relationship (so, e.g., Ehrman), I want to suggest that for Paul there is *one* soteriological model: justification is by crucifixion, specifically

9. For similar perspectives see the recent essays of Scott Schauf, Martinus de Boer, and Robert C. Tannehill discussed below. I should note that this chapter is a revision of a paper I delivered to the Pauline Soteriology Group of the Society of Biblical Literature at its November 2006 meeting. At the same meeting, Robert Tannehill delivered a paper drawing very similar conclusions (now published as "Participation in Christ: A Central Theme in Pauline Soteriology," in *The Shape of the Gospel: New Testament Essays* [Eugene: Cascade, 2007], pp. 223-37). Neither of us knew of the other's paper or referred explicitly to the published work of the other in those papers. However, we subsequently shared our papers and corresponded about them. Tannehill's work in this recent essay builds on his pioneering work in *Dying and Rising with Christ: A Study in Pauline Theology* (Berlin: Töpelmann, 1966).

10. Sanders, in his classic *Paul and Palestinian Judaism*, stresses Paul's language of participation understood as the transfer of lordships (see especially pp. 466-72, 497-500). Sanders argues that Paul did not distinguish "participatory" and "juristic" categories but kept them together (e.g., pp. 472, 502, 508, as well as 501: "Paul did not have a bifurcated mind" [see also p. 507]) as two kinds of "transfer terms" (pp. 497, 501) corresponding to two different assessments of humanity's plight, transgression and bondage (p. 508). He also insists, however, that "a supposed doctrine of 'righteousness by faith' [in Paul] . . . remains primarily a negative category, directed against the view that obedience to the law is either the necessary or sufficient condition of salvation" (p. 492), and contends that Paul "is not primarily concerned with the juristic categories, although he works with them," for "the real bite of his theology lies in the participatory categories, *even though he himself did not distinguish them this* way" (p. 502; emphasis his). Further, "[o]nce we make the [non-Pauline] distinction between juristic and participationist categories . . . there is no doubt that the latter tell us more about the way Paul 'really' thought" (p. 507). Indeed, Sanders says that Paul's "juristic" language is "sometimes pressed into the service of 'participationist' categories, but never vice versa" (p. 503). Sanders also denies the claim that righteousness was only or even primarily a forensic category (e.g., pp. 494-95, 506).

11. In *The Quest for Paul's Gospel*. Although Campbell claims to incorporate justification by faith into his own participatory model, his all-out polemical attack on justification by faith really amounts to an attempt to supplant it. For example, he finds it possible to read Rom 1:1-17 and 3:21–5:2 in a way that "removes the JF [justification by faith] model" (p. 206). His goal is that JF be "exegetically eliminated" (p. 4) — but "with integrity" (p. 7)! Even more polemical is his *The Deliverance of God*.

co-crucifixion, understood as participation in Christ's act of covenant ful-fillment.[12] This proposal is similar to, but more fully developed than, the covenantal, narrative, and participatory interpretation of justification of-fered by Richard Hays.[13] It also places the accent on slightly different aspects of such an interpretative framework.

A close reading of Gal 2:15-21 and Rom 6:1–7:6, in connection with other passages in Paul (especially Rom 5:1-11; 2 Cor 5:14-21; and, once again, Phil 2:6-11), reveals that the apostle understands faith as co-crucifixion, and "jus-tification by faith" as new life/resurrection via crucifixion with the Messiah Jesus, or "justification by co-crucifixion," and therefore as inherently partici-patory. This chapter explores several interconnected aspects of the logic of Paul's cross-centered participatory soteriology, while also making some brief constructive theological suggestions for contemporary reflection and praxis about that soteriology.

12. The reader should note that I am *not* claiming that this is a new interpretation of justification as a Christian doctrine (though it may, in some sense, be that), but rather of justification *in Paul.* (I should also note that I am building on my own previous work on Paul such that what is new here is really an extension of that work.) Relying on the historical work of Alistair McGrath (*Iustitia Dei*, 224), David Aune notes, rightly I think, that "Luther, followed by Calvin, held the personal union of Christ and the believer in justification (i.e., the *unio mystica*), a position forsaken by Melanchthon," who, Aune asserts, "was primarily responsible for developing the *forensic* conception of justification that became normative in Protestantism" ("Recent Readings of Paul Relating to Justification by Faith," in Aune, *Re-reading Paul Together,* pp. 188-245, here p. 231 n. 230). The Finnish school of Luther interpre-tation would strongly affirm Aune's position on Luther, as would Hunsinger (*"Fides Christo Formata,"* cited in n. 4 above). For the view that Calvin's understanding of justification was forensic, included the imputation of Christ's righteousness to believers, and is the source of the "standard Protestant view," see Bruce L. McCormack, "*Justitia Aliena:* Karl Barth in Con-versation with the Evangelical Doctrine of Imputed Righteousness," in McCormack, ed., *Jus-tification in Perspective,* pp. 167-96, here pp. 169-72. McCormack does not deny the presence of union with Christ in Calvin's theology but considers it a separate element of his soteriology (p. 170). McCormack himself, however, proposes a model of "covenant ontol-ogy" that is closer to mine, arguing that "at its heart, forensicism is deeply ontological" and that "[w]hat we are essentially is a divine act which establishes a covenantal relation" ("What's at Stake in Current Debates over Justification: The Crisis of Protestantism in the West," in Husbands and Treier, eds., *Justification: What's at Stake in the Current Debates,* pp. 81-117, here p. 115).

13. See Richard B. Hays, *The Faith of Jesus Christ: The Narrative Substructure of Galatians 3:1–4:11,* 2nd ed. (Grand Rapids: Eerdmans, 2001), pp. xxix-xxxiii, 210-15; and Hays, "Justification," in *ABD,* ed. David Noel Freedman (6 vols.; New York: Doubleday, 1992), 3.1129-33, especially pp. 1130-32.

To be more specific, Paul has not *two* soteriological models (juridical and participationist) but *one,* justification by co-crucifixion, meaning restoration to right covenant relations with God and others by participation in Christ's quintessential covenantal act of faith and love on the cross; this one act fulfilled both the "vertical" and "horizontal" requirements of the Law, such that those who participate in it experience the same life-giving fulfillment of the Law and therein begin the paradoxical, christologically grounded process of resurrection through death. That is, they have been initiated into the process of conformity to the crucified Christ (cruciformity, Christification), who is the image of God — and thus the process of theoformity, or theosis.[14]

Following Douglas Campbell's example of summarizing soteriological models with abbreviations or acronyms (e.g., JF for "justification by faith" and PPME for "pneumatologically participatory martyrological eschatology"),[15] we can give this model the acronym JCC — justification by co-crucifixion.

Before developing the thesis of this chapter, however, we will pause to think strategically about methodology in the study of Paul's soteriology.

A Brief Methodological Preface

It may appear presumptuous to attempt, in one chapter, to address two (or perhaps even three) of the most controverted topics in current discussion of

---

14. As noted in the introduction and in chapter one, the terms "deification" and "theosis" — the process of becoming like God — are key theological terms for the Eastern (Orthodox) churches but relatively unknown or unused terms in the West. The still lesser-known term "christification" provides the particular content to deification and is used by some Orthodox writers, such as Panayiotis Nellas, *Deification in Christ: Orthodox Perspectives on the Nature of the Human Person,* trans. Norman Russell (Crestwood: St. Vladimir's Seminary Press, 1997). As mentioned in chapter one, n. 94, Nellas stresses Christification so that deification is clearly understood as Christlikeness and is not filled with any other content; below, I will make just the opposite hermeneutical move, as I also did in chapter one, and stress that cruciformity is ultimately theosis, so that our theology (i.e., theology proper — the doctrine of God) is christologically understood. For the connection between theosis and justification, see, among others, William G. Rusch, "How the Eastern Fathers Understood What the Western Church Meant by Justification," in *Justification by Faith: Lutherans and Catholics in Dialogue VII* (Minneapolis: Augsburg, 1985), pp. 131-42; Marshall, "Justification as Declaration and Deification" (focusing on Luther); and Veli-Matti Kärkkäinen, *One with God: Salvation as Deification and Justification* (Collegeville: Liturgical, 2005).

15. See Campbell, *The Quest for Paul's Gospel,* p. 4.

Pauline (and indeed Christian) theology — Paul's understanding and experience of justification, the cross, and salvation. So we begin with five principles for the interpretation of these interrelated topics, which we can refer to broadly, together, as Paul's soteriology. The five principles are:

1. *Recognition of contextual specificity.* Following Calvin Roetzel's lead, we need to allow Paul himself to define key terms in his theology, largely by a close reading of the letters.[16] This does not mean that we ignore the Scriptures, other Jewish writings, etc. — far from it. But neither do we allow them to trump Paul's own words, or to force those words into a mold foreign to their own import in the context of his letters. We must, in other words, allow for Paul's creativity, especially in light of the cross and resurrection of Christ and the gift of the Spirit.
2. *The practice of prudent connectivity.* We may need to finish connecting the dots, so to speak, of Paul's thinking where Paul did not fully, or explicitly, connect the dots into a pattern or image. We may even have to slowly, carefully observe and connect dots to create patterns that Paul himself did not even know he was positing.
3. *Recognition of theological complementarity.* There are certainly plenty of antinomies, or antitheses, in Paul's letters.[17] We should, however, be careful about creating what may be — and I stress *may be* — false antitheses, such as divine initiative *or* human response, soteriology *or* ecclesiology, forensic declaration *or* participation, covenant *or* apocalyptic, boundary markers *or* moral effort, faith *or* obedience, obedience to death *or* sacrificial death, expiation *or* propitiation, crucifixion *or* resurrection, etc.[18]

16. In discussing Paul the "theologizer," Roetzel states that his "basic premise is that one learns what Paul means by such terms as *God, Christ, the cross, righteousness,* and so forth by observing how he uses them in their contexts" (*Paul: The Man and the Myth* [Minneapolis: Fortress, 1999], p. 97).

17. See, of course, J. Louis Martyn, "Apocalyptic Antinomies," in *Theological Issues in the Letters of Paul* (Edinburgh: Clark/Nashville: Abingdon, 1997), pp. 111-23.

18. In parallel but independent fashion, Francis Watson (*Paul and the Hermeneutics of Faith* [London/New York: Clark, 2004], pp. 323-29) also warns against the positing of "false dichotomies" in the interpretation of both Second Temple Judaism and the scriptural text itself (especially Leviticus) that has emerged since the publication of Sanders's *Paul and Palestinian Judaism.* James Dunn warns against "either-or exegesis" in discussing justification and participation (James D. G. Dunn, *The Theology of Paul the Apostle* [Grand Rapids: Eerdmans, 1998], pp. 395-96).

At the same time, moreover, I think it is imperative that we not rend asunder Paul's (so-called) "theology" and his (so-called) "ethics." As Richard Hays has said, "There is no meaningful distinction between theology and ethics in Paul's thought, because Paul's theology [we could substitute the word "soteriology"] is fundamentally an account of God's work of transforming people into the image of Christ."[19] Thus, for example, any Pauline soteriology that separates "justification" from "justice," either for theological reasons or for (allegedly) linguistic ones (e.g., Ziesler),[20] ought to be immediately suspect as an adequate reading of Paul.

4. *Recognition of the experiential character of Paul's theology.* If we can thank Richard Hays for reminding us of the symbiosis of theology and ethics in Paul, we all also owe a great debt of gratitude to Luke Johnson for reminding us time and again that the study of the New Testament cannot neglect the experience of those who wrote and who read and heard the various New Testament documents.[21] With respect to Paul, the term used by Roy Harrisville, "the pauline experiential theology," seems especially appropriate, even if a bit clumsy.[22]

5. *Recognition of flexible coherency.* Finally, I agree with interpreters such as N. T. Wright and Douglas Campbell that in our approach to Pauline soteriology we must balance careful exegesis that attends to the contingent, on the one hand, with the use of bold, broad brush strokes that at-

---

19. Richard B. Hays, *The Moral Vision of the New Testament: A Contemporary Introduction to New Testament Ethics* (San Francisco: HarperCollins, 1996), p. 46. If Hays is right, as I certainly think he is, then the real substance, not only of Pauline soteriology but also of Pauline theology more broadly, is theosis, as we have been defining it. We will see this more clearly as we progress through this chapter.

20. John Ziesler (*Pauline Christianity,* The Oxford Bible Series, rev. ed. [New York/Oxford: Oxford University Press, 1990], p. 101) drives a wedge between *dik-* terms that (allegedly) mean "justification" (relationship) and those that mean "righteousness," even in a single passage like Gal 2:15-21. He claims that Paul changes subjects from "justification" in 2:15ff. to "new life" in 2:20 — although these two supposedly different subjects, justification and new life, are both effected "by faith"!

21. See, e.g., Luke Timothy Johnson, *Religious Experience in Earliest Christianity: A Missing Dimension in New Testament Study* (Minneapolis: Fortress, 1998). My own concerns about this matter came to fruition in my *Cruciformity: Paul's Narrative Spirituality of the Cross* (Grand Rapids: Eerdmans, 2001).

22. Roy A. Harrisville, *Fracture: The Cross as Irreconcilable in the Language and Thought of the Biblical Writers* (Grand Rapids: Eerdmans 2006), pp. 104-9.

tends to the coherent, the big picture, on the other — perhaps leaning more toward the latter for a while. Yet we must do so without confusing coherency with assembly-line sameness.[23]

Having proposed these methodological principles, we may now carefully develop Paul's understanding of justification by co-crucifixion (JCC).

The Demands of the Covenant and the Meaning of Justification

The first aspect of justification in Paul to consider is this: the Law requires vertical and horizontal covenant-keeping — love of God and neighbor — for humans to experience present and/or eschatological life (justification). Paul, we will see, agrees with this.

The Demands of the Covenant

In his *Theology of the Old Testament,* Walter Brueggemann says that for Israel the demands of covenant relations may be summarized in one requirement: love for people as the expression of love for God.[24] Perhaps Brueggemann goes too far in conflating the two, but he is clearly right that both are fundamental to covenantal life, and that they are inseparable. We may refer to these two inseparable categories of covenant-keeping and covenant-breaking heuristically as the vertical (God-oriented) and horizontal (human-oriented) dimensions both of the Law and of sin: love of God and love of neighbor, sins against God and sins against neighbor. Brueggemann also claims that texts like Micah 6:8 show that in the Bible God expects not only Israel, but all human beings, to express this symbiosis of horizontal and vertical love.[25]

This way of thinking seems clearly to be related to the two tables or tablets of the Law given to Moses (Exod 31:18). It may be too much to say that

23. I sense this desire both in Campbell's *The Quest for Paul's Gospel* and in N. T. Wright's *Paul: In Fresh Perspective* (Minneapolis: Fortress, 2005).

24. Walter Brueggemann, *Theology of The Old Testament: Testimony, Dispute, Advocacy* (Minneapolis: Fortress, 1997), p. 424; cf. p. 429 and the entire discussion of "Israel's Covenant Obligation" (pp. 417-34).

25. Brueggemann, *Theology of the Old Testament,* pp. 460-61.

every Jew who read the Scriptures of Israel thought instinctively in this bipartite, interconnected, covenantal fashion, but according to the Synoptic Gospels, that is how Jesus thought (Mark 12:28-34; cf. Matt 22:36-40 and Luke 10:25-28). It is also how several noted Jewish writers of the same era thought, including the author(s) of *Jubilees* and of the *Testaments of the Twelve Patriarchs*, as well as both Philo and Josephus.[26] What about Paul?

Paul and Sin(s)

The human problem, as Paul sees it, is multifaceted. On the one hand, there is the problem of Sin (singular) as a power, from which people need liberation, or redemption (Rom 3:9, 24; 6:7; Gal 3:22). On the other hand, there is the problem of sins (plural), for which people need forgiveness (Rom 1:18-32; 3:10-18, 25). Paul's theology of the cross, as expressed in Romans 3:21-26, addresses both of these needs: redemption from Sin, and expiation for sins. Many students of Paul have tended to stress his unique understanding of Sin as a power and underestimated the significance of sins (plural) for him. But the two are closely related. A person needs both freedom *from* and freedom *for*: liberation from Sin and a new power to replace sins/transgressions with righteous/just behaviors. For Paul, the sins themselves have a basic bipartite structure or pattern to them. Like the two tables of the Law and Jewish tradi-

---

26. See *Jubilees* 20:2: "And he [Abraham] commanded them [his sons and grandsons] that they should observe the way of the Lord; that they should work righteousness, and love each his neighbor, and act on this matter among all men; that they should each so walk with regard to them as to do judgment and righteousness on the earth." The writer then proceeds to warn against "fornication and uncleanness," on the one hand, and idolatry on the other (20:3-10). Similarly, the *Testaments of the Twelve Patriarchs* contains the following texts: "[L]ove the Lord and your neighbor" (*Testament of Issachar* 5:2); "Love the Lord through all your life, and one another with a true heart" (*Testament of Dan* 5:3); "Fear the Lord and love your neighbor. . . . For he that fears God and loves his neighbor cannot be smitten by the spirit of Beliar, being shielded by the fear of God. Nor can he be ruled over by the device of men or beasts, for he is helped by the Lord through the love which he has toward his neighbor" (*Testament of Benjamin* 3:3-5). These and other texts make it clear that "fornication," or sexual immorality, is contrary to neighbor-love, but they do not limit the failure to love one's neighbor to sexual sin. On the contrary, other "horizontal" sins include anger, evil speech, lying, lawlessness, and failure to have compassion on the poor and weak. On *dikaiosynē* as integral to *eusebeia* in Josephus, see Mark A. Seifrid, "Paul's Use of Righteousness Language Against Its Hellenistic Background," in Carson, *et al.*, eds., *Justification and Variegated Nomism*, vol. 2, pp. 39-74, here pp. 45-49.

tion, Paul divides human covenantal responsibility — and covenantal failure — into two categories: those involving our relationship with God and those involving our relationships with others.[27]

Paul can refer to these two covenantal categories — the vertical and the horizontal — in a couple ways. We may begin with the negative aspect of these categories: vertical and horizontal covenant-*breaking*. Adopting a common Jewish (and early Christian) practice, Paul can summarize them as idolatry and (sexual) immorality *(porneia)*, as does *Jubilees*. This view appears in 1 Corinthians (see further below) and in Romans, where Paul seems to follow Wis 14:12-31, a text that calls idolatry "the beginning of fornication" as well as the "beginning and cause and end of every evil" (Wis 14:12, 27; cf. Rom 1:18-32).[28] It was common for Jews and Christians to stress sexual immorality as the most egregious and representative violation of the second table.[29] Paul, in fact, stresses sexual sins but clearly does not limit his understanding of horizontal covenant-breaking to such sins, as Rom 1:18-32 demonstrates.[30]

In Rom 1:18 Paul refers to the two basic categories of sin as *asebeia* and *adikia,* impiety and injustice, sins against God and sins against fellow humans.[31] These correspond roughly to idolatry and immorality, though *adikia* is broader and more inclusive than *porneia*. Although Romans 1 is often read as an indictment of Gentiles, it is clear from the text's allusions to the golden calf incident (1:23; cf. Ps 106:19-20) and from the following chapters that Paul

27. See Watson, *Paul and the Hermeneutics of Faith,* pp. 305-14, especially p. 311 and 314, for the view that Paul's scriptural interpretation suggests that he, like Philo, Josephus, and other Jews, divided the Decalogue into two parts.

28. On 1 Corinthians, see Roy E. Ciampa and Brian S. Rosner, "The Structure and Argument of 1 Corinthians: A Biblical/Jewish Approach," *NTS* 52 (2006): 205-18. They find that 1 Corinthians is "an early Christian reformulation of the traditional Jewish approach to dealing with sexual immorality [4:18–7:40] and idolatry [chs. 8–14]" (p. 218; cf. pp. 210-11). The inclusion of passages on disunity (chs. 1–4) and unjust lawsuits (6:1-11), however, suggests that Paul's vision of the horizontal sins at Corinth is more than just *porneia* and can be defined as injustice *(adikia)* more broadly (see 6:9, where *adikoi* appears).

29. See William Loader, *The Septuagint, Sexuality and the New Testament* (Grand Rapids: Eerdmans, 2004), p. 7.

30. For a brief but helpful discussion, see Joel Marcus, "The New Testament and Idolatry," *Int* 60 (2006): 152-64, here pp. 154-55.

31. So also, e.g., Keck, *Romans,* ANTC (Nashville: Abingdon, 2005), p. 59, and Charles H. Talbert, *Romans,* Smith & Helwys Bible Commentary (Macon: Smith & Helwys, 2002), p. 57.

sees idolatry, as well as injustice, as the universal (Gentile and Jewish) human predicament.[32] (That Paul can see *porneia* as a form of *adikia* and a failure to love is clear from 1 Thess 4:3-6.) Paul's division of sin, or covenant-breaking, into two basic categories is evident also from 1 Corinthians, in which he uses the imperative "flee" *(pheugein)* just two times, once of immorality (1 Cor 6:18) and once of idolatry (1 Cor 10:14). In addition, these terms summarize the concerns of 1 Corinthians 10, where Paul (as in Rom 1:23) draws upon the golden calf narrative to describe the basic existential issues facing human beings in general and God's people in particular: vertical and horizontal failure, idolatry and immorality.

The reality of sins (plural) requires, in Paul's worldview, a sacrifice that effects forgiveness. As noted above, there is also an implicit connection in Paul between the problem and solution of *Sin,* on the one hand, and *sins* on the other. Paul believes that the solution to both problems lies in the internalization of the covenant through the circumcision of the heart and the gift of the empowering Spirit (Rom 2:25-29; 8:1-8). Of course he also hopes and believes that those who are forgiven and liberated will actually refrain from the sins that characterized the pre-justified way of life and perform instead the opposites of such sins. In fact, it is only in so doing that a community (or individual) can be described as those (or one) in whom "the just requirement [*dikaiōma*] of the Law" is fulfilled (Rom 8:4). Thus justification, or "rightwising," must include forgiveness but be more than forgiveness. It must be the reversal of Romans 1, of human *asebeia* and *adikia*. In other words, there can be no justification without transformation. The justified are those who have begun the process of replacing *asebeia* and *adikia* with *pistis* and *dikaiosynē/agapē* by the power of the Spirit, thus fulfilling the two tables of the Law.[33] To this understanding of justification we now turn.

---

32. So also, e.g., Watson, *Paul and the Hermeneutics of Faith*, p. 411.

33. Francis Watson correctly makes the point that, for Paul, Lev 19:18, which the apostle cites twice (Gal 5:14; Rom 13:9), "summarizes the second table of the decalogue and indeed 'any other commandment' (Rom 13:8-10)" and that this summary text remains "normative for Christian congregations" (*Paul and the Hermeneutics of Faith,* p. 520). I am not convinced, however, of Watson's corollary claim that Paul finds Lev 18:5 (about keeping the Lord's statutes and ordinances as the way to life) to be a "summary of the law's unchristian soteriology," with two neighboring texts, one to be rejected (Lev 18:5) and the other accepted (Lev 19:18), demonstrating that Paul finds "a plurality of voices," "contradictions," and "tensions and anomalies" within Torah (pp. 520-21). (For the full argument, see his pages 314-53.) Watson also claims (mistakenly, in my view) that Paul's rejection of Lev 18:5 (Law-keeping

The Meaning of Justification

The concept of "justification" expressed in the Greek verb *dikaioō* and related words, whether in Second Temple Judaism generally or in Paul particularly, has sometimes been subjected to narrow "word studies" as if everything about this vast theological concept could be discovered simply by
analysis of the occurrences of the word itself. But any discussion of justification as a Jewish theological concept must stay connected to such overlapping
concepts as covenant,[34] life,[35] and, of course, justice/righteousness (Greek
dikaiosynē).[36]

So what is justification *for Paul?* For Paul, I would contend, justification
means the establishment or restoration of right covenant relations,[37] both

---

leads to life) is more fundamental to "the whole structure" of his reading of Torah than is his
interpretation of Lev 19:18 and that therefore the removal of the former, but not the latter,
would affect that entire structure (p. 521). Rather, I would argue, Paul finds the statutes and
ordinances of the Law summarized in concepts like self-offering to God (faith) and to others
(love), enabled by Christ and the Spirit (Rom 8:3-4). This leads Paul to the construction of
the phrase "the law of Christ" (Gal 6:2; 1 Cor 9:21), shorthand for a christologically determined reading of the second table of the Law that stresses cruciform love.

34. I am therefore in complete agreement with Simon Gathercole ("The Doctrine of
Justification in Paul and Beyond," pp. 236-37) when he insists that righteousness must be understood in covenantal terms but not merely (contra N. T. Wright) as membership in the
covenant. Instead, says Gathercole, righteousness must be understood in the Hebrew Bible,
early Judaism, and Paul as "doing what God requires," citing Deut 6:24-25 as a foundational
text. I cannot agree with Gathercole, however, that Paul understands faith simply as "trusting God's promise" (p. 240). That is a necessary but not sufficient understanding of faith in
Paul.

35. I agree with Francis Watson in stressing "life" (understood as either present or eschatological life, or both) as the goal of Law-keeping in the Torah (e.g., Lev 18:5; Deuteronomy 30) and thus, for Paul, essential to the meaning of justification (*Paul and the Hermeneutics of Faith,* e.g., pp. 53 n. 61, 437, *et passim*).

36. The English language, which has two word-groups ("just-" and "right-") available
to render the Greek word-family *dikaioō, dikaiosynē*, etc., creates enormous difficulties in
seeing the connection between God's justice/righteousness and justification, between justification and human justice/righteousness, and even between human justice and human righteousness. The various Bible translations deal with this problem in different (and sometimes
theologically biased) ways. John Reumann points out that "[o]nly English is likely to have
separate articles in a Bible dictionary on 'righteousness' and 'justification'" ("Justification
and Justice in the New Testament," *HBT* 21 [1999]: 26-45, here p. 28).

37. On this, Ziesler starts off on the right path but then takes a significant and illogical
wrong turn. He rightly stresses that justification in the LXX and Paul is not merely juridical

"vertical" or theological (toward God) and also, inseparably, "horizontal" or social (toward others) — what Paul most frequently calls *"pistis"* and *"agapē"* — with the certain hope of ultimate vindication and glory, all understood in light of, and experienced through, Christ and the Spirit.[38]

Or, as I have said more succinctly elsewhere:

> Justification for Paul may be defined as follows: *the establishment or restoration of right covenantal relations — **fidelity** to God and **love** for neighbor — with the certain **hope** of acquittal/vindication on the day of judgment.*[39]

---

but "has to do with the restoration of a relationship" — "to put wrongs right and to restore people to their proper place, no more and no less, in the covenant community" (*Pauline Christianity*, p. 88). But he still too quickly defines justification narrowly as forgiveness (justification "comes close to forgiveness," referring to Rom 4:6-8) and wrongly asserts that this means that justification is not about "the establishment of a new character." For transformation, Ziesler claims, Paul uses other language, limiting justification to "[s]trictly acceptance, restoration to fellowship, and not transformation of character (though that will follow)." But how can the restoration of people "to their proper place . . . in the covenant community" — in the symbolic world of the Bible — not involve their transformation into people who keep the covenant?

38. This understanding is a development of positions I have taken in all of my previous work on Paul, including *Cruciformity; Apostle of the Crucified Lord: A Theological Introduction to Paul and His Letters* (Grand Rapids: Eerdmans, 2004); and *Reading Paul* (Eugene: Cascade, 2008). In addition to these points, I would add also that: "Justification, then, is about reconciliation with God and membership in God's covenant community. For Paul, this takes place by God's initiative and grace, to which humans respond in faith — trust, obedience, and public confession. Faith is not merely a onetime act of response to the gospel but an ongoing covenantal relationship with God that is itself a kind of crucifixion and resurrection, so that the covenantal obligations can now be fulfilled" (*Apostle of the Crucified Lord*, p. 138). The last part of the paragraph attempts to acknowledge the insight of, e.g., N. T. Wright that all Pauline theology is Jewish theology reconfigured around Christ and the Spirit *(Paul: In Fresh Perspective)* as well as the insight of, e.g., Luke Johnson that the New Testament is a witness to early Christian experience, not just ideas. On this latter point, see also *Cruciformity*.

39. This is a slight adaptation of the definition in *Apostle of the Crucified Lord*, p. 138 (emphasis added). In *Cruciformity* I wrote that "Justification, then, may be described as (1) right relations with God (covenant) issuing in (2) right (even "godly") relations with others (virtue) and (3) acquittal on the day of judgment (vindication). In other words, justification, righteousness, and their related terms in English refer to *covenant faithfulness with respect to God and neighbor*, and *ultimate divine approval*" (p. 136). For a similar view see Hays, "Justification," especially pp. 1130-32.

This is life indeed, both present and future, the goal of every Jew, the essential substance of the covenant, and the purpose of the divine gift of the Law and, for Paul, the purpose of the divine gifts of Christ and the Spirit.

The actual language of justification is drawn from four interlocking realms:

- *theological,* referring to the divine character — God is just;
- *covenantal,* referring to the moral obligations associated with a communal, covenant relationship with God — God requires justice;
- *legal,* referring to juridical images of God as judge — God judges and pardons; and
- *eschatological,* referring to future judgment and salvation — God will judge and grant approval and life (or condemnation and death) on the day of the Lord.[40]

The just/righteous are those who are, and who will be vindicated as being, in right covenant relationship with the just/righteous God of the covenant as that God's distinctive people.[41] In Christ (or, better, in the Messiah), of course, that relationship is open to Jews and Gentiles alike.[42]

For Paul, then, justification is not merely or even primarily juridical or

---

40. See, similarly, N. T. Wright, *What Saint Paul Really Said: Was Paul of Tarsus the Real Founder of Christianity?* (Grand Rapids: Eerdmans, 1997), pp. 117-18, 131, though Wright does not note the first (divine character). I cannot agree with Wright, however, that justification for Paul "does not itself *denote* the process" (emphasis his) of being brought by grace to faith (that is what "call" means, according to Wright) but means "'how I am declared to be a member of God's people'" — how people are "given the status . . . 'righteous', 'within the covenant'" (*Paul: In Fresh Perspective,* pp. 121-22; cf. 159; see also *What Saint Paul Really Said,* pp. 113-20). For a brief but excellent overview of the scriptural background of justification/righteousness in Paul, see Joseph A. Fitzmyer, "Justification by Faith in Pauline Thought: A Catholic Perspective," in Aune, ed., *Rereading Paul Together,* pp. 77-94, here pp. 78-81.

41. Michael F. Bird (*The Saving Righteousness of God: Studies in Paul, Justification, and the New Perspective* [Carlisle: Paternoster, 2007], p. 4) defines justification as "the act whereby God creates a new people, with a new status, in a new covenant, as a foretaste of the new age." Although this is generally a very fine description, the word "status" is a bit troublesome, since it may be heard as an echo of certain theologies that wish to minimize the transformative character of justification that reconciliation and new covenant require.

42. It is misguided, however, to find the sole or even primary meaning of justification to be the welcoming of Gentiles *qua* Gentiles into the covenant community. Their inclusion is a necessary dimension of a proper understanding of justification, but it is not the totality.

judicial — the image of a divine judge pronouncing pardon or acquittal. That is part, but only part, of the significance of justification. The judicial image must be understood within a wider covenantal, relational, participatory, and transformative framework. To consider that framework, we turn to Rom 5:1-11 and 2 Cor 5:14-21.

That justification itself is first and foremost a covenantal, relational reality is demonstrated by Rom 5:1-11, where Paul places justification and reconciliation in synonymous parallelism, first in vv. 9-10:

> 9Much more surely then, now that we have been *justified by his blood,* will we be saved through him from the wrath of God. 10For if while we were enemies, we were *reconciled to God through the death of his Son,* much more surely, *having been reconciled,* will we be saved by his life.

The meaning of the phrase "justified by his blood" in v. 9 is given in the two parallel phrases in v. 10, "reconciled to God through the death of his Son" and "having been reconciled." That is, justification means reconciliation to God. This is a divine act, not a human achievement, as the three occurrences of the passive voice in vv. 9-10 demonstrate: "we have been justified," "we were reconciled," and "having been reconciled." Moreover, it is not a private act of reconciliation but one both intended by God and experienced by people in community, as a people; the subject of the verbs in Romans 5 is "we," not "I."

This equation of justification with reconciliation is also evident in the next verse (Rom 5:11), which uses an active verb with passive semantic weight ("we have now received")[43] to indicate the gift of reconciliation. This verse forms an inclusio, like bookends, with the first verse in the passage (5:1). This opening verse has already used the passive voice in speaking of justification and already indicated its relational character as "peace with God":

> 1Therefore, since we are justified [lit., "having been justified"] by faith, we have peace with God through our Lord Jesus Christ. . . .

> 11But more than that, we even boast in God through our Lord Jesus Christ, through whom we have now received reconciliation.

---

43. In this sentence, God is the semantic Actor who gives the gift of reconciliation to us, the recipients. Thus, although the form of the verb is active ("we have received"), its force is passive.

In a similar way, 2 Cor 5:14-21 suggests that what God has done in Christ is to effect reconciliation, defined as "becom[ing] the righteousness [Greek *dikaiosynē*] of God" in Christ (5:21). We will return to this text later, but for now we simply note that reconciliation (5:18-20) and righteousness/justification language (5:21) are again interconnected. The terms "justification" and "reconciliation" are, thus, essentially synonymous for Paul.[44] Justification as reconciliation includes both forgiveness of sins (plural; i.e., transgressions: Rom 3:25; 2 Cor 5:19) and liberation from Sin (singular) as a power (Rom 3:24; 5:15-21). Since both sins and Sin affect human relationships with God and with others, forgiveness and liberation are inherently realities that can only be experienced in connection with others, that is, in community and in relation to a wider world.

Moreover, 2 Cor 5:14-21 suggests that inherent within the very notion of reconciliation/justification are both participation and transformation. We see participation in the phrases "in Christ" (5:17) and "in him" (5:21).[45] These references to participation, to being in Christ, should be understood both individually and corporately. Each believer is in Christ, but Christ himself constitutes a body, a covenant community of Jews and Gentiles. To be in Christ is a corporate reality, but it is experienced as such by individuals.

We see transformation as innate to reconciliation/justification according to 2 Cor 5:14-21 in the references to "new creation" (5:17), in the phrase "become the righteousness of God" (5:21), and in the image of death and resurrection, resulting in living for Christ rather than self (5:14-15). The image of death and resurrection is especially intriguing, and it will of course reappear in Romans 6 (as well as Galatians 2), discussed below. As we will see in considering Romans and Galatians, Paul's understanding of justification is inseparable from the experience of death and resurrection, which is grounded in Christ's own death and resurrection (Rom 4:25).

For Paul, then, in light of Romans 5 and 2 Corinthians 5, justification has

1. an *objective basis,* or *means,* which is Christ's death as a gift of God's gracious initiative (Rom 5:1, 6-8, 9-11; 2 Cor 5:18, 21), together (implicitly) with Christ's resurrection as God's life-giving power;

44. So also Sanders, *Paul and Palestinian Judaism,* pp. 471-72. See additionally Dunn, *Theology,* pp. 387-88.

45. This is probably also how we should understand Paul's explanation of the source of justification as "the redemption that is in Christ Jesus" in Rom 3:24. That is, the redemption effected by Christ's death is experienced in him, by participation in him.

2. a required *subjective response,* or *mode,* that effects justification/reconciliation, which is usually (though not always) explicitly labeled *pistis,* normally translated "faith" or (in its verbal form) "believe" (Rom 5:1; 2 Cor 5:20; cf. Rom 3:21-26; 10:9); and

3. *substantive content,* which includes reconciliation, participation, and transformation (Rom 5:1-2, 9-11; 2 Cor 5:14-15, 17, 21).[46]

I have already suggested that the essential content of this transformation is fidelity to God and love for neighbor, the very heart of the covenant. But to see why that is the case, we must now address three questions that arise from these three conclusions:

- What is the distinctive meaning of Christ's death for Paul?
- What is his distinctive understanding of *pistis?* and
- What is the connection between the meaning of Christ's death and the meaning of *pistis,* on the one hand, and the significance and character of the transformation inherent in justification, on the other?

As we address these questions, we will also see the close connection between death and resurrection (Christ's and ours); indeed, justification will emerge as a participatory experience of death and resurrection.

Christ's Death as the Quintessential Covenantal Act

The next aspect of justification we must consider is Paul's distinctive interpretation of Christ's death as covenant fulfillment.[47] We shall see that, ac-

---

46. On the first two aspects (objective basis and subjective response), using the hermeneutical lens of "cause" as employed by Aristotle and Philo to mean a nexus of causes (formal, material, efficient, final), Peter Frick proposes that we see in Paul a distinction between the *means* of salvation (the nexus of causes constituted by God's gracious love in Christ) and the *mode* of salvation, the response of faith that makes salvation a reality ("The Means and Mode of Salvation: A Hermeneutical Proposal for Clarifying Pauline Soteriology," *HBT* 29 [2007]: 203-22). Frick rightly stresses that *"[w]e can only speak of salvation in the Pauline sense when both the means and mode of salvation cohere"* (p. 221). Although Frick simply means that there is no salvation without both the objective and subjective elements, we will see below that for Paul the means and the mode cohere in material, not merely formal, ways.

47. This is not to claim that "covenant fulfillment" exhausts the meaning of Christ's death for Paul.

cording to Gal 2:15-21 and Phil 2:6-11, Christ's crucifixion simultaneously manifests both vertical and horizontal covenant-keeping, thus fulfilling the two tables of the Law as the quintessential covenantal act. This aspect of Paul's interpretation of Christ's death has been largely overlooked, resulting in significantly truncated understandings of justification.

The death of Jesus is of course interpreted in the New Testament as an act of love: God's love, or Christ's own love, or both. According to Paul, Christ died as a demonstration of God's love (Rom 5:6-8; 8:31-39) and a manifestation of his own love (Gal 2:20; Rom 8:34-35 and 2 Cor 5:14, implicitly). A succinct expression of Christ's death as his act of love is found in Gal 2:20:

> . . . the Son of God, who loved me and gave himself for me. (NRSV)

Or, better translated:

> . . . the Son of God, who loved me by giving himself for me. (my translation)[48]

Paul also interprets Christ's death as an act of *obedience* (to God the Father) and similarly as an act of *"faith,"* in the sense of *"covenant faithfulness"* or "faithful obedience." The theme of obedience is stated most unambiguously in passages like Phil 2:8 ("obedient to the point of death"); Rom 5:18-19 ("one man's act of righteousness . . . one man's obedience"); and Gal 1:4 ("according to the will of our God and Father"). Recent scholarship suggests also that Christ's death is depicted as his act of "faith" or "faithfulness" *(pistis)* in seven passages within the undisputed letters of Paul where the Greek grammar is ambiguous: Rom 3:22, 26; Gal 2:16 (twice), 20; and 3:22; and Phil 3:9.

Traditionally (at least since the Reformation) the ambiguities have been rendered "faith *in* Christ," but the arguments for interpreting these phrases as examples of the so-called "subjective genitive" and thus translating them as "the faith[fulness] *of* Christ/the Son of God" are persuasive to many, including this writer.[49] If "the faith of Christ" is the correct translation, then

---

48. In Gal 2:20 the phrase "loved me and gave himself for me" is almost certainly an example of "hendiadys," literally "one through two," or two separate grammatical items (in this case linked by "and") referring to one actual thing or event. Paul is clearly not referring to two separate "events," an act of loving and a separate act of dying. Thus we should translate this text as "loved me by giving himself for me."

49. For a strong, now classic summary of the "faith of Christ" interpretation, see Rich-

Paul says that Christ's faithful death embodies the righteousness of God (Rom 3:22), constitutes the *means* of justification (Gal 2:16; 3:22; Phil 3:9) as well as the *mode* of justification (Rom 3:26), and somehow even provides the *manner* of living in the present (Gal 2:20), as the following table shows:

The Faith of Christ: Texts in the Undisputed Letters

	Objective genitive ("faith in Christ") NRSV	Subjective genitive ("faith of Christ") NRSV altered
Rom 3:21-22a	21But now, apart from law, the righteousness of God has been disclosed, and is attested by the law and the prophets, 22the righteousness of God through *faith in Jesus Christ* for all who believe.	21But now, apart from law, the righteousness of God has been disclosed, and is attested by the law and the prophets, 22the righteousness of God through *the faith[fulness] of Jesus Christ* for all who believe.
Rom 3:26	it was to prove at the present time that he himself is righteous and that he justifies the one who has *faith in Jesus.*	it was to prove at the present time that he himself is righteous and that he justifies the one who has [*or,* "shares in"] *the faith[fulness] of Jesus.*

---

ard B. Hays, "*PISTIS CHRISTOU* and Pauline Theology: What Is at Stake?" in E. Elizabeth Johnson and David B. Hay, eds., *Pauline Theology* IV: *Looking Back, Pressing On* (Atlanta: Scholars, 1997), pp. 35-60, and reprinted in Hays, *The Faith of Jesus Christ,* 2nd ed., pp. 272-97. On Galatians 2, see also especially J. Louis Martyn, *Galatians: A New Translation with Introduction and Commentary,* AB 33A (New York: Doubleday, 1997), pp. 263-75, especially pp. 269-75; Frank J. Matera *Galatians,* Sacra Pagina (Collegeville: Liturgical, 1992), pp. 100-102; and all of Hays, *The Faith of Jesus Christ,* 2d ed. For the traditional interpretation, see James D. G. Dunn, "Once More, *PISTIS CHRISTOU,*" in the volume edited by Johnson and Hay, pp. 61-81, and reprinted in Hays, *The Faith of Jesus Christ,* 2nd ed., pp. 249-71. For my own position, see especially *Cruciformity,* pp. 110-21. Paul Foster argues that Eph 3:12, which he considers deutero-Pauline, also contains a subjective genitive *pistis Christou* and that it confirms the validity of reading the undisputed texts that way ("The First Contribution to the *pistis Christou* Debate: A Study of Ephesians 3.12," *JSNT* 85 [2002]: 75-96). For the theological implications of reading the *pistis Christou* texts as examples of the subjective genitive, see David L. Stubbs, "The Shape of Soteriology and the *Pistis Christou* Debate," *SJT* 61 (2008): 137-57.

Gal 2:16	yet we know that a person is justified not by the works of the law but through *faith in Jesus Christ.* And we have come to believe in Christ Jesus, so that we might be justified by *faith in Christ,* and not by doing the works of the law, because no one will be justified by the works of the law.	yet we know that a person is justified not by the works of the law but through *the faith[fulness] of Jesus Christ.* And we have come to believe in Christ Jesus, so that we might be justified by *the faith[fulness] of Christ,* and not by doing the works of the law, because no one will be justified by the works of the law.
Gal 2:20	and it is no longer I who live, but it is Christ who lives in me. And the life I now live in the flesh I live by *faith in the Son of God,* who loved me and gave himself for me.	and it is no longer I who live, but it is Christ who lives in me. And the life I now live in the flesh I live by *the faith[fulness] of the Son of God,* who loved me and gave himself for me [*or,* "by giving himself for me"].
Gal 3:22	But the scripture has imprisoned all things under the power of sin, so that what was promised through *faith in Jesus Christ* might be given to those who believe.	But the scripture has imprisoned all things under the power of sin, so that what was promised through *the faith[fulness] of Jesus Christ* might be given to those who believe.
Phil 3:9	and be found in him, not having a righteousness of my own that comes from the law, but one that comes through *faith in Christ,* the righteousness from God based on faith.	and be found in him, not having a righteousness of my own that comes from the law, but one that comes through *the faith[fulness] of Christ,* the righteousness from God based on faith.

This newer reading of *pistis Christou* and parallel phrases has a very significant impact on one's overall reading of Paul. It is beyond the scope of this chapter to argue for this interpretation. We will assume its validity and will, in turn, help to strengthen the argument for it. It is the joining of the two interpretations of Christ's death noted above — as *pistis* and as *agapē* — in Philippians 2 and Galatians 2 that is of the most immediate interest to us.

In Gal 2:15-21 Paul makes three references to the faith of (Jesus) Christ (2:16, twice) or of the Son of God (2:20), referring in context to his death for our justification. In 2:20 this faithful act of the Son of God is described specifically as his act of love: "I live by the faith[fulness] of the Son of God, who loved me by giving himself for me." So for Paul, Christ's death on the cross was simultaneously his act of self-giving faith(fulness) toward God (2:16, 20) and his self-giving love toward humanity (2:20). It was a unified act of vertical and horizontal covenant fulfillment, of love for God and for neighbor.[50]

In Phil 2:6-11, the poetic text about Christ's self-emptying and subsequent exaltation that we considered in chapter one, Paul describes Christ's death as his obedience (implicitly, to God), the culmination of his self-humbling (2:8). The text of the poem itself does not explicitly also call the death an act of love. But clearly Paul sees it that way, for the poem is used by Paul as the basis of an exhortation to the Philippians to look out for the interests of others rather than self (with two basically synonymous texts in 2:3 and 2:4) as the joyful expression of the life of love in the Spirit (2:1-4).

> 1If then there is any encouragement in Christ, any consolation from *love,* any sharing in the Spirit, any compassion and sympathy, 2make my joy complete: be of the same mind, having the same *love,* being in full accord and of one mind. 3Do nothing from selfish ambition or conceit, but in humility regard others as better than yourselves. 4Let each of you *look not to your own interests, but to the interests of others.* (emphasis added)

The word "love" appears twice in the preface to the poem (2:1, 2), and both the structure and content of the preface, as well as the poem itself, are parallel to other Pauline texts on love, particularly in 1 Corinthians. Indeed, 1 Corinthians uses virtually the same Greek idiom as Phil 2:4 to say that love does not seek its own interests but rather the interests of others (1 Cor 13:5; cf. 10:24, 33).[51] These clear parallels between the explicit exhortation to Paul's particular understanding of love (vv. 3-4, defining the word "love" named in

---

50. For further discussion of this, see Gorman, *Cruciformity,* pp. 113-15, 162-63.

51. Phil 2:4 has *mē ta heautōn hekastos skopountes alla [kai] ta heterōn hekastos,* while 1 Cor 13:5 says that *[hē agapē] ou zētei ta heautēs,* "love does not seeks its own interests" (my translation). Similar ideas are expressed in a different idiom in Romans 14–15, where hospitality is grounded in Christ's refutation of self-interest (Rom 15:1-3).

vv. 1-2) and the Christ-narrative (vv. 6-8) mean that Paul understands the actions of Christ narrated in vv. 6-8 not only as Christ's obedience but also, simultaneously, as his love.[52]

Thus for Paul, as these two very central Pauline texts demonstrate, Christ's death is a *unified act of faith toward God and love toward others*.[53] His faith and love are inseparable — two sides of one coin. Several other interpreters of Paul have previously noted the joining of faith and love as descriptors of Christ's death.[54] But we must go on to see that this joining of faith and love corresponds, positively, to the two tables of the Law and, negatively, to the twin human failures of faithlessness and injustice, or idolatry and immorality, as discussed above. Thus Christ's death is not merely a representative, messianic act or a substitutionary act. It is, more specifically and importantly, the quintessential *covenantal* act, in which love of God and of neighbor are joined and embodied in the one act of a faithful, loving death.[55] And because Paul sees

52. For further discussion, see Gorman, *Cruciformity*, pp. 164-69.

53. This interpretation of Christ's death as both faith and love may also underlie Romans 5, in which love (especially God's love) dominates 5:1-11 and obedience 5:12-21.

54. See, e.g., Richard B. Hays, "Crucified with Christ: A Synthesis of the Theology of 1 and 2 Thessalonians, Philemon, Philippians, and Galatians," in Jouette M. Bassler, ed., *Pauline Theology* I: *Thessalonians, Philippians, Galatians, Philemon* (Minneapolis: Fortress, 1991), pp. 227-46; here pp. 232-33, 243. See also his *Moral Vision*, pp. 27, 31. See as well Bruce W. Longenecker, "Defining the Faithful Character of the Covenant Community: Galatians 2.15-21 and Beyond: A Response to Jan Lambrecht," in James D. G. Dunn, ed., *Paul and the Mosaic Law* (Grand Rapids: Eerdmans, 1996), pp. 75-98, especially pp. 88-89.

55. This interpretation of the meaning of Christ's death for Paul depends on (or is at least greatly strengthened by) reading the disputed phrase *pistis christou* as "the faith of Christ," meaning Christ's covenantal devotion or fidelity to God, a reading that James D. G. Dunn does not accept. This may explain, in part, his rejection of any significant "link between Christ's death and thought of the new covenant" in "Paul's theologizing about Christ's death" ("Did Paul Have a Covenant Theology? Reflections on Romans 9:4 and 11:27," in *Celebrating Romans: Template for Pauline Theology: Essays in Honor of Robert Jewett*, ed. Sheila E. McGinn [Grand Rapids: Eerdmans, 2004], pp. 3-19; here p. 11). In that essay, Dunn argues that although "'covenant' was not a primary category for Paul" (p. 11; cf. also pp. 7, 10, 14, 19), when he does use the term and theme "covenant," it is not to create a supersessionist gospel-versus-Law antithesis over against Judaism (pp. 14-16). Rather, Dunn argues, Paul is making "an in-house contribution to Israel's understanding of itself as God's covenant people" (p. 19) in which the theme of (new) covenant means "a more effective way of fulfilling the covenant obligation" (p. 17) by means of the Spirit within. Although Dunn is unconvincing in downplaying the importance of covenant for Paul, he is absolutely right in what he affirms about covenant-fulfillment enabled by the Spirit. That this Spirit is the Spirit of the faithful and loving crucified Christ — and thus the covenant-fulfilling Christ with whom

Christ not only as Israel's Messiah but also as Adam's antitype (Rom 5:12-21; 1 Cor 15:22, 45), such an act is also the quintessential *human* act.[56]

At the same time, we must not separate this understanding of Christ's death as his act of fidelity and love from its kenotic character discussed in chapter one. Christ — indeed God acting in Christ — made a self-renouncing decision to identify with humanity in its deepest need: sin.[57] This covenantal act of kenotic faith and love is "the divine participation in the human plight, which makes possible human participation in God's Son,"[58] as we will now see.

Justification by Co-Crucifixion (JCC)

We come, next, to Paul's distinctive understanding of faith — *pistis* — as the human response to the gospel and the instrument of appropriating justification, and therefore also once again to what Paul means by justification itself. Our focus will be on the two passages where Paul uses the Greek verb *systauroō*, "co-crucify" — each time in the passive voice. We will see that, according to Gal 2:15-21 and Rom 6:1–7:6, faith is co-crucifixion with Christ; faith is a death experience. For Paul, justification — restoration to right covenant relations with God and others — occurs, not through performance of or zeal for the Law, but through participation in Christ's quintessential act of covenant-keeping. This restoration to right covenant relations is therefore an experience of death and resurrection, or resurrection via death.

Galatians 2:15-21

In Gal 2:15-21 we have one of the two instances in which Paul uses the verb *systauroō*. Of course it also contains other key terms in Paul's theological lex-

---

believers are co-crucified — makes Paul's theology of Christ, his death, and its significance for us *covenantal at its core*.

56. We have already made this point in chapter one concerning the kenotic and cruciform character of Christ's incarnation and death versus Adam's self-seeking. Here we look at the same reality from the perspective of faith/obedience and love in contrast to Adam's disobedience.

57. E.g., 2 Cor 5:21. On this point, see Tannehill, "Participation in Christ," pp. 225, 227, 228-29, 230, 235-36.

58. Tannehill, "Participation in Christ," p. 229. Tannehill does not, however, offer the covenantal interpretation that is being developed here.

icon, including *erga nomou* ("works of [the] Law") and *pistis Christou* ("faith of/in Christ"). Most interpreters of Gal 2:15-21 would find two major claims in the text. First, they would say, Paul argues that justification is not by *erga nomou* but by *pistis Christou,* however these terms are understood. Second, they would say, Paul claims that those who are in Christ can also be described as those "crucified with Christ," perhaps referring metaphorically to their death to, or separation from, the Law, and to the subsequent life of faith. In any event, the text is understood as referring to two existential realities, justification and (metaphorical) crucifixion.

But this reading of Gal 2:15-21 as an alleged reference to two separate (even if related) experiences simply will not do. These two claims must be seen as connected aspects of the *same* reality.[59] Verses 16 and 21 are not merely parallel statements forming an inclusio (the subject being justification by faith grounded in Christ's death) around a different topic in vv. 19-20 (the experience of being crucified with Christ). Rather, vv. 19-20 show *why* justification by works of the law would render the cross null, void, and superfluous. It is because justification is by participation in the cross — by co-crucifixion. This is what Paul means, in context, by faith over against works of the Law.

Paul Redefining Justification

Three recent essays support the general thrust of this reading and argue also that the context of Gal 2:20 shows that in that text Paul is redefining justification.[60] First, in an article on Gal 2:20, Scott Schauf rightly com-

---

59. This was recognized already by both Luther and Calvin, though their later interpreters tended to disconnect faith and justification, on the one hand, from union with Christ and sanctification, on the other. See Stephen Chester, "When the Old Was New: Reformation Perspectives on Galatians 2:16," *ExpTim* 119 (2007-08): 320-29, esp. pp. 325-27, 328-29.

60. See Scott Schauf, "Galatians 2.20 in Context," *NTS* 52 (2006): 86-101; Martinus C. de Boer, "Paul's Use and Interpretation of a Justification Tradition in Galatians 2.15-21," *JSNT* 28 (2005): 189-216; and Tannehill, "Participation in Christ." In his book *The Risen Crucified Christ in Galatia,* SBLDS 185 (Atlanta: Society of Biblical Literature, 2001), Robert A. Bryant claims that "crucified with Christ" is Paul's "striking expression" for "describing how a person who is not properly related with God comes to be in a right relationship with God" (p. 169). But Bryant does not fully develop the meaning of this "striking expression," suggesting that in Galatians 2 it means abandoning the Law as the basis of a right relationship with God and instead trusting in Christ (p. 169), though it may have other nuances of mean-

plains that most interpreters bracket out this verse from Paul's discussion of justification and use it as the prime example of Paul's "mysticism" or "participationist" theology, linking it to texts like Romans 6 but not to its immediate context.[61] Schauf especially stresses the tight connection between 2:20 and 2:21:

> 20and it is no longer I who live, but it is Christ who lives in me. And the life I now live in the flesh I live by faith in the Son of God, who loved me and gave himself for me. 21I do not nullify the grace of God; for if justification comes through the law, then Christ died for nothing. (NRSV)

Schauf correctly argues that 2:21 "wraps up all of the arguments contained in 2:15-20" and that it "particularly builds on v. 20."[62] For Schauf, 2:20 is a "depiction of the Christian apart from any consideration of the Christian's Jew or Gentile status."[63] He finds four central features of this depiction of justification in 2:20: (1) Christ's loving death on the cross as the source of righteousness, (2) crucifixion with Christ as the common justifying experience of all Christians, (3) Christ's indwelling as indication of divine adoption and reception of the Spirit, and (4) the life of faith rather than works of the Law as appropriate existence in Christ.[64] Schauf's analysis of Gal 2:20 is largely compelling. However, he has not sufficiently shown the connection between faith and crucifixion with Christ to establish the synonymity of those two terms in supporting the thesis that 2:20 is about justification. We shall return to this below.

Similarly to Schauf, but a bit more cautiously, Martin de Boer argues in a careful study of Gal 2:15-21 that in 2:19-20 Paul reworks a common, even formulaic, view of justification as future and forensic that is shared by him, Cephas, and the new preachers in Galatia and expressed in 2:16a. Paul first strongly dissociates this shared view of justification from works of the Law, broadly understood (the remainder of 2:16). Here Paul's insistence that justification comes (to those who believe) from *pistis Christou* rather than works of the Law intimates what Paul makes clearer in 2:19-21: that justification is not just *future*, but also

---

ing elsewhere (p. 169 n. 14). This understanding of Galatians 2 is not inaccurate, but it is unfortunately very general and incomplete.

61. Schauf, "Galatians 2.20."
62. Schauf, "Galatians 2.20," p. 96.
63. Schauf, "Galatians 2.20," p. 97.
64. Schauf, "Galatians 2.20," pp. 98-101.

present.[65] When Paul returns explicitly to the subject of justification in 2:21, he does so having spoken of co-crucifixion with Christ, thereby associating participation in Christ with justification.[66] What de Boer calls the death of the "nomistic I"[67] — a deathlike separation from the Law and identification with the crucified Christ — means that Paul sees justification as participation, not sacramentally (as in Romans 6) but as an experience of God's rectifying power in the present, "informed and shaped by the categories and motifs native to Jewish cosmological apocalyptic eschatology."[68] Thus, not *explicitly* but *in context*, de Boer says, Paul has redefined justification as present and participatory, and the future and forensic view becomes insufficient.[69]

The thrust of de Boer's article is on target, but two additional points will strengthen and expand his thesis. First, de Boer is far too hesitant in saying that context alone suggests a redefinition of justification and that "no explicit redefinition occurs."[70] To be sure, Paul does not specifically say "justification is by co-crucifixion," but the parallel language in 2:19a and 2:19b-20a makes that claim in itself, and not just in its context:

2:19a (a) For through the Law I died to the Law [my previous source of justification]

(b) so that I might live to God.

2:19b-20a (a′) I have been crucified with Christ [my new source of justification];

(a″) and it is no longer I who live,

(b′) but it is Christ who lives in me.

(b″) And the life I now live in the flesh I live by the faith[fulness] of the Son of God.[71]

In 2:19-20, Paul is clearly not speaking about some experience *subsequent* to justification but is speaking of justification itself, understood now as

65. de Boer, "A Justification Tradition," pp. 210-11.
66. de Boer, "A Justification Tradition," pp. 211-15.
67. de Boer, "A Justification Tradition," p. 213.
68. de Boer, "A Justification Tradition," pp. 213 n. 33, 215.
69. de Boer, "A Justification Tradition," pp. 214-15.
70. de Boer, "A Justification Tradition," p. 215.
71. Or, less likely, "by faith in the Son of God."

occurring by co-crucifixion instead of Law-keeping. De Boer has corrected an error that many interpreters make, which is, ironically, to disconnect (at least implicitly) co-crucifixion in 2:19-20 from justification in 2:16-18 and 2:21. But the text of 2:19-20 itself, not just the context, also tells us that this co-crucifixion is what Paul himself means by justification — as Schauf argues.[72]

To be more precise, however, and this is my second point in response to de Boer (though it would apply also to Schauf), we should say that Paul is defining (or redefining) not only justification, but therefore also faith. Justification "by *faith*" is for Paul justification by *co-crucifixion*. Those described as "hav[ing] come to believe in [*eis*] Christ Jesus" (2:16) — meaning those who have responded affirmatively to the gospel with faith and thus moved from outside Christ into Christ — and having been justified by *pistis Christou* rather than by doing the works of the Law, are subsequently redescribed (if we assume that Paul is speaking representatively) as those who have died to the Law and been crucified with Christ in order to live. It is hard to resist the conclusion that faith is, for Paul, a death experience, a death *to* the Law (and/or to the "flesh") and a death *with* Christ.[73] (As the parallel language of transfer in Gal 3:27 suggests, this faith probably was recognized as such in baptism, though the emphasis here is on faith.[74])

Moreover, by defining faith as co-crucifixion and the result of that co-crucifixion as life — life "to God" and Christ living within (2:19-20) — Paul connects justification with the resurrection of the dead — that is, the present resurrection of the dead. The "I" has been crucified but also lives as a new "I"; the logical and implicit missing link between death and new life is, of course, resurrection. Justification by faith means resurrection

---

72. Schauf also agrees that the context strengthens the claim that 2:20 is about justification ("Galatians 2:20," p. 101).

73. Gentiles would of course not need to die to the (Jewish) Law, but they would require crucifixion with respect to the flesh and the world (Gal 5:24; 6:14). Such texts are probably to be understood as expressive of Paul's more generic images, applicable to Gentiles and Jews alike, parallel to and inclusive of the reality of death to the Law that is applicable only to Jews. For both Jews and Gentiles, faith means death.

74. The parallel between "faith into [*eis*] Christ" (2:16) and baptism is unmistakable: "As many of you as were baptized into [*eis*] Christ have clothed yourselves with Christ" (Gal 3:27).

from the dead; justifying faith is inherently both participatory and trans-formative.[75]

This line of interpretation is taken also by Robert Tannehill in his essay on participation in Paul. Tannehill argues that Paul, "while arguing fervently for justification from faith and not works of the law . . . expresses his argument in terms of participation in Christ."[76] He contends that in "two passionate passages [Gal 2:15-21 and Phil 3:2-11] Paul grounds his assertion that justification is based on faith, not works of the law, on the reality and surpassing value of participation in Christ. These same passages suggest a neglected but important dimension to the meaning of faith for Paul."[77] About Gal 2:19-20, Tannehill specifically says:

> Here Christ's death is proclaimed as a freeing and transforming event that is effective *because Paul is pulled into it and shares in it,* resulting in a continuing participation in Christ, who is the new life-power in Paul. The next sentence provides important explanation. In Gal 2:20b Paul reformulates his statement that "Christ lives in me" and does so in part in order to relate his new life to the previously introduced (see 2:16) theme of faith: "And what I now live in flesh, I live by faith, the faith of the Son of God who loved me and gave himself over for me." This is the self-renouncing Son of God that we encountered in previous passages, the Son of God who renounced his own advantages in order to identify with humanity in its need, a renunciation carried to the point of death on a cross (Phil 2:8).[78]

Although Tannehill does not use the precise language of co-crucifixion and co-resurrection, he clearly sees Paul articulating justification "from faith" (Tannnehill's rendering of the Greek *ek pisteōs*) in terms of participating in Christ's death and resurrection. Faith itself is being defined in a unique way as participation in Christ's death.[79]

---

75. We saw these elements of participation and transformation already in the discussion of 2 Cor 5:14-21 above. See also the work of Daniel G. Powers, who stresses the corporate character of participation in *Salvation through Participation: An Examination of the Notion of the Believers' Corporate Unity with Christ in Early Christian Soteriology,* Contributions to Biblical Exegesis and Theology (Leuven: Peeters, 2001), pp. 119-25.

76. Tannehill, "Participation in Christ," p. 229.

77. Tannehill, "Participation in Christ," p. 229.

78. Tannehill, "Participation in Christ," pp. 229-30; emphasis added.

79. In personal correspondence (January 25, 2008), Tannehill reacted to my proposal of

Like Hays, Wright, myself, and many others, Tannehill reads the *pistis Christou* passages here and elsewhere as examples of the subjective genitive ("the faith of Christ").[80] However, our analysis has shown that Gal 2:15-21 demonstrates clearly, no matter how one interprets the two *pistis Christou* (faith of/in Christ) texts, that Paul's understanding of both faith and justification is irreducibly connected to the cross of Christ and to participation in it. As Lutheran New Testament scholar Roy Harrisville says matter-of-factly in his book on the cross in the New Testament, "[j]ustification of the sinner is established by virtue of being crucified with Christ (Gal. 2:19)."[81] Harrisville succinctly summarizes the conclusion to which our analysis of Gal 2:15-21 has driven us. Any other understanding of faith, or of justification, is therefore less than Pauline.

The Theological Consequences of Paul's Redefinition

Justification by faith, then, is a death-and-resurrection experience. Three important theological comments on this contention must be stressed.

First, justification is not in any sense a self-generated experience. The passive voice — "I have been crucified with Christ" — implies an external agent, a divinely initiated action. As Paul says in Gal 3:1-5, he "exhibited" Christ crucified, the Galatians received the Spirit, and they responded with "faith."[82] This can only mean that the Spirit somehow effected the Galatians' experience of co-crucifixion and co-resurrection. We cannot here solve the mystery of divine initiative and human response, but we must rule out any semi-Pelagian or

---

the phrase "justification by co-crucifixion" with the words "a good summary phrase" of what each of us is arguing about Paul.

80. Tannehill ("Participation in Christ," p. 230) rightly stresses that he accepts the subjective interpretation "with this proviso: Christ's faith (= his faithful obedience) is a founding event that opens a realm of faith in which others are invited to participate. . . . When his people put faith in Christ, they enter this new eschatological reality. They participate in Christ and share his faith."

81. Harrisville, *Fracture*, p. 76. Even Mark Seifrid, who has been emphatic about the forensic character of justification, says that Gal 2:18-21 is an "explanation of justification [cf. 2:15-17] in terms of participation in the crucified and risen Christ" ("Paul's Use of Righteousness Language," p. 53).

82. Alternatively, some take the awkward phrase "hearing of faith" *(akoēs pisteōs)* in 3:2 as a reference to the Galatians' hearing about Jesus' faith(fulness). Although that reading would strengthen the point I am making here, I am not yet convinced that this text refers to Jesus' faith.

Pelagian interpretation of faith (and specifically co-crucifixion and co-resurrection) as something that initiates or effects one's own salvation.

Second, justification is not a private experience but a public and corporate one. Those who have expressed *pistis* in response to the exhibition of Christ crucified "have come to believe in [Greek *eis*, "into"] Christ" (Gal 2:16). The parallel language in Gal 3:27 suggests that this experience occurs in, or is at least expressed in, the public event of identification with Christ's death and resurrection in baptism: "As many of you as were baptized into [Greek *eis*] Christ have clothed yourselves with Christ." And baptism into Christ means incorporation into the diverse community of fellow baptized, co-crucified, co-resurrected, justified inhabitants of Christ (Gal 3:28).

Third, justification is an experience of both death and resurrection, and both must be stressed. But the resurrection to new life it incorporates is a resurrection to an ongoing state of crucifixion: I "have been" crucified means I "still am" crucified. Therefore, justification by faith must be understood first and foremost as a participatory crucifixion that is, paradoxically, life-giving (cf. 2 Cor 4:7-15). The one who exercises faith, and is thereby crucified with Christ, is resurrected to new life but always remains crucified (hence the perfect tense of *systauroō* in Gal 2:19 — as in Rom 6:6 [see below]), because he or she is animated by the resurrected Christ, who always remains for Paul (and the New Testament more generally) the crucified Christ (e.g., 1 Cor 2:2; cf. John 20:20, 27; Rev 5:6). As Miroslav Volf says in commenting on this text, the self "is both 'de-centered' and 're-centered' by one and the same process, by participating in the death and resurrection of Christ through faith and baptism. . . ."[83] Volf continues:

> By being 'crucified with Christ,' the self has received a new center — the Christ who lives in it and with whom it lives. . . . The center of the self — a center that is both inside and outside — is the story of Jesus Christ, who has become the story of the self. More precisely, the center is Jesus Christ crucified and resurrected who has become part and parcel of the very structure of the self.[84]

This understanding of faith as crucifixion is reinforced by Paul's insistence that the believer's experience (narrated representatively by Paul in

83. Volf, *Exclusion and Embrace: A Theological Explanation of Identity, Otherness, and Reconciliation* (Nashville: Abingdon, 1996), p. 70.
84. Volf, *Exclusion and Embrace*, p. 70.

first-person texts) is not only a death with Christ but also a death to the Law (Gal 2:19), to the world (Gal 6:14), and of the flesh (Gal 5:24). The mention of death of the flesh and to the world also demonstrates that Gal 2:15-21 should not be read only as a Jewish experience of liberation from the Law. Rather, *every* believer begins and continues his or her existence in Christ by co-crucifixion.[85] Gal 2:19-21 suggests that co-crucifixion is both the *way in* and the way to *stay in* the covenant.

Once again, we must stress that it is *the resurrected crucified Christ*[86] with whom believers are initially and continually crucified. This is important, both christologically and soteriologically, in two ways. First, as an experience of the risen or resurrected Christ, co-crucifixion is not merely a metaphor but an apt description of an encounter with a living person whose presence transforms and animates believers: "It is no longer I who live but Christ who lives in me. And the life I live, I live by the faithfulness of the Son of God, who loved me by giving himself for me." As Douglas Campbell says, "this is no mere *imitatio Christi!*" for "God is not asking [believers] . . . to imitate Christ — perhaps an impossible task — so much as *to inhabit or to indwell him*," such that "the Spirit of God is actively reshaping the Christian into the likeness of Christ."[87] The kenosis of the preexistent Son of God, known in the fidelity and love of the historical Jesus, continues to define the reality of the resurrected Christ and thus of those whom he enlivens.[88] Second, then, as we saw also in chapter one, the Resurrected One remains the Crucified One. As Käsemann famously said, "The cross is the signature of the one who is risen."[89] It is that christological reality that requires and per-

---

85. De Boer ("A Justification Tradition," pp. 212-15) is right to point out that even though the first few verses of 2:15-21 refer only to Jewish experience, 2:20 is universal. Wright (*Paul: In Fresh Perspective*, pp. 112-13) implies that the entire passage is only about the experience of Jewish believers.

86. This phrase, which I have used elsewhere, is more precisely Pauline than the title of Bryant's book, *The Risen Crucified Christ in Galatia,* though we are each making the same christological connection between crucifixion and resurrection.

87. Campbell, *The Quest for Paul's Gospel,* p. 93, emphasis added. Unfortunately, Campbell sometimes overemphasizes fidelity in suffering, rather than cruciformity more generally, as the work of the Spirit, as we will note again below.

88. Cf. Hays (*Moral Vision,* p. 32), commenting on Gal 2:19-20: "The faith(fulness) of Jesus Christ becomes the animating force in our lives."

89. See Ernst Käsemann, "The Saving Significance of the Death of Jesus in Paul," in *Perspectives on Paul,* trans. Margaret Kohl (Philadelphia: Fortress, 1971; repr. Mifflintown: Sigler, 1996), pp. 32-59, here p. 56. For a recent, lengthy restatement of this dictum based on a study

mits the paradoxical character of present-resurrection-as-cruciformity described above.

In summary, we may say that in Gal 2:15-21 justification is a participatory death-and-resurrection experience that

1. occurs for those who have entered into Christ by transfer of dominion from outside Christ into Christ by faith (explicitly, 2:16) and baptism (implicitly; cf. Gal 3:27): "we have come to believe in [*eis*] Christ Jesus" (2:16), and we are "justified in Christ";[90]
2. requires "death" to the Law as the means of justification: "through the law I died to the law" (2:19);
3. is by faith understood as co-crucifixion, the death of the self: "I have been crucified with Christ; and it is no longer I who live" (2:19-20);
4. is a resurrection of the self to new life, such that justification by faith means resurrection by crucifixion (co-crucifixion): "so that I might live to God. . . . And the life I now live in the flesh" (2:19-20);
5. has a present participatory, covenantal, and transformative character (2:19-20), as well as (within the larger context of the letter) a future participatory, transformative dimension;[91]
6. is specifically about a participatory relationship with the living Christ and thus a life "to" God: "so that I might live to God. . . . it is Christ who lives in me" (2:19-20); and
7. is characterized by the faith and love (self-donation to God and others) of Christ the Son of God: "I live by the faithfulness of the Son of God, who loved me by giving himself for me" (2:20, my translation).

We turn now to Romans 6, where we will find significant similarities to Galatians 2.

---

of Galatians, see Bryant, *The Risen Crucified Christ in Galatia.* For his treatment of Gal 2:15-21 (actually 2:11-21), see pp. 150-51 and pp. 166-70.

90. Hays notes that the compatibility of "participation in Christ" and "justification" "appears most clearly [at least in Galatians] in Gal 2:17," where "justification and participation in Christ are merged" (*The Faith of Jesus Christ*, 2nd ed., p. 212). It should also be noted that 3:1-5 suggests that faith itself is enabled by, or is in response to the action of, the Spirit.

91. Paul's clear emphasis throughout the text is on the present experience, though 2:16 may imply that justification also has a future dimension: "no one will be justified." Even this future dimension of justification is participatory and not merely forensic, however. The phrase "hope of righteousness" in Gal 5:5 implies a future, full transformation, not merely acquittal.

Romans 6:1–7:6

Romans 6 is, of course, where the second occurrence of *systauroō* is found (6:6). As in Galatians 2, so also in Romans 6: life comes from death, from co-crucifixion. Romans 6 (or, more precisely, 6:1–7:6) is Gal 2:15-21 writ large.[92] In fact, we should probably see Rom 3:20–8:39 as an expansion of Gal 2:15-21, discussing in more detail and for a different audience the meaning of justification by faith, that is, by co-crucifixion. The heart of this is in Romans 6, where the term *systauroō* actually appears, but ch. 6 cannot be severed from ch. 5 and chs. 7 and 8, any more than Gal 2:19-20 (with its language of co-crucifixion) can be severed from Gal 2:15-18 and 2:21 (with the language of justification). If much of the first half of Romans is essentially an expansion of Gal 2:15-21, then the absence of "participationist" language from Romans until ch. 6 is no more significant than its absence from Gal 2:15-21 until vv. 19-20. Similarly, the oft-noted absence of "justification" and "faith" language for several chapters after Rom 5:1-11 is no more significant than its absence from Gal 2:19-20.

In neither Galatians nor Romans does this variation in language mean either that Paul works with two soteriological models or that participation is an experience "added onto" justification. To be sure, interpreters have usually viewed Romans 5–8 as a discussion of the *consequences* of justification by faith. The most common approach is to see the consequences as various forms of freedom, especially freedom from wrath, sin, and death. However, these chapters are more accurately viewed as a discussion of the *meaning* of justification by faith, understood as co-crucifixion and participation in Christ. That is, *the realities narrated in these chapters (Romans 5-8) are constitutive of, not consequences of, justification.*[93]

Part of the problem, then, in the misunderstanding of justification is the misreading of Romans 5–8, particularly the relationship of ch. 6 to 5:1-11. For many interpreters, the relationship is either sequential or supplemental. That is, "sanctification" (ch. 6) follows justification (5:1-11), either chronologically or logically — or both.

Despite the lack of "justification" and "faith" language in Rom 5:12–8:29, this is a fundamental misreading of Romans.[94] We must resist the temptation

---

92. This is implicitly Tannehill's position as well ("Participation in Christ," pp. 229, 235).

93. See the discussion in my *Apostle of the Crucified Lord*, pp. 363-79.

94. Agreeing with this view over against the "traditional Protestant" reading are, e.g.,

to read Romans 5–8 in linear fashion as an *ordo salutis*. Rather, we must read it perspectivally, to use Mark Seifrid's term;[95] the chapters provide several perspectives on the same reality. For Paul, Romans 6 does not supplement justification by faith or merely explain its effects or consequences; rather, it *defines* justification by faith. Robert Tannehill draws a similar conclusion:

> When Paul shifts to participatory language in Rom 5:12-21 and 6:1–7:6, speaking of dying and rising with Christ and describing Adam and Christ as supra-individual persons, he has not moved on from soteriology to a new topic but is deepening his soteriology, providing further insight into how redemption in Christ Jesus has taken place and explaining its implications.[96]

Following 5:1-11, Paul provides three sets of quite fully developed antitheses that contrast pre- and post-justification existence: life in Adam vs. life in Christ (5:12-21), slavery to sin vs. slavery to God (6:1–7:6), and life in the flesh vs. life in the Spirit (7:7–8:39). (This Trinitarian construction corresponds to the Trinitarian character of 5:1-11.) We might call these Paul's "justification antinomies" or, better, "justification antitheses." The first part of ch. 6 is an extended definition of justification by faith as resurrection by co-crucifixion that explains what happens in baptism when one moves from Adam to Christ, from sin to God, and from the flesh to the Spirit — that is, when one is justified by faith, restored to right covenant relations, and crucified, buried, and resurrected with Christ.

The parallels between Gal 2:15-21 and Rom 6:1–7:6 support this reading of Romans. We have seen in Gal 2:15-21 that justification is a participatory death-and-resurrection experience with seven concrete dimensions, enumerated above. Similarly, what is described in Romans 6:1–7:6 is a participatory death-and-resurrection experience that has parallel dimensions; it

1. occurs for those who have entered into Christ by transfer of dominion from outside Christ into Christ by baptism (explicitly, 6:3: "baptized

---

Talbert, *Romans*, pp. 162-63; Thomas R. Schreiner, *Romans* (Grand Rapids: Baker, 1998), pp. 298-99, 319.

95. Mark A. Seifrid, "Unrighteous by Faith: Apostolic Proclamation in Romans 1:18–3:20," in Carson, *et al.*, eds., *Justification and Variegated Nomism*, vol. 2, pp. 105-45, here p. 107 n. 5 (discussing a different matter).

96. Tannehill, "Participation in Christ," p. 235.

into Christ Jesus"; cf. 6:11, 23) and faith (implicitly, in the larger context; see 5:1);

2. requires "death" to the Law as the means of justification — "you have died to the law through the body of Christ" (7:4) — and also death to Sin: "died to sin" (6:2); "so that the body of sin might be destroyed, and we might no longer be enslaved to sin" (6:6); "dead to sin" (6:11);

3. is a co-crucifixion, the death of the self: "baptized into his death" (6:3); "buried with him by baptism into death" (6:4); "united with him in a death like his" (6:5); "our old self was crucified with him" (6:6); "we have died with Christ" (6:8);

4. is a resurrection to new life: "just as Christ was raised from the dead . . . so we too might walk in newness of life" (6:4); "those who have been brought from death to life" (6:13); "died to the law . . . the new life of the Spirit" (7:4, 6);[97]

5. has both a present covenantal, transformative, participatory character (Paul's emphasis throughout) and a future participatory, transformative dimension: "we will certainly be united with him in a resurrection like his" (6:5b); "eternal life" (6:22, 23);[98]

6. is specifically about a participatory relationship with the living Christ and thus a life "to" God: "alive to God in Christ Jesus" (6:11); "so that you may belong to another, to him who has been raised from the dead in order that we may bear fruit for God" (7:4b); and

7. is implicitly grounded (in context) in the faith/obedience and love of Christ (5:19; 8:34-35), and is therefore characterized by self-presentation to God and a life of holiness and justice/righteousness: "No longer present your members to sin as instruments of wickedness *(adikia)*, but present yourselves to God as those who have been brought from death

---

97. Some New Testament scholars seem blindly, dogmatically opposed to the idea of present resurrection and insist only on a future resurrection in Paul. This is simply wrong, as both Galatians 2 and Romans 6 (plus Romans 8) show. The resurrected Christ lives in believers and gives them new life. For Paul, this is a resurrection *in* the body now that anticipates the later resurrection *of* the body (see, e.g., Rom 8:11). Helpful discussion may be found in N. T. Wright, *The Resurrection of the Son of God*, Christian Origins and the Question of God, vol. 3 (Minneapolis: Fortress, 2003), pp. 248-54. Wright correctly argues that "in baptism the Christian not only dies with the Messiah *but rises as well*" (p. 252; emphasis his). See also Campbell, *The Quest for Paul's Gospel*, pp. 205-6, who writes that "[b]y mapping Christians onto the life of the presently resurrected one, Christ, [Paul affirms that] Christians are mapped onto the preliminary stages of eschatological salvation" (p. 206).

98. Cf. Phil 3:21.

to life, and present your members to God as instruments of righteousness" (6:13);[99] "you . . . have become slaves of righteousness" (6:18; cf. 6:19b); "the advantage you get is sanctification" (6:22); cf. Rom 12:1-2.

These similarities between justification in Gal 2:15-21 and in Rom 6:1–7:6 may be summarized in the following table:

Similarities between Gal 2:15-21 and Rom 6:1–7:6 on Justification

The Features of Justification	Galatians 2:15-21 (by faith)	Romans 6:1–7:6 (by baptism)
1. Transfer into Christ	"we have come to believe in [*eis*] Christ Jesus" (2:16); "justified in Christ" (2:17); cf. 3:27	"baptized into Christ Jesus" (6:3); "alive to God in Christ Jesus"; "eternal life in Christ Jesus our Lord" (6:23)
2. Death to the Law/Law and sin	"through the law I died to the law" (2:19)	"you have died to the law through the body of Christ" (7:4); cf. "died to sin" (6:2); "so that the body of sin might be destroyed, and we might no longer be enslaved to sin" (6:6); "dead to sin" (6:11)
3. Co-crucifixion (expressed in passive voice), death of self	"I have been crucified with Christ; and it is no longer I who live" (2:19-20)	"baptized into his death" (6:3); "buried with him by baptism into death" (6:4); "united with him in a death like his" (6:5); "our old self was crucified with him" (6:6); "we have died with Christ" (6:8)

99. Cf. Rom 6:16, where the self-presentation is to obedience, which we should probably understand as synecdoche for Christ's obedience (5:19) and hence Christ himself. Even here, "righteousness" most likely refers to God's project of rightwising the world through the righteous Son and thus to Christlike obedience and love (cf. 8:29-30, where Christlikeness is the soteriological telos). I once again owe some of these connections to Andy Johnson in personal correspondence (October 2006), in which he also says, "Since Christ's own body was the very instrument through which God demonstrated his *dikaiosynē*, it is not surprising that those who are justified by co-crucifixion, baptized and sharing in his *pistis*, are called to present their own bodies as weapons/instruments through which God's apocalyptic invasion to reclaim his cosmos from the chaos of 1:18ff continues to go forward."

4. Resurrection to new life	"so that I might live to God. . . . And the life I now live in the flesh" (2:19-20)	"just as Christ was raised from the dead . . . so we too might walk in newness of life" (6:4); "alive to God in Christ Jesus" (6:11); "those who have been brought from death to life" (6:13); "died to the law . . . the new life of the Spirit" (7:4, 6)
5. Present and future dimensions	Present in 2:19-20; future: "no one will be justified" (2:16)	Present throughout; future: "we will certainly be united with him in a resurrection like his" (6:5b); "eternal life" (6:22, 23)
6. Participation with Christ and to God	"so that I might live to God. . . . it is Christ who lives in me" (2:19-20)	"alive to God in Christ Jesus" (6:11); "so that you may belong to another, to him who has been raised from the dead in order that we may bear fruit for God" (7:4b)
7. Faith and love (Christ's and ours); i.e., proper covenantal relations with God and others	"faith of Jesus Christ . . . faith of Christ" (2:16); "we have come to believe in [*eis*] Christ Jesus" (2:16); "I live by the faith of the Son of God, who loved me by giving himself for me" (2:20, my translation). Cf. 5:6 for believers' faith and love explicitly.	"No longer present your members to sin as instruments of wickedness, but present yourselves to God as those who have been brought from death to life, and present your members to God as instruments of righteousness" (6:13); "you . . . have become slaves of righteousness" (6:18; cf. 6:19b); "the advantage you get is sanctification" (6:22). Cf. 5:19; 8:34-35 for Christ's faith/obedience and love explicitly.

To be sure, there are some differences in emphasis between Romans and Galatians. Although the language of being "in Christ" occurs in both texts (Gal 2:17; Rom 6:3, 11), the specific language of Christ within (Gal 2:20a) awaits ch. 8 in Romans (vv. 9-11). Moreover, the death language of Romans is expanded to include and emphasize liberation from and death to sin. Even this idea may be implied in Gal 2:15-21, however, and it has a parallel in the notions of liberation from and crucifixion of the flesh (Gal 5:13, 24).[100] Finally, the expectation of love on the part of the justified/crucified community, so clearly implied in Gal 2:20, does not appear explicitly in Romans until Romans 12–15, where it is grounded, as in Galatians, in the love of Christ (15:1-3).[101]

These are, however, minor differences of emphasis in an expanded text for a new context. The more significant parallels, on the other hand, suggest very clearly that *Paul is describing in Rom 6:1–7:6 the same reality he describes in Gal 2:15-21:* namely, justification by faith understood as a participatory experience of co-crucifixion and resurrection with Christ. In both passages Paul is likely addressing the charge that he preached an antinomian gospel (Gal 2:17; 5:1, 13; Rom 3:8; 5:20; 6:1, 15). What happens in faith and baptism, Paul says, is the beginning of apocalyptic liberation from "the present [evil] age" (Gal 1:4) and from Sin itself (Rom 3:9; 6:6), that is, the reversal of the covenantally dysfunctional impiety and injustice that characterize human existence apart from Christ (Rom 1:18-32), and thus the beginning of individual and corporate covenantal existence for Gentiles and Jews alike, marked by faith and love. Both Romans and Galatians say that in such a community the Law, or at least its Christ-shaped (Gal 6:2) "just requirement" (Rom 8:4), is being fulfilled (Gal 5:14; 6:2; Rom 13:8-10).[102]

If that is the case, then we need once again to reexamine the relationship between faith and baptism in Paul. Galatians 2 is about faith, Romans 6 about baptism. But this is a superfluous difference. It does not and cannot mean that baptism is some kind of supplement (or alternative) to faith that somehow has the same kind of effect or structure as faith — or vice versa.

---

100. Greek *sarx*, hidden in the NRSV of 5:13, where it is rendered "self-indulgence."

101. At the same time, however, we should remember that the call to love is in fact only implicit in Gal 2:20, and it appears explicitly quite a bit later, in 5:6-15.

102. I owe the connection of Rom 5:18 to Rom 8:4 to Andy Johnson in personal correspondence. Paul's rejection of *erga nomou* or the Law itself as the basis of justification does *not* mean his rejection of the Law per se or even of the Law as something that believers perform. In fact, ironically and paradoxically, it is only believers, who do not seek justification by (works of) the Law, who actually (fulfill) the Law — or more precisely, in whom the Law is fulfilled by the action of the Spirit of Christ. Richard Hays persuasively makes this point about Paul generally in his essay "The Role of Scripture in Paul's Ethics," in *The Conversion of the Imagination: Paul as Interpreter of Israel's Scripture* (Grand Rapids: Eerdmans, 2005; originally published in 1996), pp. 143-62; here especially 148-51. Key texts, as Hays reminds us, include Rom 13:9-10, Gal 5:14, and Rom 8:3-4 (in all of which the verb "fulfill" appears), but also Rom 2:26-29a and Phil 3:2-3.

Rather, it shows that for Paul faith and baptism are theologically coterminous, and faith is the essence of baptism even as baptism is the public expression of faith. Thus what Paul predicates of faith he can also predicate of baptism, and vice versa,[103] because together they effect, at least from the perspective of the human response, transfer into Christ and thus participatory justification in him.

This clearly does not mean that faith and therefore justification are human achievements. To be sure, the response of faith and its expression in baptism are required, not optional. The faith of Christ still requires the human response of faith, as every *pistis Christou* passage demonstrates.[104] We must once again stress, however, that God is the initiator and primary actor in all this, as seen in the many passive participles and main verbs Paul uses to describe the salvation event. This important grammatical phenomenon suggests a salvific source outside the self, even an "alien" righteousness: justified (1 Cor 6:11), baptized (Rom 6:3; Gal 3:27; 1 Cor 1:13; 12:13), washed (1 Cor 6:11), crucified (Rom 6:3; Gal 2:19; 6:14), buried (Rom 6:4), and liberated (Rom 6:18). People respond in faith to the gospel, but it is God who justifies, washes (through human agents of baptism), crucifies, raises, and liberates.

While some may prefer a nice orderly *ordo salutis,* Paul sees baptism, justification, and even sanctification as theologically coterminous: "But you were washed, you were sanctified, you were justified in the name of the Lord Jesus Christ and in the Spirit of our God" (1 Cor 6:11).[105] "And at the same time," Paul would say, "you were crucified and raised by God's grace and power."

Refining Our Understanding of "Faith" in Paul

Thus far, the argument of this chapter, especially this section on Romans and Galatians, has been that justification is indeed, for Paul, by faith, but it is faith understood as co-crucifixion. For Paul, the appropriate response to the good

103. Building on the work of E. P. Sanders, Jouette M. Bassler, *Navigating Paul: An Introduction to Key Theological Concepts* (Louisville: Westminster John Knox, 2007), p. 31, briefly makes a similar point in her discussion of faith.

104. Tannehill rightly notes a pattern of Christ's faith and human responsive faith in all the *pistis Christou* texts ("Participation in Christ," pp. 232-33).

105. This is also stressed by Campbell, *The Quest for Paul's Gospel,* p. 49, referring to Dunn's *Theology.*

news of God's faithfulness, manifested in Christ's faith(fulness), is human faith. Christ's faith (reading *Christou* as a subjective genitive) is met by our faith (Gal 2:16). We need to unpack this a bit more fully because the soteriological model we are proposing takes human faith seriously, as just noted.

Paul's understanding of faith is complex. Faith is a total response of obedience to the gospel (Rom 1:5; 16:26). It is also, as we have seen, a *death experience* in which one enters into the experience of Jesus' crucifixion. Paradoxically, this death experience called faith results in life, both present and future, as the following graphic seeks to illustrate:

Faith   →   justification   =   (a) present covenantal relations and
                                     (b) future vindication/righteousness
Crucifixion   →   resurrection   =   (a) present new life and
                                     (b) future bodily resurrection

As a person enters into Christ and into the realm of his reign as living Lord (Gal 2:19-20; Rom 6:1-11), Christ (or Christ's Spirit) enters into that person (Rom 8:9-11). The Spirit of the Son (Gal 4:6) is the Spirit of love and faith(fulness) (Gal 5:22) because the Son is the embodiment of love and faithfulness (Gal 2:20).[106] Human faith, therefore, is an intimate identification with Christ's unified act of fidelity and love. The result, as we will see more fully in the next section, is that our own faith (fidelity) toward God and love toward others are *inseparable* (Gal 5:6).

This interpretation of faith is not about merit, or "salvation by works," but about what actually constitutes participation in Christ's faithful and loving death.

Paul believes that God's justification means the creation of a community of Jews and Gentiles with a new heart, by virtue of internal rather than external circumcision (Rom 2:25-29), who, enabled by the Spirit, live faithfully toward God and lovingly toward others, thus fulfilling the "just requirement of the law" (Rom 8:3-4). The very purpose of Christ's incarnation and death was to create such a community (Gal 5:6, 13-14; Rom 8:3-4; 2 Cor 5:21).[107]

But doesn't Paul's separation of faith from "works of the law" (Rom 3:28; Gal 2:16) contradict this? No, it does not. Paul's separation of faith from

---

106. For further discussion of the Spirit in Galatians, see chapter three below, pages 115-18.

107. So also Francis Watson, *Paul, Judaism, and the Gentiles: Beyond the New Perspective,* rev. ed. (Grand Rapids: Eerdmans, 2007), pp. 298-300.

works of the Law has two meanings. First, it signifies that *justification is available to all,* not just to those who possess the Law (i.e., Jews). Second, it asserts that justification is on the basis of *divine initiative* followed by *human response* rather than *human initiative* followed by *divine response.*

In other words, justification by faith apart from works means justification by *grace-enabled participatory response* rather than by *privilege* (passive) or *initiative* (active).[108] It does *not* mean justification by faith narrowly construed as assent, or even trust.[109] Justification by faith means that God justifies those who *respond appropriately to,* rather than *ignore* or *try to elicit,* God's favor (grace), whether Jew or Gentile. In the end, it is perhaps best to say that justification is by means of God's faithfulness expressed in love, demonstrated in Christ's act of faithfulness expressed in love, to which humans, moved and enabled by God's Spirit, respond in faithfulness that expresses itself in love — that is, in co-crucifixion. What matters for Paul is faith "made effective through" (NRSV margin) or "expressing itself through" (NIV) love (Gal 5:6), which corresponds to the cross of faith and love by which believers live (Gal 2:20). Once again, *there can be no separation of faith from love, of faith from action.*

At the risk of repetition, we must emphasize that this claim is not the same as saying that justification is by works, or that salvation is achieved by love. It is rather to say that sharing in this kind of death can take place in no other way than that of covenantal fidelity, because that is the nature of the Son, his death, his Spirit, and his Father. It is what the grace of the cross both requires and enables.[110]

Here we may find ourselves in frustrating partial agreement with Simon Gathercole, who argues compellingly for the importance of obedience, or doing what God requires, as inherent in Paul's understanding of justification, though not as the *basis* of God's justification of the sinner.[111] So far, so

---

108. For a study of the comprehensive and participatory character of faith in Paul, see David M. Hay, "Paul's Understanding of Faith as Participation," in *Paul and His Theology,* Pauline Studies vol. 3, ed. Stanley E. Porter (Leiden/Boston: Brill, 2006), pp. 45-76. Hay writes, "[F]aith, for Paul, is the mode by which Christians participate or live spiritually in Christ" (p. 52; cf. p. 46); it has "both individual and corporate dimensions" and "combines elements of cognitive assertion, trust, and faithfulness" (p. 46).

109. See also Watson, *Paul, Judaism, and the Gentiles,* rev. ed., pp. 212-13.

110. The misplaced fear of a "lurking Pelagianism" among advocates of a participationist soteriology is also noted by Stubbs, "The Shape of Soteriology," p. 156.

111. Gathercole, "The Doctrine of Justification in Paul and Beyond," p. 240.

good. At the same time, however, Gathercole claims that faith, understood as trusting God's promise (as the "alternative 'instrumental cause'" of justification, instead of obeying the Law), is what leads to a "divine decision":

> By divine decision, this [faith, trusting God's promise] is reckoned as righteousness. That is to say, the believer is reckoned as having accomplished all that God requires. Justification, then . . . is God's creative act whereby, through divine determination, the believer has done everything that God requires.[112]

Unfortunately, Gathercole's "minimalist"[113] definition of faith leads inevitably to the dead end of a legal fiction — the very thing Gathercole despises! — if a divine declaration allegedly creates righteousness where there is none.[114] Logically, we must reject this approach and its legal fiction and either return to the exegetically untenuous principle of the imputation of righteousness or expand our definition of faith to mean participation in Christ's righteousness, his *pistis* and *agapē* (as I think Paul says it), or *his* doing of "all that God requires" (as Gathercole describes it).[115]

At this point, Douglas Campbell's exploration of faith in Paul comes to the rescue — almost. Campbell provides a thick definition of faith in Paul as inherently participatory and Trinitarian[116] — with which I am in complete agreement. Curiously, however, he does not link this faith very directly to the cross. This is probably the case because Campbell reacts so negatively to the justification-by-faith soteriological model and its allegedly "transactional" interpretation of Christ's death (as a sacrifice), leading him to emphasize resurrection and apocalyptic categories even while claiming that "Christ crucified!" is the "critical moment that stands at the centre of [Paul's] model

---

112. Gathercole, "The Doctrine of Justification in Paul and Beyond," p. 240.

113. The term "minimalist," as noted above, comes from Gathercole himself in his critique of N. T. Wright's definition of justification ("The Doctrine of Justification in Paul and Beyond," pp. 228-29).

114. See Gathercole, "The Doctrine of Justification in Paul and Beyond," pp. 225-29, and the discussion above.

115. Francis Watson also has a rather minimalist, or thin, understanding of faith in Paul. Although he grants that for Paul there can be no faith without faithfulness (*Paul and the Hermeneutics of Faith*, p. 161), he repeatedly uses terms like "acknowledgment" and "consent" to explain "faith" as the proper response to God's salvific action (e.g., pp. 75, 160, 162, 179).

116. Campbell, *The Quest for Paul's Gospel*, pp. 200-201.

of salvation."[117] To be sure, for Campbell Christ has certain "actions and characteristics" in which we participate,[118] and Christ is the example of present "weakness"[119] and the "paradigm of fidelity," especially fidelity in suffering.[120] Moreover, Campbell, referencing Gal 2:20, rightly says that the love required in Gal 5:6 comes from God and Christ. But if our exegesis of Galatians 2 and Romans 6 is on target, then any talk of faith as participation in Paul's soteriology must place co-crucifixion — and not merely weakness or fidelity in suffering — at the center of the discussion.[121]

More helpful is the approach of Robert Tannehill discussed above. Tannehill convincingly argues that Paul sees justification from faith itself as being "pulled into" Christ's kenotic, loving death and sharing in that death, with the result being "a continuing participation in Christ, who is the new life-power in Paul" — the same kenotic, loving Christ.[122] In this chapter, and throughout this book, we are contending, with Tannehill, for a "participatory righteousness," or participatory justification by means of participatory faith — all meaning participation in Christ's death and resurrection.

To return to the opening of this chapter: our investigation has revealed that Paul has not two soteriological models but one. Coming to the same conclusion, Jouette Bassler speaks rightly of the

> coordination of two lines of thought in Paul's letters that have long been viewed as jarringly independent: the juridical concept of justification by faith (e.g., Rom 1–4) and the participatory concept of baptism into Christ (e.g., Rom 5–8). If faith involves participation in Christ, *the two lines of thought merge into one.*[123]

In view of the argument of this chapter, may we still say that justification is by faith "alone," as Luther interpreted Rom 3:28 and as most Protes-

---

117. Campbell, *The Quest for Paul's Gospel*, p. 93.

118. Campbell, *The Quest for Paul's Gospel*, p. 200; for a list see p. 205.

119. Campbell, *The Quest for Paul's Gospel*, e.g., p. 53.

120. Campbell, *The Quest for Paul's Gospel*, pp. 201, 205; cf. pp. 92-93, where the emphasis is on Christ's suffering.

121. For resurrection vs. atonement in Campbell's *Quest*, see, e.g., p. 198. Interestingly, Campbell's entire book has a few minor references to Gal 2:19-20 and Romans 6, but no sustained exegesis of either. He finds (p. 110) Romans 5–8 to be Gal 3:26-28 writ large — not Gal 2:15-21 (see above, p. 73).

122. Tannehill, p. 229.

123. Bassler, *Navigating Paul*, p. 32 (emphasis added).

tants have insisted? No, at least not with any kind of minimalist understanding of faith. But yes, as long as we accept Paul's understanding of faith as *cruciform* faith, as the response of Spirit-enabled participation in the faithful, loving death of Christ and henceforth in his cruciform resurrection life. This is why Paul can affirm that justification is by faith alone and also affirm, with utmost seriousness, that God judges and justifies on the basis of *doing* the Law (Rom 2:13).[124] This is the law of love manifested in the obedience/faith/death of Christ, the law or "narrative pattern" of the Messiah,[125] the fulfillment of which is made possible by the indwelling, living Christ.

Some would of course argue that throughout this chapter we have loaded too much onto the initial experience of faith required for justification and thereby confused or combined justification and sanctification, or some similar theological constructs. The strongest argument for this objection would be an appeal to Paul's own texts in which he discusses faith, especially the simple faith of Abraham, as the basis of justification (Galatians 3, Romans 4). Here we have, perhaps, justification simply by trust: "Abraham believed God." But of course, even those who wish to understand faith in Paul primarily as "trust" recognize that there is a difference between Abraham's faith and that of (Christian) believers. The "simple trust" of certain texts sounds more robust and more "Christian" in Rom 4:16-25 when faith is connected to death and resurrection. This is Paul's way of saying that our understanding of faith, even of Abraham-like "simple" faith, is reconfigured by his and others' own experience of faith associated with Christ.

Thus simplistic appeals to the "faith-as-trust" texts, or to the "justification-as-crediting" metaphor, will not suffice to explicate Paul's understanding of faith and justification. Yes, faith is opposed to circumcision and works; and yes, justification is like a gift and not a wage, but these truths

---

124. Kent L. Yinger arrives at the same conclusion from a slightly different angle. See his *Paul, Judaism, and Judgment According to Deeds*, SNTSMS 105 (Cambridge: Cambridge University Press, 1999). See also Watson, *Paul, Judaism, and the Gentiles*, rev. ed.: "Belief in judgment by works is indeed an integral part of Paul's theology and not simply an unfortunate remnant of a Jewish outlook that the apostle has carelessly omitted to harmonize with his own theological stance" (p. 213). See also N. T. Wright, commenting on Rom 2:6-11 (*Resurrection*, p. 245): "[T]here is no need to 'protect' Paul from speaking of the 'good works' which people perform during their lifetime, in accordance with which this final judgment will be given."

125. See Gorman, *Cruciformity*, pp. 155-77, especially pp. 172-77, and Richard B. Hays, "Christology and Ethics in Galatians: The Law of Christ," *CBQ* 49 (1987): 268-90.

alone do not exhaust the meaning of faith or even supply its essential, distinctively Pauline, content. Here it will be helpful to draw on the concept of "non-identical repetition" as developed by John Milbank and applied to Paul by Stephen Fowl, among others.[126] When Paul holds up David and especially Abraham as models of justification by faith, he is not saying "imitate them precisely," or "your own faith is a *precise* replica of theirs." Rather, he is saying that there is an essential characteristic of their response to God that is also essential to your response to God. But this absolutely essential characteristic does not *exhaust* the reality of justification by faith *post*-Christ, and cannot do so, because it was a *pre*-Christ phenomenon. Rather, Abraham and David demonstrate aspects of justification that are essential to justification by faith but that do not exhaust it. Why? Simply because they are properly theocentric but are not, and cannot be, christocentric. As soon as Christ appears, is crucified, and is raised, justification and faith are irreversibly christocentric even as they remain theocentric. This is at least because God has now been revealed in Christ.[127]

Summary: Justification by Co-Crucifixion

For Paul, just as Christ's crucifixion led to resurrection, so also faith understood as co-crucifixion leads to justification understood as co-resurrection, meaning both new life in the present and eternal life in the future. This makes sense of Rom 4:25, in which Paul says that Christ was raised for our justification — that is, for our new life with Christ and God, both present and eschatological, to which both Gal 2:15-21 and Rom 6:1–7:6 bear witness.

We must now expand our definition of justification offered earlier in this chapter to reflect the study of Galatians and Romans we have just undertaken. That is,

> Justification is the establishment or restoration of right covenantal relations — *fidelity* to God and *love* for neighbor — by means of God's grace in Christ's death and our Spirit-enabled co-crucifixion with him. Justification therefore means co-resurrection with Christ to new life within the

126. E.g., Stephen Fowl, "Christology and Ethics in Philippians 2:5-11," in *Where Christology Began: Essays on Philippians 2*, ed. Ralph P. Martin and Brian J. Dodd (Louisville: Westminster John Knox, 1998), pp. 140-53, here p. 148.

127. See also Seifrid, "Paul's Use of Righteousness Language," pp. 60-63.

people of God and the certain *hope* of acquittal/vindication, and thus resurrection to eternal life, on the day of judgment.[128]

Justification, then, is about life, present and future (eternal). Covenant is about life. This new covenantal life, in its present form, is one of cruciform faith and love because the resurrected Christ is continuous with the faithful and loving crucified Jesus. To that new life we now turn briefly.

"The Righteousness of God": The Symbiosis of Faith and Love in the Justified

Having examined both Christ's death and faith *(pistis)* according to Paul, we come now to the third of the three questions posed earlier in this chapter: What is the connection between the meaning of Christ's death and the meaning of *pistis*, on the one hand, and the significance and character of the transformation inherent in justification, on the other? We have already anticipated the answer to this question at several junctures.

One of the key overall contentions of this chapter has been the characterization of Christ's faithful and loving death as the quintessential fulfillment of the covenant and the corollary interpretation of justification by faith as participation in that death, defined as such. We have already suggested that to participate in something that is defined as the union of faith and love will have certain inevitable consequences. Specifically, those who are crucified and resurrected with Christ will, by the power of his Spirit, embody his faith and love as the covenant community. In that community will be found the symbiosis of faith and love that was found in Christ, as narrated in texts like Phil 2:6-11 and Gal 2:19-20. This symbiosis of faith and love is not an addendum to justification (such as "sanctification" or "Christian ethics") but is constitutive of justification itself — the restoration of right covenant relations.[129] Justification, as we have already seen, is inherently both participatory and transformative.

---

128. Taken from my *Reading Paul*, pp. 116-17 and 152-53, with the addition of the term "Spirit-enabled" to make it clear that this co-crucifixion is not a human achievement but the result of divine grace, expressed by Paul in the passive voice — as is justification/reconciliation elsewhere.

129. We shall return to this important point in the discussion of holiness in chapter three.

This is what we should expect if we take not only Paul's narrative account of Jesus' death seriously, but also his account of the human condition. Just as alienation from God was due to, and expressed in, both "vertical" and "horizontal" sins (Rom 1:18-32; 3:9-18), so also reconciliation to God is a matter of restoration to both vertical and horizontal wholeness in covenant relationships. It is not, after all, merely the reality of ungratefulness and idolatry that invites God's wrath and Paul's indictment of human guilt and covenantal failure. It is also the reality of "humanity's inhumanity to humanity" — up to and including lethal violence — that needs to be named, judged, and repaired.

By virtue of co-crucifixion and co-resurrection with Christ — participatory justification by participatory faith — the reign of Sin has been broken within and among those who are in Christ. They have been made participants in the power of the Spirit that makes the covenantal life of faith and love possible. Those in Christ can experience the true purpose of Christ's death and of their participation in it; in Christ they can become the righteousness, or justice, of God (2 Cor 5:21).

Paul's claim in 2 Cor 5:21 about "interchange" in Christ — that "[f]or our sake he [God] made him to be sin who knew no sin, so that in him we might become the righteousness [or justice: *dikaiosynē*] of God" — has often puzzled interpreters.[130] The language of "interchange" clearly does not mean merely some kind of legal transaction. Rather, it suggests participation in the very life of both Christ and God as human sin is transformed into divine righteousness/justice in Christ. "[T]he very purpose of the covenant community is to manifest God's righteous design for human creatures."[131]

In light of the account of the logic of Paul's soteriology developed in this chapter and summarized above, we may propose that, for Paul, becoming the "righteousness/justice of God" in Christ means becoming a people of faith(fulness) and love who embody and participate in God's reconciling/justifying work — God's new creation — (2 Cor 5:17) — as God's covenant community.[132] As Katherine Grieb says, "The 'new creation/new crea-

---

130. Or perhaps "God made him who did not know sin, sin on our behalf [or in our stead] in order that we might become the righteousness of God in him." On interchange in Paul, see the classic articles by Morna D. Hooker, "Interchange in Christ" and "Interchange and Atonement," in *From Adam to Christ: Essays on Paul* (New York/Cambridge: Cambridge University Press, 1990), pp. 13-25 and 26-41.

131. Hays, "Justification," p. 1132.

132. Against N. T. Wright, "On Becoming the Righteousness of God: 2 Corinthians

ture' that God has accomplished in Christ belongs to a spiritually empowered reality that was previously as inconceivable as it was impossible: God's own covenant righteousness enacted in community — in Corinth."[133] Although Paul does not say in any one specific verse of 2 Corinthians 5 "this means being a people of faithfulness and love," he does clearly speak of both vertical and horizontal relations in familiar ways. His notion of being "compelled" (NIV; cf. NAB) or "urged on" (NRSV) by the love of Christ as an internal power (5:14), and his notion of living to/for the Christ who died and was raised (5:15), are reminiscent of Gal 2:19-20 and Rom 6:10-11.

The Symbiosis of Faith and Love in Specific Letters

In Galatians itself, one of the focal letters of this chapter, the symbiosis of faith and love that should obtain among those in Christ is made very explicit. After joining the two christologically in Gal 2:20 while redefining justification, Paul returns to the subject of justification in Galatians 5, where he once again rejects justification by the Law (5:2-4), affirming the symbiosis among the justified of both faith and hope (5:5) and also, quite emphatically, faith and love: "the only thing that counts is faith working through love" (5:6, NRSV), a certain echo of 2:20.[134] We have already noted the significance of the connection between these two texts.

Elsewhere Paul portrays the new existence in other, but not unrelated, vertical and horizontal terms. In Romans 6, self-presentation to God and a life of righteousness/justice/holiness are inseparable, as 6:13 especially well summarizes: "No longer present [a form of *paristēmi*] your members to sin as instruments [weapons, *hopla*] of wickedness [injustice, *adikias*], but present yourselves to God as those who have been brought from death to life,

---

5:21," in *Pauline Theology*, vol. 2, *1 & 2 Corinthians*, ed. David M. Hay (Minneapolis: Augsburg/Fortress, 1992), pp. 200-208, who restricts the "righteousness of God" to Paul.

133. A. Katherine Grieb, "'So That in Him We Might Become the Righteousness of God' (2 Cor 5:21): Some Theological Reflections on the Church Becoming Justice," *Ex Auditu* 22 (2006): 58-80 (66). Grieb's entire article deserves careful attention.

134. For the connection between Gal 5:6 and 2:20, see also Hays, "Christology and Ethics in Galatians"; Martyn, *Galatians*, p. 474; Matera, *Galatians*, pp. 183, 189. Interestingly, the link between these two verses also figures prominently in the 2006 statement of the World Methodist Council when it formally agreed to the Joint Declaration on the Doctrine of Justification issued by Catholics and Lutherans in 1999.

and present your members to God as instruments [weapons] of righteousness [or justice, *dikaiosynē*]." (Cf. especially 6:19, 22, which speak of being slaves to God and to righteousness.) The reference to *adikia* both recalls and is intended to depict the reversal of the *adikia* of 1:18, while the self-presentation to God is the antithesis of the human failure to honor God described in 1:21. "[Believers] are called, in short, to allow the risen Lord to live out his continuing obedience to the Father in them as in his own extended person or 'body.'"[135]

Similarly, in Rom 12:1-2 Paul uses the same verb of self-presentation *(paristēmi)* to indicate the reversal of Romans 1 in the presentation to God of our bodies as a living sacrifice, which includes the renewal of the mind (12:2; cf. 1:21 and the explicit reversal of 1:28) and the consequent discerning of God's will for action in this world. Thus the vertical dimension of justification leads to the horizontal, which is then spelled out in detail in the ensuing three chapters (12:3–15:13) as cruciform love and hospitality. In other words, the faith of 12:1-2 expresses itself in the love described in the remainder of the letter.

We may also briefly note the Corinthian correspondence on this symbiosis of the vertical and horizontal. As noted earlier, in 1 Corinthians Paul is trying to prevent idolatry and immorality/injustice. His goal is to replace these basic covenantal failures with exclusive devotion to the Lord Jesus and with cruciform love for one another. The symbiosis of these two appears perhaps most powerfully in Paul's treatment of the Lord's Supper (1 Cor 10:1-22; 11:17-34).

In 2 Corinthians, discussing an entirely different matter, the collection for the poor of Jerusalem, Paul lauds the Macedonians as an example of cruciform generosity and justice because they "gave themselves first to the Lord and, by the will of God, to us" as a means of aiding the poor saints (2 Cor 8:5; cf. 8:9). The Macedonians are proof that a community in Christ, who first embodied God's justice, God's self-giving generosity, in incarnation and crucifixion (8:9; cf. 9:15), can fulfill the goal of that incarnation and death by becoming the justice of God. That is, the Macedonians, the Corinthians, and we can become, *in Christ, the just and righteous one,* a place where "the justice of God and the justice of church . . . overlap in an ethic of generosity toward others."[136] As Paul says in 8:13-14, such generosity, rooted in God's own

---

135. Brendan Byrne, *Romans,* Sacra Pagina (Collegeville: Liturgical, 1996), p. 193.
136. Grieb, "'So That in Him,'" p. 59; cf. p. 68.

generosity in Christ, is not some form of *noblesse oblige* but rather a small instantiation of God's gracious intention to establish a world of equality (Greek *isotēs*)[137] in which the abundance of some and the need of others are brought together.

These examples demonstrate the way in which Paul sees the inseparability of vertical and horizontal devotion — faith and love — in the lives of those who are incorporated into Christ through faith and baptism. This is what it means, concretely, to be in right covenantal relation with God and with others — to be justified. A thick understanding of faith (participatory fidelity, loyalty, obedience toward God) reverses the idolatry and hard-heartedness that plague the human race, thus fulfilling the covenant's expectations about relations with God. Love, on the other hand, reverses people's mistreatment of one another and thus fulfills the obligations of the covenant toward others in the form of cruciform justice.[138] But the two, *pistis* and *agapē*, are inseparable, because they were and are joined in Christ, the image and manifestation of God.

Justification as Theosis

It is now time to connect this chapter more explicitly to chapter one and to anticipate chapter three. Our contention is this: Because the faithful and loving crucified Christ is the image and self-revelation of God, the paradoxical process of justification by co-crucifixion, or resurrection through conformity to the crucified Christ, means that the *pisteuontes* ("believers") are those who are becoming like God and thus experiencing the process of theosis inasmuch as they embody the symbiosis of fidelity and love found in the Son of God.

What does that mean? Inasmuch as Christ's faithful and loving death reveals the faithfulness and love of God, and justification is participation in that death, justification is participation in the faithfulness and love of God. It is,

137. "Equality" in NIV, NAB; poorly translated "fair balance" in NRSV.

138. We should not, however, think that the language of "covenant" means that for Paul justification is only a Jewish phenomenon. In Romans 1 Paul reads the plight of the world with covenantal lenses. Yet he describes the failed human project with allusions to Genesis and creation as well as Exodus and the covenant (the golden calf incident), both in concert with the Wisdom of Solomon. So it is the plight of the whole world that Paul describes — as covenantally dysfunctional.

thus, a process of deification or theosis.[139] The cruciformity that is constitutive of justification is actually theoformity, or theosis, as we saw in the previous chapter. This means also that to become the righteousness or justice of God in Christ is theosis.[140] This is not primarily an individual experience, but a corporate one of *communal* theosis — *we* become, in Christ, the righteousness/justice of God.[141] This communal theosis is, of course, no different from the communal kenosis we described at the end of chapter one. Because this process of kenosis/theosis is never complete, the very process reinforces the significance of hope as an equally essential aspect of justification.

As we will see in more detail in the next chapter, the process of deification is the process of becoming like the God revealed in the cross, and none other.[142] As Joel Marcus notes, building on the work of C. Kavin Rowe on iconography, in the Pauline literature a common term for pagan images and statues, *eikōn,* is transferred to Jesus as the image of the invisible God (2 Cor 4:4; cf. Col 1:15). It is given over also to believers as those who bear the image of Christ and God "at least *in nuce,* and as an eschatological pledge" and who therefore "seek God's likeness not in the religious statuary that crowds their world but in the moveable icons that are their brothers and sisters, '. . . predestined to be conformed to the image of his [God's] Son' (Rom 8:29).'"[143]

The paradox in Paul's theology — or, better, his spirituality — is of

139. See the introduction to this book for helpful overviews of theosis. For a persuasive argument that Luther understood justification as deification as well as declaration, see Marshall, "Justification as Declaration and Deification." Marshall's arguments and responses to possible objections are also instructive for the interpretation of Paul.

140. Although neither Paul himself nor Katherine Grieb (in the discussion above) uses the word theosis to describe the transformation about which Paul speaks in 2 Cor 5:21, Stephen Finlan suggests that that is precisely what Paul is discussing ("Can We Speak of *Theosis* in Paul?" in *Partakers of the Divine Nature: The History and Development of Deification in the Christian Traditions,* ed. Michael J. Christensen and Jeffery A. Wittung [Grand Rapids: Baker, 2007], pp. 68-80; here p. 75).

141. This is also Grieb's contention, emanating from the way she formulates the question: "in what sense could *the very human church* possibly become 'the righteousness of God'?" ("'So That in Him,'" p. 58, emphasis added).

142. If the cross is indeed the self-revelation of God, then the supposed choice between soteriologies of incarnation and of cross/atonement is a false dichotomy. When we participate in the cross we participate in the incarnate one, and vice versa. The two are inseparable, as even Phil 2:6-11 suggests. The story of Christ narrated there has two phrases describing two stages in Christ's selflessness: incarnation and death ([z¹] and [z²] in the graphic in chapter one).

143. Marcus, "Idolatry in the New Testament," p. 158.

course that because believers now gaze on the image of God manifested in the exalted Christ, who remains forever the crucified one, their ongoing metamorphosis into the image of God, or the image of the Son (2 Cor 3:18), is a participation in his cruciform narrative identity and a transformation into his cruciform image.[144]

The appropriate eschatological reservation to which Marcus refers should not cause us to think that this transformation, this theosis, does not actually occur. Of course it is incomplete, but the claims of Lutheran theologian David Brondos that for Paul the transformation is not in any sense present and ontological but is completely future and eschatological (with a little foretaste thanks to the Spirit), and that believers do not participate in Christ's faith/faithfulness, death, or resurrection, simply do not do justice to the texts.[145] Fellow Lutheran Roy Harrisville is much closer to the mark when he speaks of Paul's conviction that "by his [Christ's] divine power . . . the risen and exalted one makes his epiphany in those who are his, and in cruciform shape." Believers are thus "the epiphany of the Incarnate Christ."[146]

Another possible critique of theosis in Paul (or more generally with respect to the church) comes from John Webster. Webster argues for the church's "*alien* sanctity," over against social interpretations of the Trinity and the church's life in it, against "ontological participation in the divine holiness."[147] He argues that the church's holiness is "by virtue of its calling by

144. On Paul as *merkabah* Jew gazing on the resurrected (and crucified) Christ as the glory of God, see Alan Segal, *Paul the Convert: The Apostolate and Apostasy of Saul the Pharisee* (New Haven: Yale University Press, 1990), pp. 334-71.

145. David A. Brondos, *Paul on the Cross: Reconstructing the Apostle's Story of Redemption* (Minneapolis: Fortress, 2006), especially pp. 151-89. Brondos (e.g., pp. 170, 173, 179) attempts to argue that Paul simply communicates in different language (with no different concept) the "take up your cross" and "deny yourself" language of the Synoptic tradition. There are of course similarities between the Synoptics and Paul, but the differences are significant — and conceptual, not just semantic. At the very least, the Synoptic writers report words spoken by and/or about a tangible, pre-resurrection, historical figure, whereas Paul's experience is of the resurrected-exalted crucified Christ, known by his Spirit. For a convenient summary of the entire Brondos book, see pp. 191-95.

146. Harrisville, *Fracture*, pp. 122, 124. This notion is of course close to my own work on "cruciformity," though Harrisville is a bit too individualistic, ignoring the communal dimension of the "epiphany," in contrast to the notion of "communities of cruciformity" (see Gorman, *Cruciformity*, pp. 349-67).

147. John Webster, *Holiness* (Grand Rapids: Eerdmans, 2003), pp. 56-57; emphasis his.

God, its reception of the divine benefits, and its obedience of faith."[148] There is much to affirm in Webster's work on holiness, especially divine holiness (see chapter 3 below). But he has unfortunately set up an unnecessary and false dichotomy between "ontological participation in the divine holiness" and the "obedience of faith." If, in fact, the human response of obedience/faith is co-crucifixion with (and indeed mutual indwelling with)[149] the faithful and loving Jesus, who is in turn the revelation of God's own fidelity, love, and holiness, then is it not the case that the obedience of faith is inherently a participation in the being — or at least the narrative identity (which implies of course the essence[150]) — of God?

How does this transformation into Godlikeness — this theosis — take place? We may summarize it as follows, leaving a fuller discussion to the next chapter:

For Paul theosis takes place in the person and especially the community that is in Christ and within whom/within which Christ resides, as his Spirit molds and shapes the individual and community into the cruciform image of Christ. But this process of transformation takes some human cooperation, including especially contemplation of the exalted crucified One (2 Cor 3:18).[151] For Paul, this is not merely a form of ancient, perhaps vacuous, mysticism, but a sustained reflection on, and identification with, the narrative pattern of Christ crucified and of its paradoxical power to bring life out of death (2 Cor 4:7-12), all enabled by God himself at work in the individual and community (Phil 2:12-13). This sustained reflection and identification begin in the public act of faith and baptism and continue throughout one's life in Christ, and for this reason the traditional Protestant distinction between justification and sanctification is, in some very essential ways, deeply problematic. The corollary separation of faith from love (or works/deeds), and specifically justification from justice, is no less problematic, and to its reunion we now turn.

---

148. Webster, *Holiness*, p. 57.

149. I.e., Christ in us and we in Christ, as in Romans 8. The technical theological term for this mutual indwelling or reciprocal relationship is perichoresis, used first of all to refer to relations among the persons of the Trinity but also to refer to the divine-human relationship.

150. As Webster himself persuasively argues (pp. 39-43).

151. Matera, *2 Corinthians*, p. 97.

Cruciform Justice: The Ethics and Politics of Justification by Co-crucifixion

In Christian theological parlance, "righteousness" and "justice" are sometimes separated, the former referring to personal dealings and holiness, the later to public affairs and what we Methodists call "social holiness." Both the biblical tradition (e.g., the prophets and Jesus) and the biblical lexicon (which often treats "righteousness" and "justice" as near-synonyms) stand against this dichotomy, as many have noted. Few, however, have applied those insights to Paul. But because of the inseparability of faith and love in Paul's theology of justification, justification is ethical as well as spiritual, corporate as well as personal, and public rather than private.

Paul himself exemplifies this reality. He was a public persecutor of the church, most likely attempting to secure his justification before God through imitating the violent priestly hero Phinehas, who purified Israel and stayed God's wrath by killing an Israelite and his Midianite consort (Num 25:6-13). According to Ps 106:31 (LXX 105:31), Phinehas was justified by his violent zeal: his act was "reckoned to him as righteousness" *(elogisthē autǭ eis dikaiosynēn)*. The Greek phrase is exactly the same as the parallel text in Gen 15:6 (about Abraham's justification) and in Rom 4:3, 5, 9, 22-24.[152]

When he was justified, reconciled to God, Paul's oppressive, violent public behavior changed dramatically. He would later describe such behavior as precisely the manifestation of Sin (Rom 3:9-18) that caused God to deal with his rebellious people and the wider human family, now established as enemies of God. Of course, God did not deal with those enemies in retaliation or violence, but in reconciliation and love — enemy love (Rom 5:6-8, 10). That is, God acted with restorative rather than retributive justice. Justification, therefore, has a public, observable, social face by virtue of the divine action in which it is rooted (Christ's crucifixion) and the life-story of the apostle who first articulated the meaning of justification in light of that divine action. Moreover, as a rejection of justification by killing and the embrace of reconciliation and restoration, justification manifests itself publicly as nonviolence and reconciliation.[153]

---

152. We will explore the relationship between Phinehas and Paul, as well as the nonviolent character of justification/theosis in Paul, more fully in chapter four.

153. See, *inter alia*, Miroslav Volf, "The Social Meaning of Reconciliation," *Int* 54 (2002): 158-72. See also chapter four below.

sinners through the blood of his Son, but rather that God [we should add "also"] offers the opportunity to transform this upside-down world . . . by raising up the One who was condemned for his practice of justice.[161]

We cannot be naïve about the difficulty of this demand for cruciform justice. It requires more than the declaration of forgiveness or even a call to imitation; it requires *participation,* as Paul Bischoff asserts: "[O]nly a personal, loving crucified God who suffers with and for humanity creates space for a theological view of participation incarnated by a cruciform community in the world led by a powerless Christ."[162]

Miroslav Volf approaches the language of theosis in making a similar point about what we might call cruciform hospitality, or the cruciform embrace of the other:

> Through faith and baptism the self has been re-made in the image of "the Son of God, who loved me and gave himself for me." No "hegemonic centrality" closes the self off [from the other]. . . . For Christians, this "de-centered center" of self-giving love — most firmly centered and most radically open — is the doorkeeper deciding the fate of otherness at the doorstep of the self. . . . The Spirit enters the citadel of the self, de-centers the self by fashioning it in the image of the self-giving Christ, and frees its will so it can resist the power of exclusion in the power of the Spirit of embrace.[163]

The social meaning of justification grows not only out of the reality of transformation into the image of Christ, but also out of the more traditional emphasis on unmerited grace.[164] If God's response to enemies is to love them (Rom 5:6-8), and if this is the heart of Paul's gospel, then the claim of John Howard Yoder seems inevitable: Paul preaches "Good News that I and my enemy are united, through no merit or work of my own, in a new humanity that forbids henceforth my ever taking his life in my hands."[165] Positively,

---

161. Tamez, "Justification as Good News for Women," p. 184.

162. Paul Bischoff, "Participation: Ecclesial Praxis with a Crucified God for the World," *JCTR* 8 (2003): 19–36, here p. 20.

163. Volf, *Exclusion and Embrace,* pp. 71, 92.

164. I do not mean here to set up a false antithesis between grace and transformation but simply to suggest that even a more traditional reading of Paul should prompt a social, or horizontal, interpretation of justification along with the vertical dimension.

165. John Howard Yoder, *The Politics of Jesus: Behold the Man! Our Victorious Lamb,* 2nd ed. (Grand Rapids: Eerdmans, 1994 [orig. 1972]), p. 226.

that means that reconciliation and peacemaking — not just God's but ours, as ethical and political practices — are integral to Paul's gospel.[166] These practices manifest justification now in anticipation of the realization of complete justice when the kingdom of God is realized in its fullness.[167]

Paul provides a concrete example of becoming the righteousness, or justice, of God in Christ in 1 Cor 6:1-11, and in so doing he shows the inseparable connection between justification and justice. Addressing the problem of Corinthian believers taking one another to court, Paul makes it clear that this practice is an injustice and needs to be replaced by practices of christologically informed justice. Unfortunately, the NRSV masks some of the most important links in the passage by using "unrighteous" and "wrong" to translate the word-family *dik-* while never using a form of "just" except for the word "justification":

> 1When any of you has a grievance against another, do you dare to take it to court before the unrighteous [**unjust**, *adikōn*], instead of taking it before the saints? . . . 7In fact, to have lawsuits at all with one another is already a defeat for you. Why not rather be wronged [**treated unjustly**, *adikeisthe*]? Why not rather be defrauded? 8But you yourselves wrong [**practice injustice**, *adikeite*] and defraud — and believers at that. 9Do you not know that wrongdoers [the **unjust**, *adikoi*] will not inherit the kingdom of God? Do not be deceived! Fornicators, idolaters, adulterers, male prostitutes, sodomites, 10thieves, the greedy, drunkards, revilers, robbers — none of these will inherit the kingdom of God. 11And this is what some of you used to be. But you were washed, you were sanctified, you were justified [**made part of the just ones**, *edikaiōthēte*] in the name of the Lord Jesus Christ and in the Spirit of our God. (NRSV)

It is clear from a close reading of the Greek text that Paul sees taking fellow believers to pagan courts, which are the courts of the unjust/unjustified (v. 1), as an act of injustice (v. 8) that betrays the Trinitarian divine action of

166. See further Willard M. Swartley, *Covenant of Peace: The Missing Peace in New Testament Theology and Ethics* (Grand Rapids: Eerdmans, 2006), pp. 189-253.

167. On the connection between justification and the future kingdom of God, to include the entire cosmos, see Peter Stuhlmacher, *Revisiting Paul's Doctrine of Justification* (Downers Grove: InterVarsity, 2001), especially pp. 33-53, 71-73, as well as N. T. Wright's claim (developed more fully elsewhere) that "[j]ustification is ultimately about justice, about God putting the world to rights" ("New Perspectives on Paul," in McCormack, ed., *Justification in Perspective*, pp. 243-64, here 264).

rescue from that sort of injustice that Paul calls justification (v. 11). To practice such injustice is effectively to annul the justification wrought by God, to return to the realm of the unjust, and to jeopardize one's future inheritance of the kingdom of God (v. 9). The justified are expected to suffer injustice (v. 7) and not to inflict it.

Thus the linguistic connections among the various *dik-* terms in these verses express a fundamental theological conviction that is basic to Paul's soteriology but is often overlooked by his interpreters: justification means a *transfer* from the realm of the unjust/unjustified into the realm of the just/justified, which simultaneously means a *transformation* from being unjust people to being just people and thus a *transition* from practices of injustice to practices of christologically informed, or cruciform, justice. Such cruciform justice means, first of all, the absorption rather than the infliction of injustice. Justification makes the unjust into the just; that is, justification is the divine act of transforming people into the righteousness/justice of God. They become capable, by God's grace and power, to practice the justice of God displayed on the cross.

To the extent that the justified continue to practice injustice, they demonstrate, at the very least, their need for ongoing transformation into the righteousness/justice of God to which they have been called in justification. Should they resist that transformation, their fate will be that of those who have never experienced the justifying justice of God. On the other hand, should they permit that transformation to occur, they will more fully embody the justice of God in the world, both as individuals and as a community, and thereby fulfill the very purpose for which God acted in Christ: to create a people that lives in loving faithfulness toward God and loving justice toward others.

A Brief Excursus: Faith, Hope, and Love and the Origin of Justification

The mention of faith and love in connection with justification naturally makes a reader of Paul wonder also about hope. What is the relationship between the dyad of faith and love, on the one hand, and the triad of faith, hope, and love, on the other?

That justification by God's grace is ultimately about faith, love, and hope (or perseverance) is suggested by the appearance of this quintessential

Pauline triad (e.g., 1 Thess 1:3, 5:8; 2 Thess 1:3-4; 1 Cor 13:7, 13; cf. Col 1:4-5) in the discussion of justification in Rom 5:1-11 and Gal 5:2-6.[168] If this is correct, then we do not have to look for the word "justification" to identify passages in which the topic of justification appears. This means, among other things, that Paul's earliest extant letter (in all probability), 1 Thessalonians, not only mentions justification at least twice, but does so for the first time in the letter's very first paragraph: Paul reminds the Thessalonians of their faith, hope, and love (1:3; cf. 5:8). That is to say, the first substantive words by Paul that have been preserved for us are essentially about justification.[169] Furthermore, if these observations about 1 Thessalonians are correct, then it is clear that the very-oft-held thesis that the problem in Galatia prompted Paul's formulation of the doctrine of justification is very wrong, and we must now search for another, earlier source for that key aspect of Paul's theology.[170] In light of everything I have said, I suggest that that source is his

---

168. The terms are highlighted here: "You who want to be justified by the law have cut yourselves off from Christ; you have fallen away from grace. For through the Spirit, by *faith*, we eagerly wait for the *hope* of righteousness. For in Christ Jesus neither circumcision nor uncircumcision counts for anything; the only thing that counts is *faith* working through *love*" (Gal 5:4-6); "Therefore, since we are justified by *faith*, we have peace with God through our Lord Jesus Christ, through whom we have obtained access to this grace in which we stand; and we boast in our *hope* of sharing the glory of God. And not only that, but we also boast in our sufferings, knowing that suffering produces endurance, and endurance produces character, and character produces *hope*, and *hope* does not disappoint us, because God's *love* has been poured into our hearts through the Holy Spirit that has been given to us" (Rom 5:1-5). In Rom 5:6-11 faith, love, and hope reappear in references to Christ's death as his own act (5:6-7; which death Paul likely calls Christ's "faith" in 3:22, 26), Christ's death as God's love (5:8), and the certain hope of future salvation from God's coming wrath (5:9-10). The occurrence of these three terms has often been noted, but their connection as a triad to justification has not been developed much if at all.

169. It is interesting that the second occurrence of the triad in 1 Thessalonians (1 Thess 5:8), an admonition to faith, hope, and love, is followed by the words, "For God has destined us not for wrath but for obtaining salvation through our Lord Jesus Christ, who died for us . . ." (5:9-10a), words that clearly foreshadow Rom 5:6-10. Even the first occurrence (1 Thess 1:3) is linked to a reference to salvation from the coming wrath (1:10) that anticipates the discussion of justification/salvation in Rom 5:1-11. This strongly suggests that the notion of justification, if not the term, is present in 1 Thessalonians from beginning to end (literally). This is precisely the point of Douglas Harink (*Paul among the Postliberals: Pauline Theology beyond Christendom and Modernity* [Grand Rapids: Brazos, 2003]) in his chapter on justification, which includes a discussion of 1 Thessalonians (pp. 32-38; cf. p. 64).

170. This is not to say that the situation Paul faced in Galatia, or later in Rome, did not help to sharpen his theology of justification.

early understanding of Jesus' crucifixion as the Messiah's quintessentially covenantal, nonviolent, righteous act of simultaneous fidelity and love that generates our fidelity, love, and hope in return.

Conclusion

Does a participatory understanding of justification rule out its juridical dimension? By no means! Rather, it says that in Pauline theological forensics, God's declaration of "justified!" now is a "performative utterance,"[171] an effective word that does not return void but effects transformation. Thus God's declaration now of "justified!" accompanies the divine crucifixion and resurrection of the believer and effects, by the Spirit, a real, existential process of transformation, which is nothing like a legal fiction. "This declaration has a quasi-legal dimension, but there is no question here of a legal fiction whereby God juggles his heavenly account books and pretends not to notice human sin"[172] — or fails to do something transformative about it. Furthermore, therefore, God's declaration of "justified!" at the final judgment is based on an existential, even an objective, reality — initiated and empowered by God — rather than on anything resembling a legal fiction.[173] According to Joseph Fitzmyer, even Melanchthon — normally blamed with making the juridical view of justification the exclusive view — believed this.[174]

171. The term is Luke Timothy Johnson's, commenting on Rom 1:16-17 and referring to the gospel as the power of God to effect salvation (*Reading Romans: A Literary and Theological Commentary* [New York: Crossroad, 1997], p. 25).

172. Hays, "Justification," p. 1131.

173. Simon Gathercole makes a similar point in arguing for a forensic but also ontological interpretation of justification in Paul, especially in Romans 4–5: "The principal trouble is if one supposes that God can declare something to be the case . . . but that in reality the opposite state of affairs persists. . . . We should more properly consider that God's 'speech-acts' are what *determine* reality; they do not merely create an alternative, Platonic reality" ("The Doctrine of Justification in Paul and Beyond," p. 226; for the full discussion, see pp. 225-29). Gathercole continues (p. 229): "God's act of justification is not one of *recognition* but is, rather, closer to *creation*. It is God's *determination* of our new identity rather than a recognition of it [arguing here specifically against N. T. Wright's view but also against more traditional Protestant views]. . . . The category of 'alien' righteousness is vital in capturing the truth that our righteousness comes only from God and not from ourselves. But it should not be misinterpreted to mean that we are thereby not really righteous."

174. Fitzmyer, "Justification by Faith in Pauline Thought," p. 85, in Aune, ed., *Rereading Paul Together.*

This transformative character of justification is the corollary of its participatory character, as we have repeatedly seen in this chapter. There is therefore no need to affirm two soteriological models in Paul. In the words of Robert Tannehill, "our study of Pauline passages shows that we cannot draw a sharp line between Paul's participatory concepts and his juridical concepts, centering in the theme of justification, for Paul argues for justification from faith with participatory language."[175]

Does a participatory view of justification rule out a sacrificial understanding of Christ's death? Again, by no means! Rather, the polyvalent character of Christ's death as sacrifice for sins *and* redemption from Sin *and* fulfillment of the covenant (and more) is affirmed; the justified are able to fulfill the law and do the works of love because they are forgiven *and* liberated *and* restored *and* filled with the Spirit. There is no need to posit two or more basic soteriological models, however, one that deals with sins as transgressions, another that deals with Sin as power, and yet another that focuses on participation.[176] Rather, by participating in Christ's sacrificial (forgiving), apocalyptic (liberative), and covenantal (law-fulfilling) crucifixion, believers are forgiven, freed from Sin, and empowered to fulfill the vertical and horizontal requirements of the covenant instead of continuing in the various transgressions that previously characterized their existence and that manifested, inseparably for Paul, both their slavery to Sin and their covenantal dysfunctionality.[177]

---

175. Tannehill, "Participation in Christ," p. 235.

176. As Tannehill ("Participation in Christ," p. 225) has argued, "Paul proclaims that Christ died for us or for our sins, and he proclaims that we have died with Christ. These are not alternative and competing views of Christ's saving death. For Paul these affirmations fit together, as we see from Paul's logical inference in 2 Cor 5:14: 'One died for all, therefore all died' (followed by a reference to the new life that results). This statement follows the pattern of dying and rising with Christ: participation in Christ's death leading to a new kind of life. But here Paul shows that, for him, this is a logical implication of — and perhaps Paul's distinctive explanation of — the affirmation that 'one died for all.'" Building on the work of Harmut Gese and Otfried Hofius, Tannehill suggests that sacrifice and participation are inherently connected because in a priestly sacrifice the sacrificial victim "represents and includes the one who benefits" (p. 226).

177. N. T. Wright says rightly that in Galatians (especially 3:24-29, which mentions faith, baptism, and putting on Christ) the two soteriological categories, juridical and participationist, are "happily jumbled up" (*What Saint Paul Really Said*, p. 121). He implies that this is true for Paul in Romans as well. But his rather minimalist definition of justification (with special reference to Rom 3:21-26) as God's declaration in the present that believers

This chapter has attempted both to enlarge and to clarify our understanding of justification by connecting it *materially*, not just *formally*, to Christ's crucifixion and our crucifixion with him. This results in one coherent soteriological model, justification by faith understood as crucifixion with Christ — justification by co-crucifixion (JCC). It is appropriate, therefore, to refer to faith as the *formal* principle (or perhaps instrument) of justification and to co-crucifixion as the *material* principle (or instrument) of justification.

This chapter has also reformulated the relationship between "faith" and "works" by redefining *pistis* — Christ's and therefore ours — as inherently in symbiotic relationship with *agapē*. Justification includes both the vertical and the horizontal dimensions of God's covenantal requirements, Christ's embodiment of them, and our life in him as those who together practice faith expressing itself in love.[178] For Paul, the charge of antinomianism is answerable only with a thick understanding of justification by faith (JF) as justification by co-crucifixion (JCC), of the justified community as thereby the crucified community, raised to new life.[179]

---

in Christ are now what they will be in the future — the true, righteous covenant people of God — forfeits the "happy jumbling" of the participationist and juridical models in favor of the latter (see *What Saint Paul Really Said*, p. 129).

178. The Lutheran theologian Hartmut Schönherr, working in Africa, argues that the vertical soteriology of theosis and the (antithetical) horizontal theology of liberation find their synthesis in the complementarity of justification, understood as cruciform in its basis and shape, as the most complete soteriology ("Concepts of Salvation in Christianity," *Africa Theological Journal* 12 [1983]: 159-65). Though I agree with his view of justification as a synthesis of the vertical and the horizontal, I would obviously suggest that theosis, properly understood via Paul, incorporates the horizontal. The symbiosis of faith and love in Paul means, additionally, that George Hunsinger's interpretation of participation/theosis/divinization fails to incorporate the heart of the Pauline witness (see his *"Fides Christo Formata,"* noted early in this chapter). Hunsinger asserts (p. 79) that "as Luther and Barth both affirm, faith does not need to be formed by love in order to be saving faith" because it is formed by Christ from the beginning, and thus (citing Luther) faith "is not, therefore, deficient 'until love comes along to make it alive' (LW 26, 129)." Hunsinger adds, "Certainly, faith needs love in order to be genuine. But it does not need love to preserve, recover, or increase the justification it freely receives, nor does it need it to merit eternal life." The issue, however, is not merit; it is what constitutes participation in the quintessential covenantal act of unified faith and love.

179. "This sanctification and justification by co-crucifixion represent a pattern of activity empowered by the Holy Spirit that takes one up into an analogous pattern [analogous to that of Christ the image of God] of cruciform activity and therefore takes one up into the life of God" (Andy Johnson, personal correspondence, October 2006).

As noted earlier, in the end, it is perhaps best to say that justification is by means of God's faithfulness expressed in love, demonstrated in Christ's act of faithfulness expressed in love, to which humans, enabled by the Spirit, respond in faithfulness expressed in love — i.e., in co-crucifixion. What matters for Paul is faith "made effective" (or "working") through love (Gal 5:6), which corresponds to the cross of faith and love of the Crucified, by whom and in whom believers live together. *There can be no separation of faith from love, of faith from action, of justification from justice.*[180]

With this broader and, hopefully, clearer and more accurate understanding of justification as an "exegesis of the crucifixion,"[181] which includes a *living* exegesis of the doctrine in the community of believers growing into the image of the Son, we can once again affirm with conviction and joy both that the doctrine of justification is central to Paul and, indeed, that it is the doctrine by which the church stands or falls. At the same time, we can affirm that justification, precisely as an exegesis of the crucifixion, where God is revealed in the Son as kenotic and cruciform, is theosis. In justification we become the righteousness of God, the embodiment of God's covenant fidelity and love, God's generosity and justice. In a word, God's holiness — the subject of the next chapter.

---

180. One of the strengths of Campbell's argument in *The Quest for Paul's Gospel* is his emphasis on this same point, or what he calls Paul's gospel and his ethics; see, e.g., p. 115. The major difference from the present argument is that he sees participation and justification as antithetical rather than integrated. This emphasis on the horizontal dimension does not mean, however, that justification or theosis is reduced to ethics. The following observation about Africa may also be true for the West and Western churches: "[A] theology which does not take the vertical dimension of life — which is the religious dimension par excellence — strongly into consideration may have a chance at African theological faculties but has no chance whatsoever in the African peoples" (Schönherr, "Concepts of Salvation in Christianity," 160).

181. Paul Varo Martinson ("Learning Its Meaning amidst the Religions," in Stumme, ed, *The Gospel of Justification in Christ*, pp. 141-59) says, "I think it is fair to say that for the Christian, and certainly for Paul, the doctrine of justification is an exegesis of the crucifixion" (pp. 152-53). I should add that I do not wish to say that my exegesis of the cross as covenant fulfillment rules out additional exegesis of the cross as sacrifice or even punishment for sin (on the latter, see Simon J. Gathercole, "Justified by Faith, Justified by His Blood: The Evidence of Romans 3:21–4:5," in Carson, *et al.*, eds., *Justification and Variegated Nomism*, vol. 2, pp. 147-84, especially pp. 175-83). For Paul, the cross is polyphonic.

CHAPTER 3

"You Shall Be Cruciform, for I Am Cruciform"

Paul's Trinitarian Reconstruction of Holiness as Theosis

The biblical text "You shall be holy, for I am holy" (Lev 11:44-45; 19:2) issues both a fundamental theological claim about Israel's God and a corollary, equally fundamental claim on Israel as God's people.[1] Although Paul does not explicitly cite that Levitical injunction in his letters, there is ample evidence that he, like any good Jew, knew and contemplated it.[2] To be holy is to be set apart, to be like God *(imitatio Dei)* and thus different from other people — but precisely how?

Paul's understanding of holiness was not completely new, for his gospel was a narrative in continuity with Israel's story. Thus Paul affirms certain basic Jewish understandings of holiness as difference from Gentiles (e.g., avoidance of sexual immorality and idolatry). Yet he also offers a radically new interpretation of holiness molded by the gospel of the Messiah who was crucified by Rome but raised and exalted by God. As Stephen Barton says, "[T]he reinterpretation of holiness and its corollaries represented by the claim that 'God was *in Christ*' (2 Cor. 5.19) signifies a development of momentous proportions."[3]

---

1. See also Lev 20:7-8, 26; 21:6-8.

2. For example, in 1 Thessalonians Paul's frequent admonitions to holiness are "more than a distant echo of the Levitical command to 'be holy as I am holy'" (Calvin Roetzel, *Paul: The Man and the Myth* [Minneapolis: Fortress, 1999], p. 36). 2 Cor 6:16 does cite a related Levitical text (26:11-12), but some scholars think it is part of a non-Pauline interpolation.

3. Stephen C. Barton, "Dislocating and Relocating Holiness: A New Testament Study," in *Holiness Past and Present,* ed. Stephen C. Barton (London: Clark, 2003), pp. 193-213, here p. 197.

This chapter proposes that Paul's understanding of holiness is grounded in his gospel, particularly (1) in his unique conviction that the crucified Messiah Jesus, the Son of God, is the revelation of the *holiness* of God the Father, and (2) in the corollary conviction that the justified — those co-crucified with Christ — are called to be holy through ongoing "co-crucifixion" with Christ by the power of the *Holy* Spirit, who is the Spirit of both the Father and the Son. In other words, Paul's distinctive understanding of human holiness is grounded in the cross, which reveals three interconnected realities: the narrative identity of Christ the Son, the essential character of God the Father, and the primary activity of the Spirit. Paul's experience of Son, Father, and Spirit resulted in his radical reconstruction of holiness as both a counterintuitive divine attribute/activity (or attribute-in-relation)[4] and a countercultural human imperative and process that is inherently communal. This unique, cruciform and Trinitarian vision of holiness may be summarized in a paraphrase of Leviticus: "You shall be cruciform, for I am cruciform."[5]

This understanding of holiness, therefore, is a participatory one. It puts additional flesh on the bones of this book's earlier discussions of

- God's kenotic, cruciform identity revealed in the cross and leading to the practice of cruciformity, which is in fact theoformity, or theosis (chapter one), and
- participatory and transformative justification as theosis, understood as the symbiosis of faith and love and the practice of restorative justice (chapter two).

In this chapter, then, we will develop more fully the claim that, because of Paul's participatory understanding of the cruciform life of faith and love that characterizes the community of the justified, the term "theosis" is especially appropriate to characterize his view of holiness. Indeed, theosis, we will suggest, is a helpful alternative term (and perhaps even a more appropriate one) for what has usually been called sanctification or holiness in Paul — a theme that has been sometimes misunderstood or neglected.

---

4. On divine holiness as a relational, covenantal reality, see John Webster, *Holiness* (Grand Rapids: Eerdmans, 2003), pp. 43-52.

5. This chapter will again limit its analysis to the seven letters universally considered to be authentic: Romans, 1 and 2 Corinthians, Galatians, Philippians, 1 Thessalonians, and Philemon. Notes will contain occasional references to the disputed letters.

Paul's Preoccupation with Holiness

"The river of holiness ran wide and deep through the traditions of Israel," Calvin Roetzel eloquently writes.[6] However, Roetzel rightly remarks, holiness is a "neglected feature of Paul's theological grammar."[7] This neglect is rather ironic, since Paul himself is preoccupied with holiness, as several aspects of his lexicon and letters indicate.[8]

The Holy Ones

The first piece of evidence is the term *hagioi* (singular *hagios*), or "holy ones," which is normally — unfortunately — translated "saints."[9] Paul takes over a term applied to Israel, as God's people, in the Scriptures and other Jewish writings.[10] *Hagioi* is one of Paul's two favorite terms for believers (the other being *adelphoi*, "brothers [and sisters]"). Paul addresses believers as *hagioi* at the beginning of four letters (Rom 1:1, 7; 1 Cor 1:2; 2 Cor 1:1; Phil 1:1)[11] and also refers to them as such on twenty other occasions.[12] By placing the designation *hagioi* in the opening of his letters, Paul shows his ability to direct special attention to the church's holiness,[13] and by using *hagioi* else-

6. Roetzel, *Paul*, p. 36.

7. Roetzel, *Paul*, p. 36.

8. Jeffrey A. D. Weima suggests that we should not be surprised that Paul, as a member of the Pharisees — whose name meant "separated ones" — was passionate about holiness as the "boundary marker" of God's covenant people ("'How You Must Walk to Please God': Holiness and Discipleship in 1 Thessalonians," in *Patterns of Discipleship in the New Testament*, ed. Richard N. Longenecker [Grand Rapids: Eerdmans, 1996], pp. 98-119 [p. 102]).

9. Usually or always so in the NRSV, NIV, NASB, and KJV. The NAB uses "holy ones." On these terms, see my article in the *New Interpreter's Dictionary of the Bible*, ed. Katherine Doob Sakenfeld, *et al.* (Nashville: Abingdon, 2009), vol. 5, s.v. "Saint."

10. See James D. G. Dunn, *The Theology of Paul the Apostle* (Grand Rapids: Eerdmans, 1998), p. 44 n. 90, for instances of this usage. Dunn stresses the inclusion of the Gentiles in Paul's use of this epithet (pp. 44-45).

11. See also Col 1:2, 4; Eph 1:1, 4.

12. Rom 8:27; 12:13; 15:25, 26, 31; 16:2, 15; 1 Cor 6:1, 2; 14:33; 16:1, 15; 2 Cor 8:4; 9:1, 12; 13:12; Phil 4:22; 1 Thess 3:13; Phlm 5, 7; singular "every saint" in Phil 4:21. Thus the term occurs 25 times in the undisputed letters and another 15 in the disputed (mostly in Colossians and Ephesians).

13. Holiness language especially pervades the opening of Romans (1:1-7) and 1 Corinthians (1:1-9).

where — in what appear to be less deliberate ways — Paul also reveals that this way of speaking of the church is second nature to him. Holiness is, therefore, essential to the identity of the church as a whole and to each individual in it.[14]

A second piece of evidence is related to the first. In two letter openings, Paul uses *hagioi* in connection with God's calling. In Rom 1:7, he says either that the Roman believers are "called holy ones" or, perhaps, "called to be holy ones" (so NRSV, NIV, NAB; Greek *klētois hagiois*). Does he mean that the church already *is* holy or that it is called to *become* holy? Similar language in 1 Cor 1:2 suggests that the answer is both: Paul defines "the church of God that is in Corinth" as those who have already been "made holy [*hēgiasmenois*, from the verb related to *hagios*] in Christ"[15] and who are also "called to be holy" *(klētois hagiois)*. The purpose of God, in Paul's view, is to call out a people into Christ, which in itself sets this new community apart as God's holy people, and also to form them into a people that sees holiness as its mandate and its goal, or *telos*. Holiness *(hagiasmos)*, for Paul, is both gift and task.[16] The meaning of this holiness, according to 1 Cor 1:2, derives its shape and substance only "in Christ."

The Call to Holiness

A third piece of evidence for the centrality of holiness in Paul is its appearance in programmatic statements in his letters. Perhaps the clearest example of this is 1 Thessalonians, in which "holiness is the most important theme."[17] At two key junctures in the letter (the middle and the end), Paul summarizes his basic message to the Thessalonians as a call to holiness:

14. This is further confirmed elsewhere; for example, Paul identifies both the community (1 Cor 3:16-17; 2 Cor 6:16) and the individual (1 Cor 6:19-20) as God's (holy) temple.

15. NRSV, NIV, and NAB all have "sanctified."

16. The word *hagiasmos*, "holiness/sanctification," appears in Rom 6:19, 22; 1 Cor 1:30; 1 Thess 4:3, 4, 7; cf. 2 Thess 2:13; 1 Tim 2:15. The similar term *hagiōsynē* appears in Rom 1:4; 2 Cor 7:1; 1 Thess 3:13. Dunn (*Theology*, p. 330) notes that Paul can use *hagiasmos* to mean both the *beginning* of salvation, when "individuals were set apart to discipleship," and the *process* of salvation. Cf. Webster: "Holiness is indicative; but it is also imperative; indeed, it is imperative *because* it is the indicative holiness of the triune God whose work of sanctification is directed towards the renewal of the creature's active life of fellowship with him" (*Holiness*, p. 87).

17. Weima, "'How You Must Walk,'" p. 98.

[May the Lord] strengthen your hearts to be blameless in holiness *(hagiōsynē)* before our God and Father at the coming of our Lord Jesus with all his holy ones *(hagiōn)*." (3:13)

"May the God of peace himself make you entirely holy *(hagiasai hymas holoteleis)* . . . and may your spirit, soul, and body be kept blameless at the coming of our Lord Jesus Christ." (5:23)

In addition, at the beginning of his ethical instruction in 1 Thessalonians, Paul identifies the essential will of God as the Thessalonians' "holiness" *(hagiasmos,* 4:3a). While sexual holiness is particularly in view (4:3b-8, where "holiness" appears twice and "Holy Spirit" once), this countercultural sexual holiness — believers are not to be "like the Gentiles who do not know God" (4:5) — is clearly seen as part of a larger call to holiness. Paul relates that holiness to Father, Son, and Spirit: God (the Father) calls in holiness (4:7), the Spirit effects holiness (4:8), and the Son ("the Lord") judges the unholy (4:6b).[18] Holiness is, implicitly, an experience of the Trinitarian God, as we will see in more detail below.[19]

Holiness is also the focus of 1 Corinthians. Not only does the letter's

18. Weima, "'How You Must Walk,'" p. 110.

19. Calling Paul's experience or theology of God "Trinitarian" is still occasionally subject to criticism, but it is clear to many that this adjective (referring at least to incipient or proto-Trinitarianism) is the most adequate descriptor. See, among others, Ulrich W. Mauser, "One God and Trinitarian Language in the Letters of Paul," *HBT* 20 (1998): 99-108; and Francis Watson, "The Triune Divine Identity: Reflection on Pauline God Language, in Disagreement with J. D. G. Dunn," *JSNT* 80 (2000): 99-124. Watson rightly affirms that "Paul's texts everywhere assert or assume a distinctively Christian view of God. Traditional Jewish God-language is relocated within a framework in which the word 'God' is misunderstood and misused if it is not always and everywhere accompanied by reference to Jesus and to his Spirit. That is also the framework of the classical doctrine of God as 'triune' . . ." (pp. 104-5). Responding to the oft-heard charge that reading Paul as Trinitarian is anachronistic, Watson deftly and correctly counters that "it is exegesis itself which leads to the simple conclusion that, for Paul, the word 'God' is rightly used only when accompanied by reference to Jesus and his Spirit" (123). See also chapter four of my *Cruciformity*, "The Triune God of Cruciform Love: Paul's Experience of the Trinity," (pp. 63-74), and the literature cited there, as well as Douglas A. Campbell, *The Quest for Paul's Gospel: A Suggested Strategy* (London/New York: Clark, 2005), pp. 41, 61, 78, *et passim.* Campbell refers to a "'Trinitarian dynamic'" in Paul, "a set of relationships into which the Christian is born, and by means of which recreated," involving "the three divine persons of the Spirit, Christ, and God the Father" (p. 41). Paul's soteriology is "proto-trinitarian in its actual saving mechanism" (p. 61). It is "incorporation of people into the story" of Father, Son, and Spirit (p. 78).

opening (1:2; see above) name holiness as the Corinthians' status and goal, but the thanksgiving — which sets the letter's agenda — echoes the concern of 1 Thessalonians that believers be blameless at Christ's coming (1 Cor 1:8). Paul then returns to the theme of God's call to holiness by reassuring the Corinthians (and maybe himself) that God is faithful and will indeed complete the call (i.e., effect the Corinthians' blamelessness at the coming of the Lord). This call is specified as "fellowship *(koinōnian)* with his son Jesus Christ our Lord" (1:9). We see then that for Paul holiness means participation or sharing (the root meaning of *koinōnia*) in Christ.[20] We may justly see 1 Corinthians, therefore, as Paul's attempt to explain to the Corinthians what this programmatic call of God to participatory holiness in Christ means for them in the midst of all the complex issues the community is facing.

More specifically, it is clear from the letter that the Corinthians see themselves as a "spiritual" community, heavily endowed with gifts of the Spirit. Paul recognizes the community's charismatic character (1:5-7; chs. 12–14) as well as its holy character (1:1-9; 6:11). However, the community's sanctification does not match its abundance of spiritual gifts; the people's growth in holiness — their conversion — seems incomplete.[21] Their values are still shaped more by the spirit of their Greco-Roman age than by the Holy Spirit. Throughout 1 Corinthians, Paul calls them to three dimensions of holiness: avoiding sexual immorality and embodying an appropriate sexuality (5:1-13; 6:12-20; 7:1-40), avoiding idolatry and embracing exclusive allegiance to Jesus (10:1-22), and above all avoiding self-serving behavior and practicing Christlike, cruciform love that seeks the good of the other and the community (ch. 13, esp. 13:5; 16:14; cf. 8:1-13; 9:1-26; 10:23–11:1; 14:1-40).[22]

This countercultural, cruciform (holy) love pays special attention to the weaker members of the community (11:17-34; 12:14-26) and special honor to apostles who exhibit Christlike power-in-weakness (4:1-13), and it has a counterintuitive commitment to absorbing injustice rather than inflicting it

---

20. This reinforces the interpretive principle we noted earlier: for Paul, holiness is inseparable from Christ. Paul makes this claim explicitly also in 1 Cor 1:30: Christ has become for us holiness *(hagiasmos)* from God.

21. See Stephen J. Chester, *Conversion in Corinth: Perspectives on Conversion in Paul's Theology and the Corinthian Church* (London: Clark, 2003).

22. Even Paul's vision of sexual holiness is related to a larger vision of holiness linked explicitly to the cross (or cross and resurrection) in chs. 5 and 6 (5:6-8; 6:19-20), and implicitly in ch. 7. There Paul advocates mutual, kenotic marital love (7:1-7) and honors bearing with an unbelieving spouse (7:12-16).

(6:1-11). Such cruciform holiness stands in marked contrast to the dominant Roman cultural values of promoting the self by seeking honor and of honoring the powerful. Paul's primary goal is to turn a *charismatic* community into a *cruciform* and therefore truly *holy* community, one in which all believers are in proper relationship to one another and to God the Father, Christ the Lord, and the Holy Spirit — the triune God at work among them.[23] This is not a call to something new and different from Paul's earlier message or the Corinthians' experience, but rather a summons to embody the washing, justification, and sanctification (1 Cor 6:11) that God's grace has already inaugurated. That is to say, holiness, or sanctification, *is not an addition to justification but its actualization.*

Space does not permit much discussion of holiness in the other letters.[24] It must suffice simply to mention Romans briefly.[25] Paul claims that God's loving act of justification/reconciliation in Christ, known by the presence of the Spirit (5:1-11), liberates people from the idolatry and immorality of this age (1:18-32; 12:1-2) in order to be co-crucified and co-resurrected with Christ, presenting themselves to God as his slaves who obey him in a life of holiness (6:1-23, with "holiness" or "sanctification," *hagiasmon*, in 6:19 and 6:22). Once again, holiness is not a supplement to justification but its actualization. That this holiness is in fact Christlikeness is clear from the assertion that the *telos* of salvation in Romans is conformity to "the image of his [God's] Son" (8:29)[26] rather than conformity to this age (12:1-2), from allusions to Jesus' teaching on love and non-retaliation (12:9-21), and from an explicit call to Christlike love for the weak (15:1-3).

---

23. For the Trinitarian activity of God in 1 Corinthians, see especially 6:15-20 and 12:4-6. On the purpose of 1 Corinthians, see my *Apostle of the Crucified Lord: A Theological Introduction to Paul and His Letters* (Grand Rapids: Eerdmans, 2004), pp. 227, 236-37, 239. I do not mean that Paul wishes the Corinthians to stop being a charismatic community; rather, he wishes them to become a *cruciform* charismatic community, guided by the Spirit of the cruciform Son of God (and thus the Spirit of the cruciform God, as we will see further below).

24. Several thorough treatments of holiness in the Pauline letters may be found in Kent E. Brower and Andy Johnson, eds., *Holiness and Ecclesiology in the New Testament* (Grand Rapids: Eerdmans, 2007). The present chapter is adopted from an essay in that volume.

25. Galatians and Philippians will be treated below under a different heading.

26. Dunn (*Theology*, p. 502) notes the "cluster" of terms related to election/sanctification in 8:27-33.

Three Fundamental Features of Holiness in Paul

We may now make three general observations about holiness in Paul that are suggested by the foregoing survey: (1) holiness is difference from the life of Gentile nonbelievers, (2) holiness is both the character and the activity of the triune God, and (3) holiness is essentially Christlikeness. We will consider each of these in turn.

First of all, human holiness in the Jewish (and therefore also early Christian) tradition is, first and foremost, difference from those who do not participate in God's call or character. This differentness, for Paul, is radical, and he can use very stark apocalyptic language to express the contrast (e.g., 1 Thess 5:4-11; Rom 13:13-14). Nonconformity to this age, however, does not mean escape from the world, which Paul flatly rejects as preposterous (1 Cor 5:9-10).[27] Unlike, say, the community at Qumran, holiness for Paul means being different from but still located within the host environment. In fact, the community's difference enables it to bear witness to its surrounding culture (Phil 2:14-16). This dynamic tension of "in but not of the world" appears, for example, in Romans 12–13, which begins with Paul's famous call for nonconformity to this "world" or "age" (Rom 12:1-2) and which deals nonetheless with life in this real, dangerous world where people have enemies (12:9-21) and must interact with imperial authorities (13:1-7) — who may, in fact, be the enemies.

Secondly, for Paul holiness is Trinitarian in structure. It is the unified, collaborative activity of Father, Son, and Spirit. Holiness is the call and will of God the Father; it occurs in Christ, who defines holiness for the church; and it is effected by the Spirit, who is the *Holy* Spirit. One word Paul uses to describe the result of this triune divine activity is *koinōnia* — sharing, or participation. God calls people to a countercultural, communal, participatory experience of the Son (1 Cor 1:9) that is brought to fruition by the Spirit (Phil 2:1). Human holiness is participation in divine holiness. Holiness is, therefore, both the property and the activity of the Father, the Son, and the Spirit. God not only sets people apart, but also conveys to humans the very character of God. Thus human holiness is not merely a human imperative; it is a divine product, or "fruit" (Gal 5:22).

---

27. Paul does want believers to disassociate from unholy believers (1 Cor 5:9-13). If 2 Cor 6:14–7:1 is authentic, then the "holiness" (7:1) Paul advocates probably means disassociation from such pseudo-saints, including so-called apostles who (unlike Paul — 2 Cor 6:3-10) fail to practice cruciform holiness.

Thirdly, holiness is Christlikeness. In both apocalyptic passages noted above (1 Thess 5:4-11; Rom 13:13-14), the alternative to being in the darkness of unholiness is "putting on" Christ (Rom 13:14) or "living with Christ" by practicing faith, love, and hope (1 Thess 1:2-10). That is, Christlikeness, or *koinōnia* with Christ (1 Cor 1:9), is the opposite of unholiness and thereby constitutes holiness itself. Thus the reality of "putting on Christ" and henceforth being "in Christ" — a favorite Pauline expression — is not a private mystical experience but a corporate *koinōnia* of transformation. The eschatological goal of conformity to Christ (Rom 8:17, 29; Phil 3:11-12, 21; 1 Cor 15:49) begins now through an ongoing experience of sharing in Christ's status as a slave or servant of God and others, one characterized by non-retaliatory, other-centered love. This *koinōnia* is therefore above all a participation in Christ's cross, which is inaugurated through faith and baptism (see chapter two), remembered and re-experienced in the Lord's Supper (1 Cor 10:16), and embodied existentially in both cruciform love for others (Phil 2:1-4) and suffering with Christ (Phil 3:10).[28]

We will have more to say about the shape of this Christlikeness below. For now, however, the very notion raises a crucial issue. As a Jew, Paul knows that to be holy is to be *Godlike*;[29] as a Jew in Christ, he knows that to be holy is to be *Christlike*. The question is then raised, What is the connection between these two necessary understandings of holiness? The answer for Paul, as we saw in chapter one, is that *Christ is Godlike, and God is Christlike.* That is why Paul can speak of the (Holy) Spirit as the Spirit of both the Son and the Father.

---

28. All three texts mentioned in this sentence use the word *koinōnia*.

29. L. Ann Jervis argues that "a common theme running through the religious reflections and moral deliberations of antiquity was the desire to achieve likeness to God," that this desire was found both inside and outside Judaism, that the phenomenon created a bridge for Paul to the Gentile world, and that for Paul and the ancients more generally discipleship meant achieving Godlikeness. See her "Becoming like God through Christ: Romans," in *Patterns of Discipleship in the New Testament*, ed. Richard N. Longenecker (Grand Rapids: Eerdmans, 1996), pp. 143-62, here p. 145.

The Holy Spirit[30]

The Activity of the Holy Spirit (1 Thessalonians)

In Paul's earliest letter, 1 Thessalonians, the Holy Spirit is mentioned early in the letter and associated with both power and joy (1:5-6). But the Holy Spirit is also associated with holiness per se in Paul's exhortation to holiness, especially sexual holiness. Holiness is both the property (4:8) and the activity (4:3, 4, 7) of the Spirit. As Gordon Fee says in commenting on the phrase "Holy Spirit" in this text: "the Spirit is none other than the Spirit of God, himself 'holy.' . . . we are here dealing with the character of God, and with Paul's understanding of the Christian ethic as the Spirit's reproducing that character in his people."[31]

It would be a mistake, therefore, to conclude that for Paul in 1 Thessalonians the Holy Spirit is merely the spirit of holy sexuality. The activity of the Holy Spirit is equally visible in the faith, love, and hope that Paul offers as proof of the Thessalonians' reception of the gospel and the Spirit (1 Thess 1:2-10). This experience included becoming imitators of Paul and Jesus by being persecuted (1:6; 2:14-16), and Paul associates this suffering particularly with the Thessalonians' faith, or faithfulness (*pistis*, 1:3; 3:2-7), as well as their love (3:6) and their hope/steadfastness (3:13).[32]

Thus we may conclude that Paul believes that the work of the Holy Spirit, and thus human holiness, consists in large measure of faith(fulness), hope/steadfastness, and love. Furthermore, this holiness includes becoming like Jesus (and other holy examples) through steadfast faithfulness in the face of adversity. The traditional meaning of holiness, therefore, is being expanded by Paul, in his earliest extant letter, to mean something like sharing in the story of Jesus the crucified.[33] Holiness is taking on a cruciform shape,

---

30. In Paul's undisputed letters, there are more than one hundred references to the Spirit, of which twelve or thirteen specify the Spirit as the *Holy* Spirit: Rom 5:5; 9:1; 14:17; 15:13, 16; 1 Cor 6:19; 12:3; 2 Cor 6:6; 13:13[14]; 1 Thess 1:5, 6; 4:8; and possibly also Rom 15:19 (some mss.). See also Rom 1:4: "Spirit of holiness."

31. Gordon D. Fee, *God's Empowering Presence: The Holy Spirit in the Letters of Paul* (Peabody: Hendrickson, 1994), p. 51.

32. As we saw in the excursus at the end of the previous chapter, these features of the Thessalonians' existence in Christ should be seen as signs of their justification.

33. For a full exposition of the cruciform character of holiness in 1 Thessalonians, see Andy Johnson, "The Sanctification of the Imagination in 1 Thessalonians," in Brower and Johnson, *Holiness and Ecclesiology in the New Testament*, pp. 275-92.

without thereby losing other, more traditional meanings such as sexual virtue, which itself now becomes infused with a cruciform shape. The identity and activity of the Spirit, therefore, are also being reshaped by being associated with the Son. This identification of the Spirit as the Spirit of the Son becomes explicit in Galatians, discussed below.

It is also worth noting that Paul identifies the recipients of this letter as "the church of the Thessalonians in God the Father and the Lord Jesus Christ" (1 Thess 1:1), a phrase that appears in the Pauline corpus only here and, with a minor change ("God our Father"), in 2 Thess 1:1. This phrase indicates that there is no sharp dichotomy for Paul between being "in Christ" and being "in God the Father";[34] rather, existence in Christ is existence in God, and vice versa.[35] To be in Christ is to be in God and to be the ongoing recipient of God's Holy Spirit (4:8); this is, in Paul's earliest letter, an indication of his experience of a Trinitarian participatory holiness.[36] Paul's concern is inhabiting God — inhabiting the cruciform God.

The Activity of the Spirit of the Son (Galatians)

The word *hagios* and its cognates do not appear in Galatians. This absence is rather ironic, since the core issue in this letter is the meaning of holiness: What are the essential distinctive "marks" of the Israel of God (Gal 6:17)?

---

34. Thus the conclusion of Jouette M. Bassler, in an otherwise helpful sketch of participation in Paul, is both unwarranted and misleading: "Paul's mysticism was Christ-mysticism; he did not focus, as later mystics did, on mystical union with God (but see Phil 2:13)" (*Navigating Paul: An Introduction to Key Theological Concepts* [Louisville: Westminster John Knox, 2007], p. 43). Not only does Bassler ignore 1 Thess 1:1, but she apparently fails to recognize the existential significance of Paul's assertions that Christ is the image and revelation of God. S. A. Cummins better understands Paul's position: "For the apostle Paul, an integral aim and outworking of God's self-disclosure in Jesus Christ is the incorporation of the whole of humanity into Messiah Jesus and his Spirit, and thereby into the divine life that is eternal communion with the triune God" ("Divine Life and Corporate Christology: God, Messiah Jesus, and the Covenant Community in Paul," in Stanley E. Porter, ed., *The Messiah in the Old and New Testaments* [Grand Rapids: Eerdmans, 2007], pp. 190-209, here p. 190).

35. A text somewhat parallel to these opening words in the two Thessalonian letters is Col 3:3: "for you have died, and your life is hidden with Christ in God." "In Christ" language appears in Colossians in 1:2, 28.

36. As noted in this book's introduction, the "in" language in Paul points to a Trinitarian, not merely a christocentric and/or pneumatic, spirituality.

The thrust of the letter is to reject separate table fellowship, circumcision, or even Sabbath-keeping as the true meaning of holiness. Instead, Paul proposes, participation in God the Father's gift of the Son and Spirit is the root meaning of holiness. The Israel of God is marked by the cross and the Spirit. And that Spirit is, in fact, the Spirit of the Son (Gal 4:4-6).[37] This identification of the Spirit as the Spirit of the Son is crucial to understanding Galatians in general and the meaning of holiness in Galatians in particular.

In Gal 1:4 Paul summarizes the entire letter in three phrases. The letter will focus on the promises of God (chs. 3–4) fulfilled in the crucified Messiah, who "gave himself up for our sins" (chs. 1–2) "to deliver us from the present evil age" (chs. 5–6) — that is, to create a holy, Spirit-filled people. Gal 1:4 shows that the meaning of holiness will be related to the inextricable bond between the cross and the Spirit as the outworking of God's eschatological salvation. The entire letter says that the salvation process — holiness — is crucifixion: *to* the flesh and the world (5:24; 6:14) and *with* Christ (2:19-20).

As we saw in chapter two, Gal 2:19-20 reveals the focal point of Paul's gospel in the death of Christ and in believers' participation in it. Paul speaks representatively, using "I" and "me." Echoing and expanding 1:4, in 2:20 he describes Christ's death on the cross as his unified act of self-giving love and faith, or faithfulness *(pistis)*, toward God: "I live by the faithfulness of the Son of God [rather than "faith *in* the Son of God"], who loved me by giving himself for me."[38] This means that Paul sees the identity of Christ the crucified Son of God revealed in a story of faith (toward God) and love (toward others). In the last chapter we argued that Christ's faithful, loving death on the cross is therefore the quintessential act of covenant fulfillment. We may now also say that for Paul it is the quintessential *holy* deed; it is the *definitive revelation of holiness.* This symbiosis of faith and love is what marks Christ as the Son of God who can and does indwell those who live in him, making them the holy Israel of God marked by covenant fidelity and love.

---

37. The Spirit is also referred to as the Spirit of Christ as well as of God (the Father), in Rom 8:9.

38. Author's translation, taking the Greek phrase *pistis tou huiou tou theou* as a subjective genitive, "the faithfulness of the Son of God," and the word *kai,* usually translated "and," as explanatory, "by giving." See further discussion of this text in my *Cruciformity,* pp. 110-21 and in chapter two above. It will be recalled that this interpretation does not neglect the importance of the believer's faith; see, for example, 2:16: "even we have believed in [literally, *into*] Christ."

This is so because believers are those who, by virtue of the Spirit's activity, identify so fully with Christ's cross that they, with Paul, can say, "I have been crucified with Christ" and this same crucified (but now obviously resurrected) Christ lives "in me." That is, as we saw in chapter two, believers experience a kind of resurrection by means, paradoxically, of co-crucifixion. Paul thus implies that the life of believers will also be characterized by Christlike faith and love (see 5:6) as they are "guided by the Spirit" (5:25).

Gal 4:4-6 narrates the Father's dual gift of the Son and the Spirit as the fulfillment of the promise to liberate the people of God and incorporate the Gentiles into God's family (4:5). It is both surprising and extraordinarily significant that Paul in this context describes the Spirit sent into our hearts as "the Spirit of his [God's] Son" (4:6). Not only does this demonstrate once again an intimate link among Father, Son, and Spirit, but it also connects believers simultaneously to both the Father and the Son through the Spirit. Because the Spirit is the Spirit of the Son of God who displayed faith and love on the cross (2:20), the mark of God's children, indwelt by that Spirit, is not circumcision but "faith expressing itself through love" (5:5-6, clearly echoing 2:20). This constitutes the essential holiness of the Spirit-led community. Believers live by faith and love in conjunction with a Spirit-inspired hope for righteousness (5:5), that is (as similar texts in 1 Thessalonians suggest[39]), the hope for Godlikeness (holiness) — and thus vindication — at the eschatological judgment.[40]

Finally, two points about Gal 5:22-25, on the "fruit of the Spirit," are worth noting. First, the language of "fruit" suggests the kind of natural consequence discussed above that is implied by the presence of the Spirit of God's Son. At the same time, however, human cooperation with the Spirit is required (5:25; cf. 5:16). Second, although the fruit of the Spirit includes both love and faith(fulness) (*agapē* and *pistis*), the list in 5:22-23 is obviously more extensive than these. The "crucifixion" of the flesh and its desires (5:24) means the birth of new desires and practices that "flesh out" the root meaning of cruciform holiness as self-giving, other-serving love of God and neighbor (5:13-14).

In Galatians, then, the implicit association of the Spirit with the cross of

---

39. See 1 Thess 3:13; 5:23 and the discussion above.

40. Similar ideas appear in Romans 6, though without direct reference to the Spirit (who appears in Rom 1:4 as the Spirit of holiness, and also awaits ch. 8). See also Andy Johnson, s.v. "Sanctification," *New Interpreter's Dictionary of the Bible*, vol. 5.

Christ in 1 Thessalonians has become explicit. The work of the Spirit — holiness — is, in essence, cruciformity. But this work of the Spirit is ultimately the work of the Father, who gives believers the Spirit of the Son. As in 1 Thessalonians, in Galatians Paul implies that Spirit-enabled cruciform holiness is ultimately not only Christlikeness but also Godlikeness.

We will now look briefly at three other letters that continue this association of cross and Spirit and also connect both more directly to God the Father.

Christ Crucified as the Holiness of the Cruciform God

Christ Crucified, the Holiness of God (1 Corinthians)

Sometimes called the "kerygmatic paradox," 1 Cor 1:18–2:5 declares boldly that "Christ [is] the power and wisdom of God" (1:24). In context, the reference to Christ is clearly to Christ *crucified* (1:23; cf. 1:18; 2:2). Traditional divine attributes — wisdom and power — are turned topsy-turvy by being associated with the foolishness and weakness of crucifixion. Paul infers that *Christ crucified both reveals and redefines God.* Unlike the broader Jewish tradition, in which God's power and beneficence (the "paradox of holiness")[41] were held in *tension,* Paul holds them in *concert.* As we noted in the theological conclusions to chapter one, in Christ Paul does not know a God of power *and* weakness but the God of power *in* weakness. God is cruciform.

In 1 Cor 1:30 Paul repeats the divine attribute of wisdom and adds three others: "[Christ] became for us wisdom from God, and righteousness and holiness [NIV; "sanctification" in NRSV, NAB] and redemption."[42] At first glance, these three may seem more like divine *activities* than divine *attributes:* God's right-wising, sanctifying, and redeeming. But this differentiation between divine activity and divine attribute is a false one. God's actions

41. Hannah K. Harrington, *Holiness: Rabbinic Judaism and the Greco-Roman World* (London/New York: Routledge, 2001), p. 43.

42. The phrase "for us" in 1:30 does not mean that Paul is a relativist who believes that the revelatory character of Christ crucified is a function of our belief and that non-belief voids its revelatory reality. Rather, Paul simply acknowledges the counterintuitive character of this revelation, which explains why so many reject it despite its salvific value for those who perceive it correctly (cf. 1:18-25).

are self-revelatory, the expression of God's essence or character.[43] The context once again demands that we understand Paul to be referring to Christ in 1:30 as Christ *crucified*. This means that in Christ crucified, and only in Christ crucified, God acts to make humans holy (activity). It also means that *the cross reveals the holiness of God* (attribute, essence), just as it reveals the wisdom and power of God. But this is not normal deity: "For execution by crucifixion to become the criterion of holiness, and of God's holiness at that, became the supreme scandal."[44]

A scandal, yes, but also true holiness. In 1 Cor 11:1 Paul refers to the actualization of this Christlike holiness as becoming like him (Paul) inasmuch as he is like Christ — by which Paul again means Christ crucified, Christ who did not exercise his rights but gave them up as an act of love for others. And if Christ is God's holiness for us, then becoming like the crucified Christ is sharing in God's holiness and thus becoming like God — theosis.

This strange notion of divine holiness, revealed in Christ crucified and thereby cruciform in character, is confirmed by passages from two additional letters.

Christ Crucified, the Image and Glory of God (2 Corinthians)

In 2 Cor 3:17-18 Paul comments on his interpretation of Exod 34:34 as a reference to turning to the Lord that gives "unveiled" access to God:

> "The Lord" is the Spirit, and where the Spirit of the Lord is, there is freedom. And all of us, with unveiled faces, seeing the glory of the Lord as though reflected in a mirror, are being transformed into the same image from one degree of glory to another; for this comes from the Lord, the Spirit. (NRSV, slightly altered)

These verses seem in part to distinguish and in part to conflate "the Lord" and "the Spirit" while they raise the question, Who or what is "the glory of the Lord?"

---

43. For example, the Bible stresses that God is faithful to the covenant and thereby acts to save in ways that express that unchangeable faithfulness. Cf. Webster, *Holiness*, pp. 39-40, and Colin Gunton, *Act and Being: Towards a Theology of the Divine Attributes* (Grand Rapids: Eerdmans, 2002).

44. Paul S. Minear, "The Holy and the Sacred," *Theology Today* 47 (1990-91): 5-12, here p. 8.

A few verses later, Paul makes it clear that his gospel is "the gospel of the glory of Christ, who is the image of God" (4:4), that he and his colleagues proclaim "Jesus Christ as Lord" (4:5), and that God the creator of light has now "shone in our hearts to give the light of the knowledge of the glory of God in the face of Jesus Christ" (4:6). Thus Christ is the glory and image of God, but he is also "Lord," a title associated with the Spirit in the text from 2 Corinthians 3 cited above. What are we to make of all this?[45]

First, Paul has become so convinced that Christ is the self-revelation of God that he attributes to Christ the scriptural divine epithet "Lord." He also identifies Christ with two scriptural word-pictures that speak of the likeness of God in the heavenly realm: the "glory" and the "image" of God.

Second, Paul attributes his certainty that Christ is God's self-revelation to his experience of God's Spirit. Thus, Paul concludes, it must be none other than God's Spirit who is calling him and others to experience the very glory of God in the Son. This is the essence of believing existence, to "see" the glory of the Lord (i.e., Christ) and be gradually transformed by the Spirit into the image of Christ, the image of God (2 Cor 3:18). Though Paul does not use the word "holiness" here, he is describing the process of becoming holy, of becoming like Christ and thus like God. For later Christian writers, this text would rightly become foundational for the doctrine of theosis. In fact, M. David Litwa convincingly argues, with special emphasis on the phrase "the same image" in 3:18, that Paul here presents a Christian version of *theosis*, or "sharing in God's reality in Christ."[46]

Third (and this is absolutely crucial), we must not forget that through-out this discussion of "the gospel of the glory of Christ" (2 Cor 4:4), Paul assumes that his Corinthian readers remember that the only gospel he pro-claims (1 Cor 1:18-25) and the only Christ he knows (1 Cor 2:2) is Christ *crucified*. Christ *crucified* is the image and glory of God. Commenting on this passage, Victor Paul Furnish says, "For Paul, it is precisely *as* the cruci-fied one that Christ is 'the Lord of glory' (1 Cor. 2:8 . . .)."[47] To be sure, it is Christ crucified and resurrected/exalted, but the two are inseparable in Paul's mind. Paul reminds his readers that the glory and image of God about

45. For a thorough study, see Timothy B. Savage, *Power through Weakness: Paul's Under-standing of the Christian Ministry in 2 Corinthians*, SNTSMS 86 (Cambridge: Cambridge University Press, 1996).

46. M. David Litwa, "2 Corinthians 3:18 and Its Implications for *Theosis*," *JTI* 2 (2008): 117-34 (quotation from p. 117).

47. *II Corinthians*, AB 32A (Garden City: Doubleday, 1984), p. 248.

which he writes, and into which all believers are being transformed, is the paradoxical glory of power in weakness, of life in death (2 Cor 4:10; cf. 12:1-10).

Fourth, and finally, the bottom line: if the crucified Christ is the glory and image of God, what does that say about God, and what does it say about the process of becoming Godlike? As in Phil 2:6-11 (the focus of chapter one), the answers are implicit but nonetheless clear: God is like Christ crucified. To become like God is to become like that kind of God. As Timothy Savage concludes in his study of Christ as the glory and image of God in 2 Corinthians, Christ demonstrates, in his repudiation of the pursuit of his own glory and "his act of consummate self-sacrifice on the cross . . . not only what God is like but also, dramatically, what humans ought to be like."[48] Savage continues, "They [humans] ought to manifest the same self-emptying character which Christ displayed on the cross. They ought to be 'transformed into the same image.'"[49] That is, God is Christlike, and transformation into Christlikeness is theosis.

In chapter one we came to similar conclusions from a different angle from a discussion of Philippians, to which Savage makes reference[50] and to which we now briefly return.

Christ Crucified, the Story of God (Philippians)

As we saw in chapter one, the well-known text Phil 2:6-11 is both the centerpiece of Philippians and Paul's "master story." Paul's master story begins, "Although/because Christ Jesus was in the form of God, he did not regard this equality with God as something to be exploited for his own advantage" (Phil 2:6, my translation[51]). The phrases "the form of God" and "equality with God" are synonyms indicating something Christ already possessed but did not use for his own advantage. The background of this language is probably both the scriptural language of the divine image and glory and the competing Roman language of claims to imperial divinity.[52] Thus Christ is like the God

48. Savage, *Power through Weakness*, p. 152.
49. Savage, *Power through Weakness*, p. 152.
50. Savage, *Power through Weakness*, pp. 150-51.
51. For the justification of this translation, see chapter one and the literature cited there.
52. See chapter one and, e.g., John Dominic Crossan and Jonathan L. Reed, *In Search of*

of Israel and is truly divine, unlike the emperor, who is a pseudo-god. This opening verse sets up a contrast between normal expectations of deity and Christ's actual actions, which are narrated in the following two verses (2:7-8) as a two-stage self-emptying, or *kenōsis,* in "incarnation" and obedient death by crucifixion. The text says that although normal human expectations would be for a god to exercise power and privilege, to seek status and honor, and to perpetually "climb upward" as proofs of divinity, *this* "form of God" did just the contrary. This divine abnormality constitutes the holiness — the distinctiveness — of the God displayed in Christ incarnate and crucified.

As we saw in chapter one, this narrative of abnormal divinity provides a narrative structure in Philippians and elsewhere for a cruciform life in contrast to "normalcy" — a narrative structure of holiness.[53] Paul's use of the story of Christ in its immediate context in Philippians suggests that he is describing the very meaning of life in and with the triune God. He urges the Philippians to pattern their lives after Christ (2:1-5), which is life "in Christ" (2:1, 5), "participation *(koinōnia)* in the Spirit" (2:1),[54] and the intimate activity of God (the Father) within the community that enables intentions and acts that please God (2:13).[55] To be like Christ is to participate in the Spirit and to embody the activity of God. It is, in other words, to be like God, to be holy, to participate in God's very life. And that only makes sense if the story of Christ is the story of God, if the counterintuitive kenosis of the Son reveals the way God really acts and really is — which was the argument of chapter one.

Phil 2:6-11 reveals, then, not only the narrative identity and holiness of Christ the obedient Son, but also the narrative identity and holiness of God the Father. As we stressed in chapter one, this is a *counterintuitive,*

Paul: How Jesus's Apostle Opposed Rome's Empire with God's Kingdom — A New Vision of Paul's Words and World (San Francisco: HarperSanFrancisco, 2004), esp. pp. 235-57, 270-91; and Gorman, *Cruciformity,* pp. 278-81.

53. See, e.g., 1 Thess 2:7; 1 Cor 9:12-23 (esp. 9:19); 2 Cor 8:9; and my *Cruciformity,* pp. 88-91, 164-75, 181-99, 209-12, 230-61. "Normalcy" is from Crossan and Reed, *In Search of Paul,* pp. 242, 284, *et passim.* Cf. chapter one above.

54. "Fellowship" (NIV) is a weak and potentially misleading translation of *koinōnia* because of its colloquial usage and significance. Better is "sharing" (NRSV) or "participation" (NAB).

55. Cf. N. T. Wright (*The Climax of the Covenant* [Minneapolis: Fortress, 1993], p. 87), who says that Philippians 2 is "not merely [about] the imitation of Christ: it is the outworking of the life of the Spirit of God." Even Bassler (*Navigating Paul,* 43) seems to see a union with God implicit in this text.

countercultural, and counter-imperial form of deity. Yet, for Paul, this is what Christ as the "form of God" is all about. And that means *Paul wants us to rethink God.*[56]

Paul does clearly imply that what Christ did, though counterintuitive and extravagantly unorthodox, was ultimately not a *violation* of divinity but an *expression* of it and thereby an expression of God's holiness. Otherwise, how could Christ be "equal with God" if he betrayed the character of God?[57] As we argued in chapter one, this means that "Although he was in the form of God," in the larger thought-world of the apostle, also means "*Because* he was in the form of God." As N. T. Wright puts it:

> The real theological emphasis of the hymn . . . is not simply a new view of Jesus. It is a new understanding of God. . . . [I]ncarnation and even crucifixion are to be seen as *appropriate* vehicles for the dynamic self-revelation of God.[58]

Furthermore, according to Phil 2:9-11 (recapping the discussion in chapter one), the obedient Christ is exalted because in manifesting true *divinity* as the form of God taking the form of a slave (by becoming human and offering himself in death), he also manifested true *humanity* (unlike Adam) — as the obedient Son of the Father.

Thus we see what is for Paul a crucial and inextricable link between divine and human holiness: kenosis is the *sine qua non* of both divinity and humanity, as revealed in the incarnation and cross of Christ, the one who was truly God and truly human. That is, the real subject of Phil 2:6-11 is divine holiness understood as kenosis, and the real subject of this poem in its larger context is human holiness understood as participation in God's holy, kenotic, cruciform life — what we may appropriately call theosis.

---

56. For a fuller discussion of Paul's notion of a kenotic or cruciform God, see chapter one and my *Cruciformity*, pp. 9-18.

57. See further Wright, *Climax*, pp. 86-87, on the exaltation as God's endorsement of Christ's kenosis as "the proper expression of divine character" (p. 87), and Stephen Fowl, "Christology and Ethics in Philippians 2:5-11," in *Where Christology Began: Essays on Philippians 2*, ed. Ralph P. Martin and Brian J. Dodd (Louisville: Westminster John Knox, 1998), pp. 140-53, here p. 142.

58. Wright, *Climax*, 84.

Summary: Theosis and The Shape of Holiness in Christ

Drawing on his Jewish heritage, Paul assumes that the people of God are called to be a countercultural, holy people, restored to right covenantal relations with God — justified.[59] Traditional Jewish holiness is both affirmed (avoidance of sexual immorality and idolatry) and challenged (circumcision, separate table fellowship), but above all it is recomposed in a new key. Paul's experience of Christ as the faithful, obedient, loving, self-donating, crucified Son of God leads him to reconstruct his understanding of both God's holiness and human holiness as embodied in the story of Christ's kenosis in incarnation and death. As Ann Jervis has written, "Paul interprets Jesus' death and resurrection as the means by which one becomes like God, and this in two ways: by conformity to Christ and by the manifestation of 'righteousness of God' received by faith."[60]

Living out this story is a communal, countercultural affair. Cruciform holiness stands in marked contrast to key Roman values (which can infiltrate the body of Christ), especially those values associated with the libertine and status-seeking lifestyle of the elite, and those related to the power and domination predicated of imperial divinity. This cruciform holiness means, in sum, becoming like Christ by the power of the Holy Spirit of the Father and the Son, and thus also becoming like God — for God is Christlike. "You shall be cruciform, for I am cruciform," says the Lord. Paul speaks to the ancient (and contemporary) desire for Godlikeness by claiming that through participation in Christ's death and resurrection we "can become like God through conformity to God's son."[61]

It is significant that the letter to the Ephesians (whether written by Paul or by his disciple or colleague) sees the imitation of the cruciform God as the imitation of the crucified Christ, and vice versa:

> [B]e kind to one another, tenderhearted, forgiving one another, as God in Christ has forgiven you. Therefore be imitators of God, as beloved chil-

---

59. This fundamental *covenantal* understanding of holiness also applies to justification (i.e., the restoration of right covenantal relations by means of God's initiative in Christ), as we saw in the previous chapter, demonstrating the inextricable connection between justification and holiness. Cf. Webster: "Holiness is restored covenant fellowship" (*Holiness*, p. 92).

60. Jervis, "Becoming like God," p. 151. The "two ways" are better understood, however, as one existential reality.

61. Jervis, "Becoming like God," p. 154. Cf. Litwa, "2 Cor 3:18," p. 132 n. 46: "Paul's doctrine of *theosis* is determined by the *theos* revealed in Jesus Christ."

dren, and live in love, as Christ loved us and gave himself up for us, a fragrant offering and sacrifice to God. (Eph 4:32–5:2)

That is, Christification is deification, or theosis.

We have suggested that "theosis" is an appropriate term for the participatory cruciform holiness we find in Paul.[62] We may now, by way of summary, offer a definition of theosis as it applies to Paul:[63]

> *Theosis is transformative participation in the kenotic, cruciform character and life of God through Spirit-enabled conformity to the incarnate, crucified, and resurrected/glorified Christ, who is the image of God.*[64]

This is not something different from justification; it is, as we have said, the actualization or embodiment of justification by faith because it is life by participation, co-resurrection by co-crucifixion. It is a life characterized by Godlike faithfulness and love; it is the life of the justified.

Participatory Holiness Today

Stanley Hauerwas rightly says that "Wesley was right to hold that the peculiar contribution of Methodists [and thus the entire Wesleyan tradition] to the church universal lies in our struggle to recover the centrality of holiness as integral to the Christian life."[65] At the same time, we must acknowledge that even in the Wesleyan tradition (in which I stand), and more broadly in the West as well, holiness has not always been healthily or fully understood. The Orthodox tradition, with its focus on participation in the life of God and on the process of deification, may enrich Wesleyan and Western notions of holi-

---

62. In a forthcoming dissertation on theosis in the Eastern Fathers and Paul, Ben Blackwell shows how some Fathers, particularly Cyril of Alexander, interpreted theosis as holiness, with particular reference to Paul.

63. This definition appears also in the introduction to this book.

64. Cf. Litwa, "2 Cor 3:18," pp. 132-33: "[F]or Paul the life 'unto death' [Phil 2:8] is no less the divine life. Why? Simply because it was the life of Christ, the divine human being. . . . The divine existence of Christ — and for those transformed into Christ's image — is not the life of ecstatic megalomania. It is the life of absolute humility and obedience to God — unto death. And this death does not separate redeemed humanity from God; rather, it makes them share in divine righteousness, enabling them to be (in the present partially, in the future fully) transformed, justified, glorified, and thus even 'divine.'"

65. Stanley Hauerwas, *Sanctify Them in the Truth: Holiness Exemplified* (Nashville: Abingdon, 1998), p. 124.

ness.[66] This will especially be the case if we take Paul's own interest in, and understanding of, participation in God seriously. In our context, Paul may help us understand both human and divine holiness, and therefore theosis, in many ways. Here we briefly consider three aspects of holiness today.

The Holiness of the Individual and the Church

Paul's notion of holiness challenges privatistic, self-centered, therapeutic, and sectarian notions of holiness. Cruciform holiness is inherently other-centered and communal. It is differentness of character but continued existence in the world. It is public participation in the story of God in Christ by the Spirit.

Both modern and postmodern persons have tended to look for meaning by pursuing "the reflexive project of the self,"[67] with postmoderns, of course, eschewing any meta-narrative, or master story. Even Christians are tempted to look at holiness as just another version of self-help and self-realization. But as Christians, John Webster writes, we discover our identity by entering a process of becoming holy; to be sure, this process varies from person to person by his or her "fulfilling a vocation through time."[68] However, Webster insists, "[t]he becoming is, precisely, discovery, not invention; it is not our generation of a self-narrative . . . but the enactment of an office: 'You shall be holy, for I, the Lord your God, am holy.'"[69] To continue Webster's use of narrative language, but with a Pauline emphasis: we enter into a story of Another, the divine master story of cruciform holiness. This can happen only in a community that performs the story and thereby participates in the very life of God that this story narrates.[70]

The performance of this holy story is, by definition, a countercultural act that shapes (among other things) our sex lives and our political lives.

66. See, e.g., the Wesleyan-Orthodox dialogue in S. T. Kimbrough, Jr., ed., *Orthodox and Wesleyan Spirituality* (Crestwood: St. Vladimir's Seminary Press, 2002).

67. The phrase "the reflexive project of the self" is from Anthony Giddens, *Modernity and Self-Identity: Self and Society in the Late Modern Age* (Stanford: Stanford University Press, 1991), p. 231, quoted in Webster, *Holiness*, p. 104.

68. Webster, *Holiness*, p. 104.

69. Webster, *Holiness*, p. 104.

70. On this, see the essays in Samuel M. Powell and Michael E. Lodahl, eds., *Embodied Holiness: Toward a Corporate Theology of Spiritual Growth* (Downers Grove: InterVarsity, 1999).

Holy Sex

The experience of the Spirit, for Paul, is always also the experience of the crucified Christ; any other experience, no matter how (allegedly) "spiritual" it may be, is not an experience of the Spirit of the God revealed in the cross.

We must be quick to add here, however, that an apparent actualization of cruciformity (e.g., self-giving) is not necessarily the work of the Holy Spirit. For Paul, cruciform self-giving is the distinctive dimension of holiness, its *sine qua non*, but not its totality. In particular, as we have seen, for Paul cruciformity without sexual holiness is not holiness at all; it is pseudo-holiness. The "self-giving" of someone to another in exchange for money or another form of payment is not truly an act of self-giving. Moreover, Paul shows us that sexual libertinism/immorality is the denial of cruciform existence, for it fails to appropriate the work of the triune God in redeeming the human body through the cross and to express the kind of obedience to God that marks off God's people from the "Gentiles."[71] For Paul, sexual immorality (Greek *porneia* — "'unlawful sexual intercourse' . . . including homosexual practice and sexual immorality in general"[72]) and cruciform love cannot coexist, for *porneia* is at best a form of self-love, of self-indulgence that harms others and diminishes the holiness of both the individual and the community.[73]

Thus an alleged instance of self-giving, covenantal love outside the bounds of licit sexual relations is not, Paul would argue, an example of either cruciformity or holiness; it is *not* the work of the Holy Spirit. Furthermore, neither eroticism nor erotic love is synonymous with the divine Spirit, as some have suggested. Rather, the divine gift of sex is properly used only when it is linked to the other-regarding, community-regarding kind of love that can be expressed within the covenantal bonds and bounds of marriage.

Holy Politics

As we have seen in this chapter and especially in chapter one, Paul challenges our notion of God and God's attributes. The kenotic, cruciform character of

---

71. Unholy sex is also an existential denial of the reality and significance of the resurrection of Christ and of the human body (1 Cor 6:12-20), and thereby also a denial of the significance of theosis.

72. Dunn, *Theology*, p. 690.

73. See Dunn's concise but insightful discussion in his *Theology*, pp. 119-23. See also my brief essay "Romans 13:8-14," *Int* 62/2 (April 2008): 170-72.

God is the substance of divine holiness. The embedded theology of most Christians still revolves around a non-cruciform model of God's holiness, character, and power, and a crucial corrective is needed.

This brings us inevitably back (see also the end of chapter one) to politics, to the "normal" god of civil religion that combines patriotism and power. Nationalistic, military power is not the power of the cross, and such misconstrued notions of divine power have nothing to do with the majesty or holiness of the triune God known in the weakness of the cross. In our time, any "holiness" that fails to see the radical, counter-imperial claims of the gospel is inadequate at best. Adherence to a God of holiness certainly requires the kind of personal holiness that many associate with sexual purity. That is one dimension of theosis. But participation in a *cruciform* God of holiness also requires a corollary vision of life in the world that rejects domination in personal, public, or political life — a mode of being that is often considered realistic or "normal." Kenotic divinity and a corollary kenotic community constitute "both the best possible commentary" on Paul and a "frontal assault" on "normalcy."[74]

In our context, this frontal assault will require from Christians a rejection of the normal sequence of piety, war, victory, and peace that pervaded ancient Rome and pervades much early twenty-first-century politics and religion around the world — a sequence that plays out, not only in the strategies of powerful nations, but in the minds and hearts of Christians who have found in the god of military power a seductive alternative to the cruciform God of Paul.[75] Participation in that image of God is also a dangerous pseudo-holiness, pseudo-theosis, and pseudo-Christianity.

Conclusion

Paul's vision of participatory Trinitarian cruciform holiness, or theosis, is still relevant today. It challenges our contemporary spiritualities, immoralities, and idolatries. In the next chapter we explore one particular aspect of Paul's countercultural experience of God in Christ that we have looked at more generally in this chapter.

---

74. Crossan and Reed, *In Search of Paul*, p. 296.

75. The sequence of piety, war, victory, and peace is taken from Crossan and Reed, *In Search of Paul*, pp. xi-xii; cf. pp. 412-13.

CHAPTER 4

"While We Were Enemies"

Paul, the Resurrection, and the End of Violence

What might theosis have to say about the problem of violence? Can Godlikeness, or theosis, understood via Paul, incorporate violence and make it sacred violence? Or is theosis inherently nonviolent?

Religiously based, or "sacred," violence is of course no stranger to the Christian tradition or to our postmodern interreligious world. Some have contended that religion itself, or Christianity more specifically, or a Christian figure more specifically yet — Augustine or Bernard of Clairvaux, or Luther — is responsible for such violence.

One practitioner of sacred violence was, of course, the pretransformation Saul/Paul of Tarsus. If one were looking for a malevolently inspiring figure for the practice of sacred violence, he would be a superb candidate. But in a brief yet provocative essay, historian of early Christianity John Gager suggests that the *post*-transformation Paul, even as an apostle, was a violent figure who, by implication, has inspired and can continue to inspire violence among those who read his letters as Scripture.[1] That is,

---

1. John G. Gager, with E. Leigh Gibson, "Violent Acts and Violent Language in the Apostle Paul," in *Violence in the New Testament*, ed. Shelly Matthews and E. Leigh Gibson (New York: Clark, 2005), pp. 13-21. Despite the presence of an assistant (not a co-) writer, Gibson, I will refer to this article and its author as "Gager" because the first person singular pronoun is used throughout the essay. The introduction to the book states that its goal is not merely to address a neglected theme and thereby "redress a serious gap" in New Testament scholarship, but also to scrutinize the New Testament texts "for their violent content and effects" (p. 1); the author(s) of the introduction is (are) unnamed, but one of course suspects the editors.

Paul may be an ambassador of violence as a (perverse) form of theosis.[2]

While there are details of Gager's proposal that are insightful, this chapter challenges his overall thesis and seeks to show that Paul's experience of the resurrected crucified Messiah Jesus results in his conversion away from zealous violence and toward nonviolence and nonviolent forms of reconciliation. Because of the resurrection of Christ, Paul comes to see the cross, not merely as a means of death, but as a means of life. He also sees Christ's resurrection by God as God's pronouncement that covenant fidelity, justification, holiness, and opposition to evil are not achieved by the *infliction* of violence and death but by the *absorption* of violence and death. For Paul, the communities to which he wrote, and us, his gospel of cross and resurrection defines the ongoing identity of Christ present among us and thus a fundamental characteristic of cruciform existence in Christ: a life of nonviolence and reconciliation. That is, for Paul this kind of life is an integral part of his vision of justification and of participatory holiness — theosis.

Paul: A Violent Personality?

John Gager uses the work of Robert Hamerton-Kelly, a Girardian interpreter of Paul, as a springboard for his own interpretation of Paul vis-à-vis violence.[3] Gager agrees with Hamerton-Kelly that Paul was "an eccentric precisely in his attraction to violence" but disagrees with Hamerton-Kelly's belief that the post-conversion Paul is less violent. Rather, Gager sees "the post-conversion Paul as still very much entangled in the coils of violence," for Paul is a "violent personality in his actions, in his language, and in his ideology of Gentiles and their world as a world of violence."[4]

The evidence offered for this personality assessment is Paul's allegedly pervasive language of violence toward others (perpetrated by both God and Paul himself) and violence toward himself and other believers in the form of literal suffering as well as metaphorical death with Christ.[5] Gager refers to Paul's "violent christology of the cross," which, he claims, results in Paul's own commitment to "participation in the violent act of crucifixion" as "his

2. This way of formulating the problem is mine, not Gager's.

3. See Robert G. Hamerton-Kelly, *Sacred Violence: Paul's Hermeneutic of the Cross* (Minneapolis: Fortress, 1992).

4. Gager, "Violent Acts and Violent Language," p. 16.

5. Gager, "Violent Acts and Violent Language," pp. 17-19.

way of participating in Christ" and is rooted in Paul's "own personality, his own predilection for images and symbols of violence, his 'excessive zeal.'"[6] That is, for Gager, Paul's participatory cruciformity is not a virtue, but a vice, and a violent one.

While Gager has identified language of violence, suffering, and death in Paul, his basic observations are not new, and his speculation about a personality type is unprovable. Nevertheless, Gager's thesis provides us with an opportunity to reconsider Paul the violent persecutor and his conversion and to offer an alternative interpretation of Paul.

Paul the Violent Persecutor

Paul's Violent Zeal

How do we explain, either philosophically and theoretically or historically and practically, the violent zeal of Saul/Paul, the persecutor of the early Jesus movement?

By his own admission, Paul was a zealous persecutor (1 Cor 15:9-11; Gal 1:13-17, 23; Phil 3:6-7; cf. 1 Tim 1:12-13). His goal was to destroy the fledgling Jesus-as-Messiah movement, using violence as needed. Paula Fredriksen suggests that perhaps the most common form of this persecution was flogging Jewish believers in Jesus with the forty lashes less one that Paul himself would later receive on multiple occasions (2 Cor 11:24).[7] That he would have eventually resorted to murder, as Acts hints he at least threatened (Acts 9:1), may be less likely,[8] but it is not impossible.

At the theoretical level, there are perhaps two major contenders to help us better understand Paul's persecution of the church: mimetic violence and the will to purity.[9]

---

6. Gager, "Violent Acts and Violent Language," p. 19.

7. Paula Fredriksen, "Judaism, the Circumcision of Gentiles, and Apocalyptic Hope: Another Look at Galatians 1 and 2," *JTS* n.s. 42 (1991): 532-64, here pp. 549, 556; and "Paul and Augustine: Conversion Narratives, Orthodox Tradition, and the Retrospective Self," *JTS* n.s. 37 (1986): 3-34, here p. 10. She follows the lead of Arland Hultgren, "Paul's Pre-Christian Persecution of the Church," *JBL* 95 (1976): 97-112.

8. So, strongly, Fredriksen.

9. I do not mean to imply that any theory can fully explain a concrete historical phenomenon, but theories can sometimes help us better understand historical phenomena, including this one.

Some, especially Hamerton-Kelly, have followed René Girard's lead and argued that Paul was trapped in the "system of sacred violence"[10] that is driven by "mimetic [imitative] violence and surrogate victimage"[11] and rooted in the experience of "desire" understood as "acquisitive and conflictual mimesis" — "copying someone's else's desire for an object."[12] Hamerton-Kelly argues that there existed a particularly Jewish form of the universal phenomenon of sacred violence — which for him is the original or fundamental sin[13] — that consisted of "misusing the [Jewish] Law as a weapon of exclusion and persecution"[14] and that expressed itself both in the killing of Jesus and in the scapegoating of Gentiles.[15] Hamerton-Kelly claims that "obedience to the Law as interpreted in his Jewish community made . . . [Paul] a persecutor."[16] Paul's experience of Christ, especially Christ's cross, transformed him, as he perceived the violence in himself and inherent in obedience to the Law, coming to the conclusion that Christ's cross is an "epiphany of the violence of the primitive Sacred in Judaism,"[17] "the deconstruction of sacrifice,"[18] and the paradigm of generosity or "nonacquisitive divine desire."[19] Hamerton-Kelly believes that Paul concluded that he could "identify mimetically with the crucified" in accepting the Christian gospel,[20] thereby being "liberated from the realm of mimetic rivalry and sacred violence."[21] "The mimesis of violence has become a mimesis of faith, hope, and love."[22]

Although there are aspects of the Girardian interpretation, via Hamerton-Kelly, that are quite satisfying in respect to Paul, especially its placing of violence and nonviolence front and center in the interpretation of

10. Hamerton-Kelly, *Sacred Violence,* p. 15.

11. Hamerton-Kelly, *Sacred Violence,* p. 17.

12. Hamerton-Kelly, *Sacred Violence,* p. 19.

13. Hamerton-Kelly, *Sacred Violence,* pp. 88-119.

14. Hamerton-Kelly, *Sacred Violence,* p. 10.

15. Hamerton-Kelly, *Sacred Violence,* e.g., pp. 68, 71, 75.

16. Hamerton-Kelly, *Sacred Violence,* p. 10.

17. Hamerton-Kelly, *Sacred Violence,* p. 65; cf. pp. 63-87. He also refers to the "sacred violence of Judaism" (p. 66).

18. Hamerton-Kelly, *Sacred Violence,* p. 60.

19. Hamerton-Kelly, *Sacred Violence,* p. 69; cf. pp. 167-69.

20. Hamerton-Kelly, *Sacred Violence,* p. 65. He also refers to this as entering into "mimetic fellowship with the crucified and in resurrection hope" (p. 61), one of the few references to resurrection in the book.

21. Hamerton-Kelly, *Sacred Violence,* p. 69.

22. Hamerton-Kelly, *Sacred Violence,* pp. 60-61.

the apostle, there are many dimensions that need significant nuancing or supplementing and still others that are deeply problematic. New Testament scholars have not come to any kind of consensus that either Girard's theory or Hamerton-Kelly's application of it to Paul best illuminates Paul's persecution or his transformation.[23]

One main problem with Hamerton-Kelly's thesis is that it attributes violent zeal to Judaism per se, a zeal allegedly rooted in Judaism's adherence to the Law.[24] Another is that Hamerton-Kelly claims that Paul "move[s] out of Judaism definitively and deliberately," transferring into the "life of the Christian community."[25] And yet another is that Paul's vision of Christ led to his identifying his "persecuting violence as the work of the Mosaic Law in his life."[26] But this view of Judaism as inherently violent is both historically and theologically untenable, this interpretation of Paul the apostle as an ex-Jew has rightly been rejected by nearly every other biblical scholar, and this understanding of Paul's conversion owes more to Girardian theory than to rigorous textual and historical analysis. Such careful analysis may, however, lead us to another theory, which concerns the will to purity.

New Testament scholars have looked for historical causes for Paul's persecution and have proposed several possibilities.[27] One long-standing theory is that Paul opposed the church because it preached a crucified Messiah, whereas Judaism would find such a figure both oxymoronic and unscriptural, for "anyone hung on a tree is under God's curse" (Deut 21:23, referenced in Gal 3:13).[28]

---

23. Nonetheless, Girard's influence in New Testament studies (and biblical studies more generally) has been significant in some circles. See, e.g., *Violence Renounced: René Girard, Biblical Studies, and Peacemaking*, ed. Willard M. Swartley (Telford: Pandora, 2000).

24. While it is true that Hamerton-Kelly argues that Judaism's violence is the expression of a universal phenomenon, he does in fact say that Judaism per se, not some aspects of Judaism or some (mis)interpretations of Judaism, is exclusive and violent. See especially the conclusion to *Sacred Violence*, pp. 183-87.

25. Hamerton-Kelly, *Sacred Violence*, p. 61. Hamerton-Kelly goes so far as to say that Paul calls us "to live no longer in the Jewish way, which he [Paul] describes as living 'for oneself,' but in the Christian way, which is living for Christ (2 Cor 5:15)" (p. 125; cf. p. 129).

26. Hamerton-Kelly, *Sacred Violence*, p. 66.

27. For a brief overview, with special emphasis on possible social and political factors, see Calvin Roetzel, *Paul: The Man and the Myth* (Minneapolis: Fortress, 1999), pp. 39-42.

28. For one relatively recent example of this view, see Richard N. Longenecker, "A Realized Hope, a New Commitment, and a Developed Proclamation: Paul and Jesus," in *The Road from Damascus: The Impact of Paul's Conversion on His Life, Thought, and Ministry*, ed. Richard N. Longenecker (Grand Rapids: Eerdmans, 1997), pp. 18-42, here pp. 23-24.

Despite some objections to this interpretation,[29] it is actually very plausible in light of Paul's post-transformation passion for and interpretation of the cross. At the very least, as Paula Fredriksen suggests in criticizing the standard interpretation of Paul's alleged problem with a crucified Messiah, the pre-conversion Paul would have strongly objected to any *dead* Messiah as an oxymoron.[30]

Two interrelated proposals to explain Paul's persecution that merit careful consideration are (1) that Paul was seeking to purify Israel by punishing Jews who were improperly receiving Gentiles into the community of Israel (thereby hoping to end the impurity and stay the wrath of God)[31] and (2) that, as heir to the tradition of violent zeal begun with Phinehas (Numbers 25), he was prepared to do so with violence if needed.

Paul, Phinehas, and Purity

In his article on violence in Paul, John Gager says that his "own best guess" as to the cause of Paul's "murderous violence" is that "it must have had something to do with his [Paul's] sense that Gentiles were being allowed into the community of Israel in a way that threatened Paul's sense of Israel's integrity."[32] By "integrity," Gager appears to mean Israel's freedom from impurity and thereby its distinctiveness, or holiness, vis-à-vis the rest of the world.

This proposal is on the right track as to the cause of Paul's consternation, but insufficient to explain Paul's radical, potentially violent solution — which Gager rightly counsels us not to "play down" for apologetic purposes.[33] Gager also rightly notes that Paul describes himself as an atypical

29. Especially Fredriksen, "Judaism, the Circumcision of Gentiles, and Apocalyptic Hope," pp. 551-52; "Paul and Augustine," pp. 10-13.

30. I am using the term "conversion" throughout the chapter, not in the sense of a change of religions, but in the sense of a radical transformation in belief, behavior, and belonging. For justification of applying the term "conversion" to Saul/Paul, see Alan Segal, *Paul the Convert: The Apostolate and Apostasy of Saul the Pharisee* (New Haven: Yale University Press, 1990).

31. There are two ways to understand the notion of "improper reception of Gentiles," either receiving them *tout simple* or receiving them without requiring their circumcision or adherence to the Law. There is insufficient information about the earliest first-century churches to know precisely what was happening and therefore precisely what Paul opposed.

32. Gager, "Violent Acts and Violent Language," p. 17.

33. Gager, "Violent Acts and Violent Language," p. 17.

Jew, more zealous than his contemporaries. This means (against Hamerton-Kelly) that Torah-centered Judaism does not have to be zealously violent, but it does *not* mean that Paul had no Jewish precedent for his own violence. As other scholars, such as N. T. Wright, James Dunn, and Richard Longenecker have noted, that precedent is in figures such as (moving backward in the story of Israel) the Maccabeans taking on the Seleucids, Elijah confronting the prophets of Baal, and especially Phinehas, the grandson of Aaron, killing the Israelite man and his Midianite consort to stay the wrath of God. The importance of Paul's extreme zeal has been noted but underexploited.[34]

Numbers says this of Phinehas:

10The LORD spoke to Moses, saying: 11"Phinehas son of Eleazar, son of Aaron the priest, has turned back my wrath from the Israelites by manifesting such zeal among them on my behalf that in my jealousy I did not consume the Israelites. 12Therefore say, 'I hereby grant him my covenant of peace. 13It shall be for him and for his descendants after him a covenant of perpetual priesthood, because he was zealous for his God, and made atonement for the Israelites.'" (Num 25:10-13)

For this act of zeal and atonement, Num 25:13 says, Phinehas and his lineage were given a permanent priesthood, and his heroic, violent zeal was the focus of great admiration in later Jewish texts (e.g., Ps 106:30-31; Sir 45:23-24; 1 Macc 2:50-54).

It seems likely that the pre-conversion Paul — like Phinehas, his unnamed but very real spiritual hero — believed his violent zeal would contribute to the purification of Israel and bring about his own justification before God (see further below). Moreover, Paul may also have represented the kind of theology of "ethnic cleansing" we find in texts like Deuteronomy 20 (especially vv. 12-18).

We do not need to choose between the "opposing a dead/crucified Messiah" option and the "purifying Israel à la Phinehas" option; in fact, the for-

---

34. On Phinehas as Paul's precedent in particular, see, *inter alia,* N. T. Wright, *What Saint Paul Really Said: Was Paul of Tarsus the Real Founder of Christianity?* (Grand Rapids: Eerdmans, 1997), pp. 26-28 (and the larger discussion on pp. 25-35); James D. G. Dunn, *The Theology of Paul the Apostle* (Grand Rapids: Eerdmans, 1998), pp. 350-53, 368-71, 375-76; Longenecker, "A Realized Hope," p. 23; and my *Reading Paul* (Eugene: Wipf and Stock, 2008), pp. 13-14, 120-22.

mer may have been a contributing factor to the latter.[35] But for the moment we will focus on the "purifying" explanation and then return to the subject of a crucified Messiah below.[36]

The Pursuit of Purity

The historical explanation of Paul's violent zeal in the interest of purifying a community can be understood more fully by considering the historically rooted but more theoretical work of Miroslav Volf in *Exclusion and Embrace*.[37] Both Hamerton-Kelly and Volf analyze the phenomenon of exclusion. Volf's work, however, is a more satisfactory way to help us understand Paul the persecutor, both historically and theologically, than the Girardian approach (manifested in Hamerton-Kelly or elsewhere).

In his analysis of the phenomenon of exclusion, Miroslav Volf asks us to "[c]onsider the deadly logic of the 'politics of purity.'"[38] He first defines "the *pursuit of false purity*" as "the enforced purity of a person or community that sets itself apart from the defiled world in a hypocritical sinlessness and excludes the boundary[-]breaking other from its heart and its world." "Sin," he continues, "is here the kind of purity that wants the world cleansed of the other rather than the heart cleansed of the evil that drives people out by call-

35. Justin Taylor ("Why Did Paul Persecute the Church?", in *Tolerance and Intolerance in Early Judaism and Christianity*, ed. Graham N. Stanton and Guy G. Stroumsa [Cambridge: Cambridge University Press, 1998] pp. 99-120) argues that Paul was a Zealot, a member of Josephus's "Fourth Philosophy" — a zealous "Jewish religious nationalist" (p. 110) — inspired by Phinehas, *et al.*, who opposed the early followers of Jesus for not supporting his nationalist, anti-Roman agenda. Although a crucified Messiah could have been seen as a martyr in this cause, there is no evidence for this and plenty of evidence that a crucified Messiah was problematic to Jews (pp. 111-12).

36. It should be noted that Hamerton-Kelly also appeals convincingly to Phinehas as a model for Paul's zealous violence (*Sacred Violence*, pp. 71-77). The mistake Hamerton-Kelly makes is to assume (from Girard) that the root problem is sacred violence and then to equate zeal, or "the curse of sacred violence," with "[obedience] to the Mosaic Law" (p. 76; cf. p. 141). It is more historically accurate to say that for Paul sacred violence was his particular interpretation of the requirements of obedience to the Law, and that this violence was for him the means to an end — his own life and justification before God (see below).

37. Miroslav Volf, *Exclusion and Embrace: A Theological Exploration of Identity, Otherness, and Reconciliation* (Nashville: Abingdon, 1996).

38. This paragraph, including all quotations, is drawn from Volf, *Exclusion and Embrace*, p. 74.

ing those who are clean 'unclean' and refusing to help make clean those who are unclean." Drawing on the work of Bernhard-Henri Lévy in his 1995 book *Dangerous Purity*, Volf speaks also of the "'will to purity.'"

Naming a variety of particular manifestations of the lethal will to purity, from Nazi Germany to Serbia and Bosnia to Rwanda, Volf suggests that the goal of this will is "a world of total virtue" that depends on purity: "plurality and heterogeneity must give way to homogeneity and unity."[39] This purity is achieved by reduction, ejection, and segregation, and, in extreme (but not uncommon) situations, by "exclusion as *elimination*."[40]

Volf rightly refuses to equate the will to exclude or to eliminate with the most fundamental form of human sin ("original sin").[41] Nevertheless, with him we must recognize that the will to purity is both a very basic and a very pervasive form of human sin. Moreover, the phenomenon of a basic will to purity insightfully describes and helps to explain Paul's pre-conversion persecution as reflected in Paul's own letters and in the echoes of Phinehas they contain. The will to exclusion and violence was for Paul a means to achieve the more fundamental will to purity.[42] In effect, Paul wanted both to purify his community and to justify himself, or to put it in soteriological terms, he wanted to save both his people and himself. He would later find, of course, that his zeal was misguided, not "enlightened" (Rom 10:2, speaking of his fellow Jews but implicitly also of his past self).

Paul the Convert to Nonviolence

There can be no doubt that Paul stopped persecuting the church after Jesus the Lord and Son of God appeared to/in him, as he himself says (1 Cor 9:1; 15:8; Gal 1:15). He was converted, at the very least, away from that form of violence. But too often, descriptions of Paul as the former persecutor who be-

---

39. Volf, *Exclusion and Embrace*, p. 74.

40. Volf, *Exclusion and Embrace*, pp. 74-75 (quoting p. 75). Volf names a total of three forms of exclusion: exclusion as elimination, domination, and abandonment (p. 75). His analysis of exclusion, we should note, is not totally at odds with Girardian theory. Volf, for example, suggests that one of the reasons for the hatred that leads to exclusion is the desire for what others (the excluded) have (p. 78). Volf also acknowledges the reality of scapegoating, but he significantly nuances Girard's interpretation (p. 292).

41. Volf, *Exclusion and Embrace*, p. 72.

42. That is, Volf explains Paul better than do Girard and Hamerton-Kelly.

came a member of the Jesus movement and a proclaimer of its gospel do not attempt to account theologically for Paul's conversion away from this violence. It does not suffice simply to say that anyone will of course stop trying to "annihilate" (Gager's word)[43] a movement or group that one decides to join. We must press beyond this obvious observation to the fruit of Paul's transformation, namely his own preaching, teaching, and ministry. Specifically, we need to look at the theological and Christological affirmations of his gospel and their personal and ecclesial consequences (that is, their soteriological consequences) to see why violence as the divine instrument of community purification, or salvation, became abhorrent to Paul.

The Resurrection and Paul's Conversion Away from Violence

Paul's encounter with the resurrected Christ created for him cognitive, emotional, and behavioral dissonance as his misguided theology, zeal, and sacred violence were all unmasked. In James Dunn's memorable words, the resurrection became "the key term by which all reality was to be conjugated."[44] The movement Paul had been seeking to terminate for its impurity suddenly appeared as the locus of God's activity and the source of God's good news. The resurrection was therefore a vindication of the early Christian community and its gospel. Prior to that, however, it was a vindication of the crucified Messiah as God's way of purifying and saving Israel and the world. Upon his conversion, says N. T. Wright, Paul came to realize what others had also concluded:

> The resurrection of the person who had done and said these [potentially messianic] things, and who had been put to death as a messianic pretender, said it all. Israel's God, the creator, had reversed the verdict of the court, in reversing the death sentence it carried out. Jesus really was the king of the Jews; and, if he was the Messiah, he really was the lord of the world, as the psalms [referring to Psalms 2, 72, and 89] had long ago insisted.[45]

43. Gager, "Violent Acts and Violent Language," p. 17.
44. Dunn, *Theology*, p. 239.
45. N. T. Wright, *The Resurrection of the Son of God*, Christian Origins and the Question of God, vol. 3 (Minneapolis: Fortress, 2003), p. 244.

This realization (what Paul would call revelation) became central to the apostle's message. "The resurrection and exaltation of Jesus proclaim and install him as the world's true lord and savior; in other words, according to Paul's gospel it is because of the resurrection that Jesus is lord and Caesar is not."[46]

Moreover, the resurrection was therefore inherently a critique of any and all other ways of attempting to purify and save the world, including Paul's way of sacred violence. The resurrection means that the *mode* of Jesus' salvation has been vindicated by God as the way of true salvation, and the violent modes of ethnic cleansing, imperial domination, and the like are pseudo-soteriologies.[47]

Although Paul does not explicitly make this link between the resurrection and nonviolence (or between the resurrection and, say, the character of God as power-in-weakness — 1 Cor 1:18–2:5), it is nonetheless true that the resurrection is the cornerstone of Paul's theological and Christological affirmations, for without the resurrection the crucifixion of Jesus would be non-salvific (1 Cor 15:17). The resurrection both provides and vindicates the church's unique claims about the connection between God and Jesus in general, and between God and the cross of Jesus in particular. This connection is the foundation of the multiple theological and existential affirmations Paul makes in 1 Corinthians 15 and, I would argue, of every other significant claim that he makes as well.[48]

Most importantly, without the *resurrection* of Christ, the *cross* of Christ is simply the shameful but appropriate death of a messianic pretender and possible threat to the Roman status quo — not the death of the Son of God

---

46. Wright, *Resurrection*, p. 233.

47. It has become a commonplace (with some notable exceptions) in Pauline scholarship to speak of Paul's gospel of Christ's death and resurrection as counter-imperial, which, in my view, is quite true. But his gospel is also counter-violent, and that dimension has, surprisingly, received far less attention. Imperial salvation is almost always attained and maintained by violence or the threat of violence. The critique of violence is therefore always at least implicit in a counter-imperial stance. See Sylvia C. Keesmaat, "Crucified Lord or Conquering Saviour: Whose Story of Salvation?" *HBT* 26 (2004): 69-93.

48. Although Paul has much to say about the resurrection in 1 Corinthians 15, it would be foolish to think that that chapter, addressed to a concrete ecclesial situation, exhausts either the theological or the pastoral significance of the resurrection for him. Speaking of Romans specifically, but implicitly also of Paul more generally, N. T. Wright says, "The bodily resurrection of Jesus is the foundation of this letter, the heart of the gospel of Jesus' Lordship, the centre of Paul's implicit critique of Caesar, and the source of his doctrines of justification and salvation" (*Resurrection*, p. 245; cf. p. 266).

or Lord of glory.[49] Indeed, Christ's cross is *meaningless* for Paul without the resurrection. With the resurrection, however, the cross-Jesus-God connections become both possible and necessary. Paul is very fond of describing the resurrection as an act of God, either explicitly or implicitly (through use of the "divine passive": "he was raised").[50] Among several sources for this language is Isaiah's fourth servant hymn. Just as God willed the servant's sin-bearing death (Isa 53:4-10),[51] so also God willed and effected his exaltation and vindication:

> See, my servant shall prosper; he shall be exalted and lifted up, and shall be very high. (Isa 52:13)

> Therefore I will allot him a portion with the great. (Isa 53:12)

In the hands of Paul, such texts, given a Christological interpretation, become the foundation for associating God, via resurrection, with the cross and thereby not only with the divine *vindication* of Jesus but also with the divine activity in the *death* of Jesus the Servant-Messiah. This divine activity is characterized by Paul as nonretaliatory, nonviolent, reconciling love.

We may identify five interrelated themes in Paul's theology that show how God's resurrection of Christ confirms for Paul the nonviolent saving action of God in Christ and the corresponding call to nonviolence on the part of those who live in Christ and thereby in God. Throughout the discussion, we will also consider some possible objections, from Paul's own theology and practice, to the thesis that he was a nonviolent peacemaker.

1. The Resurrection Reveals the Cross as a Divine Act of Inclusion and Embrace

If Paul's persecution was an attempt to do the will of God by exclusion, specifically exclusion of uncircumcised Gentiles and/or those who welcomed

---

49. See also Wright, *Resurrection*, p. 248.

50. See Rom 4:24; 6:4-9; 7:4; 8:11, 34; 10:9; 1 Cor 6:14; 15:4; 15:12-20; 2 Cor 4:14; 5:15; Gal 1:1; 1 Thess 1:10. Cf. Col 2:12; Eph 1:20; 2 Tim 2:8. (1 Thess 4:14 is the only exception ["Jesus . . . rose again"], and that may reflect a pre-Pauline acclamation.)

51. This is the most natural reading, in context, of these verses, despite the desires of some interpreters to dissociate God from the servant's death.

them, then the resurrection demonstrated to Paul a divine predilection for inclusion, and specifically inclusion of the Gentiles.

For Jews, especially Pharisees, the resurrection of the dead was an *eschatological* event.[52] And for some Jews, at least, the eschatological restoration of Israel was expected to be a salvation that would be inclusive of Gentiles, as certain prophetic texts indicate.[53] The earliest followers of Jesus concluded that since God has raised Jesus from the dead *now*, then in some sense the eschatological age of salvation has begun. And if that is the case, they seem to have also concluded (taking the more positive, universal approach), then the Gentiles must be about to come to the knowledge of the true God. And if *that* is the case, excluding Gentiles (or perhaps excluding them unless they become Jews) is contrary to the eschatological activity and will of God. At some point very early on, this kind of resurrection logic must have hit Paul squarely in the face.

The corollary human response to such an act of divine inclusion and embrace is, self-evidently, to embrace and embody this divine predilection oneself. James Dunn argues persuasively that Paul's "doctrine" of justification by grace originated at his conversion, and that this teaching was fundamentally not about grace versus effort but about inclusion versus exclusion.[54] Justification is at the root of some of Paul's most basic assertions about inclusivity, oneness, and acceptance of cultural differences. This is seen especially in his repeated references to "Gentile and Jew," most succinctly in Gal 3:28 and most dramatically in Romans, where it is constitutive of both the letter's stated theme (Rom 1:16-17) and its pastoral goal (Rom 14:1–15:13).

The experience of justification by grace through co-crucifixion results in a new life — a co-resurrection with Christ — that welcomes *all* who participate in that same death to Sin, including the sin of exclusivity and the will to purity. Paul's experience of the resurrected Christ has transformed his ethnic, even tribal, identity and violent personality into what Volf calls a

---

52. See Wright, *Resurrection*, 85-206.

53. On Jewish views of the eschatological fate of Gentiles, see Terence L. Donaldson, *Paul and the Gentiles: Remapping the Apostle's Convictional World* (Minneapolis: Fortress, 1997), pp. 51-78, especially pp. 69-74. For prophetic texts about the inclusion of the Gentiles in salvation, see, e.g., Isa 2:2-4 = Mic 4:1-3; Isa 25:6-10a; 56:6-8; Zech 8:20-23.

54. For a succinct exposition of his view, see James D. G. Dunn, "Paul and Justification by Faith," in Longenecker, ed., *The Road from Damascus*, pp. 85-101, and his *Theology*, pp. 346-54. While I do not concur fully with Dunn and the "new perspective" on the meaning of justification, it clearly means the inclusion of Gentiles, even if that is not the full significance of the concept.

"catholic personality," which is a "personality enriched by otherness" and which requires a similarly catholic community for its sustenance.[55] The inclusion of those Paul has excluded, having previously deemed them impure, will become his life's vocation. This conversion to inclusivity does not eliminate Paul's commitment to communal holiness, as we saw in the previous chapter, but it revolutionizes both the way in which that holy community is defined and the way in which communal holiness is practiced. It also radically affects the way in which non-members of the community are treated.[56]

Paul's practice of ecclesial discipline, however, is sometimes said to be a form of violent behavior, or at least of unacceptable exclusion.[57] The most obvious case in point is the situation described in 1 Cor 5:1-13, where a man is described as living/sleeping with his father's wife, and Paul urges the Corinthians to drive him out of the community. In fact, however, this case demonstrates just the opposite of a violent response. Not only does Paul act and hope for the good of both the community and the individual, but he also urges excommunication rather than the death penalty — as the Torah requires (Lev 18:7-8; 20:11; cf. Deut 17:1-7) — as ways to "purge the evil from your midst" (Deut 17:7, referenced by Paul in 1 Cor 5:13). This is a remarkable rereading of Torah enabled by Paul's transformation.[58]

Paul knew that exclusion may sometimes be necessary and even salutary; it is not inherently violent. Miroslav Volf warns against the danger of "falling into the abyss of nonorder in which the struggle against exclusion implodes on itself because, in the absence of all boundaries, we are unable to name what is excluded or why it ought not to be excluded."[59]

Inclusion as a fundamental disposition, even if not unqualified, is quite obviously the opposite of exclusion, and therefore also implies the termination of exclusion's handmaidens, especially violence.

---

55. Volf, *Exclusion and Embrace*, p. 51.

56. That is, of course, believers may not exercise the will to purity toward those outside Christ and treat them with hatred or violence. Paul's ethic of nonviolence and peace is to be practiced toward all (Gal 6:10; 1 Thess 3:12; 5:15).

57. E.g., Gager, "Violent Acts and Violent Language," p. 18.

58. "The man who lies with his father's wife has uncovered his father's nakedness; both of them shall be put to death; their blood is upon them" (Lev 20:11). I do not mean to suggest that the death penalty was practiced in such cases in first-century Judaism, but that is what the text calls for, and Paul does in fact reject it. On the possible theological problems associated with rereading Scripture, see n. 74 below.

59. Volf, *Exclusion and Embrace*, p. 64.

2. The Resurrection Reveals the Cross
as God's Nonviolent Reconciliation in Christ

Paul's goal in persecuting the church, we have argued, was to purify Israel and save it from God's wrath by eliminating the perceived enemy. But the resurrection has revealed that the *modus operandi* of God in the salvation of both Israel and the world is to love rather than destroy enemies, to absorb rather than inflict violence.

No passage in Paul states this more clearly or powerfully than Romans 5:

> 5. . . . God's love has been poured into our hearts through the Holy Spirit that has been given to us. 6For while we were still weak, at the right time Christ died for the ungodly. 7Indeed, rarely will anyone die for a righteous person — though perhaps for a good person someone might actually dare to die. 8But God proves his love for us in that while we still were sinners Christ died for us. 9Much more surely then, now that we have been justified by his blood, will we be saved through him from the wrath of God. 10For if while we were enemies, we were reconciled to God through the death of his Son, much more surely, having been reconciled, will we be saved by his life. (Rom 5:5b-10)

It would be difficult to find a more sober account of the human condition in relation to God — weak, ungodly, sinners, enemies — or of the utter, and counterintuitive, compassion and grace found in God's reconciling response.[60] God takes the initiative, responding not in kind to humanity's rebellion and self-generated enmity toward God, but in extraordinary grace. The normal human temptation to squash enemies, to eliminate the impure other, is not the response of God in Christ. Instead, God reaches out to reconcile: people to God, and people to people. Willard Swartley therefore rightly argues that

> the notion of making peace between humans and God and between formerly alienated humans is so central to the core of Pauline doctrinal and

---

60. Leander E. Keck's argument that Rom 5:6-7 is a later interpolation simply does not make sense (*Romans*, ANTC [Nashville: Abingdon, 2005], pp. 139-40). Not only is the vocabulary describing the human condition similar to that found both earlier and later in the letter (1:18–3:20 and 8:26), but the verses provide the fulcrum of a beautifully constructed chiasm in 5:1-11.

ethical thought that it is impossible to develop a faithful construal of Pauline thought without peacemaking and/or reconciliation at the core.[61]

The appropriate human response to such grace is first of all simply to embrace it — or, to be more Pauline, to be embraced by it. But there is of course much more. Since God's love

> is extended in Christ even to God's enemies, to those who are insurgents against the divine order, an inevitable corollary of love for Paul is non-retaliation and nonviolence. . . . This is pacifism rooted in Paul's gospel of divine love and reconciliation, and it comes into play especially when dealing with those outside the community who may persecute believers (Rom 12:14-21), but God knows — and Paul knows — that non-retaliation and peacemaking are needed within the church as well (1 Thess 5:11-15).[62]

The "passive" dimension of this response, nonviolence, must of course be complemented by the "pro-active" response of peacemaking. In this chapter we are placing emphasis on nonviolence because it has been a neglected dimension of the study of Paul. Although violence is not the "original" sin in Paul, he is clear that it is a central part of the human situation apart from Christ.[63] Richard Hays has been one of the few students of Paul to note the nonviolent fruit of the apostle's conversion: "There is not a syllable in the Pauline letters that can be cited in support of Christians employing violence."[64] The experience of the *resurrected* crucified Jesus leads Paul to an ethic of dying rather than killing. Paul is willing to die daily (1 Cor 15:31) and to be poured out as a libation (Phil 2:17), both dramatic metaphors for a cruciform existence that hint, at least, at the possibility of literal death for others.[65] Paul sees this as

---

61. Willard M. Swartley, *Covenant of Peace: The Missing Peace in New Testament Theology and Ethics* (Grand Rapids: Eerdmans, 2006), p. 192. His entire treatment of Paul (pp. 189-253) repays careful reading. "Paul's gospel, from beginning to end," Swartley writes, "is a gospel of peace and reconciliation" (p. 211).

62. The quotation is from my *Reading Paul*, p. 159.

63. See, e.g., Rom 1:29 ("murder") and 3:15-17 ("swift to shed blood . . . and the way of peace they have not known"), quoting Isa 59:7-8.

64. Richard B. Hays, *The Moral Vision of the New Testament: A Contemporary Introduction to New Testament Ethics* (San Francisco: HarperCollins, 1996), p. 331. The contrast to the position of Gager could not be more stark.

65. For Paul's cruciform existence more generally, see my *Cruciformity: Paul's Narrative Spirituality of the Cross* (Grand Rapids: Eerdmans, 2001).

life-giving dying, like that of Jesus (2 Cor 4:8-12). And he is willing to absorb violence, but not to inflict it (1 Cor 4:11-13).

We must not, however, mistake this human response for mere ethics, even *imitatio Christi*. Paul has been caught up into the nonviolent, reconciling love of God in Christ and is being transformed by the Spirit into the image of God known in the resurrected crucified Messiah. That is, as we have argued throughout this book, Paul's concern is about a different way of being, a different *modus operandi,* one of participation in the cross and resurrection. The resurrection, as we will see further below, makes theosis — transformation into the image of the loving God of the cross — possible.

Some have asked, however, if the God of the cross is really a God of love.

The Violent Cross?

We have been arguing for a nonviolent God and a nonviolent apostle. However, the description of God's response to human sin in the form of the cross strikes some as violent rather than nonviolent, and that in at least two ways. First, it seems violent to hand one's Son over to death by crucifixion — "divine child abuse," as some have called it. Second, it seems violent to speak of participating in that event, to describe one's life as "co-crucifixion" (especially Gal 2:19).[66]

Although Paul hardly denies the reality of the cross as a *human* and perhaps even demonic instrument of violent exclusion and elimination (1 Cor 2:8), it is not for him a symbol of *divine* violence that permits or even encourages violent acts and language (so Gager, at least by implication[67]). Rather, it is above all the reality and symbol of divine inclusion and love. For that reason it is absolutely crucial for Paul and for us that the cross of Christ is not merely the loving action of God the Father (Rom 5:8) but also the loving action of Christ the Son (2 Cor 5:14; Gal 2:20). Indeed, Paul beautifully ties the two together in Rom 8:31-39. To die with the Son in faith and baptism (Gal 2:15-21; Rom 6:1–7:6; see chapter two above), and subsequently in a life of ongoing cruciform holiness, is not to actively do something violent but to actively do something loving and grace-filled for the benefit of others.

This kind of love for others may, in fact, be couched in the language of

---

66. This is Gager's complaint ("Violent Acts and Violent Language," p. 19).
67. See n. 1 above.

self-sacrifice and even of crucifixion.[68] However, these are powerful meta-phors, rooted in Christ's own experience and in the language of Scripture and early Christian tradition, that express selfless concern for others rather than some form of self-harm.

It will be useful here, therefore, to return for a moment both to Jesus himself and to the hymn of the suffering servant. It has often been said that Paul either knows or says little of the life and teachings of the historical Jesus. Whether or not this is true, what he does seem to know well is material from the so-called Jesus tradition that stresses the non-retaliatory, nonviolent features of Jesus' teaching (especially Rom 12:14-17 and 1 Cor 4:12-13).[69] This important dimension of Jesus' teaching also manifests itself in Jesus' re-action to his own persecutors that the gospel tradition narrates and that Isaiah 53 foreshadows (Isa 53:7: "yet he did not open his mouth; like a lamb that is led to the slaughter, and like a sheep that before its shearers is silent, so he did not open his mouth"). The crucified servant of God, narrated as the ulti-mate peacemaker and pacifist, is the One who now resides, as the Resur-rected One, in and among believers.

Before we develop that theme more fully, however, we must consider one additional theme related to Paul's experience of the resurrection as di-vine inclusion and nonviolent reconciliation.

3. The Resurrection Provides an Alternative Basis for Justification and Life with God

If Paul's persecution of the early church can be explained historically as a continuation of the Jewish tradition of Phinehas and theoretically as an instantiation of the human will to purity through violent exclusion, it must also be further described as one expression of the Jewish tradition of seeking justification before God, understood as being in right covenant relationship with God and receiving divine approval.

The concept of "justification" in Jewish and Pauline soteriology is the subject of major scholarly debates, as we saw in chapter two. As we briefly noted there, however, we can be fairly certain from the Phinehas texts cited

68. Rom 6:6; Gal 2:19; 5:24; 6:14.
69. On this point I disagree with the otherwise fine work of Gordon Zerbe, discussed below.

above, read in connection with the Pauline texts about zeal, that the pre-conversion Paul found the key to right covenantal relationship with God and therefore also approval by God — vindication in the divine court — in his own zeal for the Law, particularly as expressed in his violent persecution of the early church. This was, for Paul, the way to life, both now (temporal life) and later (eschatological life); it was his salvation. Or, to put it more philo-sophically, in his zeal Paul found justification for his existence, a raison d'être. He would not only make an impression on God, but would also make a mark in history, like Phinehas of old.

The Old Testament refers to two people being justified (with Greek *logizomai* in the LXX) by some act: Abraham (Gen 15:6; 1 Macc 2:52) and Phinehas (Ps 106 [LXX 105]:31).[70] The Greek texts describing Abraham's and Phinehas's justification are parallel to each other and to Paul's own language of justification, which comes directly from Gen 15:6 (cf. Rom 4:3, 5, 9, 22-24). According to Gen 15:6, Abraham was justified by faith; he believed the prom-ise of God: "And he [Abraham] believed the LORD; and the LORD reckoned it to him as righteousness." According to Psalm 106, Phinehas was justified by his violent zeal: it was and is "reckoned to him as righteousness":

> 30Then Phinehas stood up and interceded, and the plague was stopped.
> 31And that has been reckoned to him as righteousness [Greek *elogisthē autō eis dikaiosynēn*] from generation to generation forever. (Ps 106:30-31)

The Greek phrase in Ps 106:31 is exactly the same as the parallel text in Gen 15:6, later repeatedly quoted and echoed in Romans 4.

Is this antithetical parallel between Abraham and Phinehas, and Paul's quotation of the former rather than the latter, merely coincidental? Or does Paul know full well that justification has two paradigms in the Scriptures, one based on violent zeal for the Law and the purity of Israel, the other on faith? As Francis Watson says, "Abraham is, so to speak, a photographic neg-ative of Phinehas."[71] Furthermore, James Dunn claims that the pre-

---

70. Francis Watson discusses Phinehas and Abraham at length (*Paul and the Herme-neutics of Faith* [London/New York: Clark, 2004], pp. 174-82), also noting the existence of just these two examples of righteousness being "reckoned" (p. 177). Most who have noted this pairing omit the 1 Maccabees text (but see Hamerton-Kelly, *Sacred Violence*, p. 74). Gen-esis highlights Abraham's trust in God's promise, 1 Maccabees his faithfulness; both stand in contrast to the violence of Phinehas.

71. Watson, *Paul and the Hermeneutics of Faith*, p. 179. Watson discusses these two con-

conversion Paul knew about justification à la Phinehas,[72] and everything we have seen so far in this chapter makes that view not only likely but strategically more important than most people have recognized. In finding his justification no longer in (violent zeal for) the Law but in grace and faith, Paul simultaneously replaces Phinehas with Abraham as the prototype of justification — and finds a new raison d'être.[73]

The importance of this for Paul has been almost universally underestimated, but it is the corollary of the experience of justification by grace through faith. Grace and faith replace violent zeal. In the God seeking him in the resurrected Christ (Gal 1:15-16; cf. Acts 9:1-9), Paul is confronted with gracious, di-

---

trasting exemplars of righteousness being reckoned (pp. 178-79) but sees the contrast only as an heroic act (Phinehas) versus "consent" to God's promise and self-commitment. Surprisingly, Watson does not note the parallel between Phinehas and Paul on the matter of zeal.

72. Dunn, *Theology*, pp. 368-71, 376.

73. A similar interpretation of Paul and Phinehas in my book *Reading Paul* led one reviewer of that book to accuse me of taking "tremendous liberties with the Old Testament text," "unfair[ly] reading" the Old Testament as the source of an "exclusivistic impulse in Judaism that is categorically rejected within the terms of the New Covenant," and turning Paul into a Marcionite by alleging that Paul, a believer in Scripture as "the revealed word of God," made a biblical personage praised by Scripture (Phinehas) a "paradigm of evil" (Gary Anderson, review of Michael J. Gorman, *Reading Paul, First Things* 184 [June-July 2008]: 52-53, here p. 53). As I have insisted in this chapter, over against Hamerton-Kelly, Paul did not (and I do not) see Judaism as inherently or necessarily violent. And I certainly am not, and do not think Paul was, a Marcionite. (See, e.g., my explicit criticism of Marcion in *Reading Paul*, p. 65.) In fact, in my work I have stressed the Jewishness of Paul (e.g., *Apostle of the Crucified Lord: A Theological Introduction to Paul and His Letters* [Grand Rapids: Eerdmans, 2004], p. 40). It is the case, nonetheless, that Paul's encounter with the resurrected crucified Messiah transformed his understanding of the Law, including its demands and the God who makes those demands. To say that Paul abandons the Phinehas approach to justification is *not* to say that he abandons Scripture as the revealed word of God, but it is to say — as I think Anderson would agree — that Paul reinterprets all of Scripture, and reevaluates all interpretations of Scripture, in light of Christ. It is not Marcionite, for example, to stop offering animal sacrifices because Christ died once for all, or to stop pursuing an eye for an eye because Christ taught and practiced another way that truly embodies God's will and thus "fulfills" Scripture. In fact, I would argue that it is precisely because Paul, unlike Marcion, believes that the God of Israel's Scriptures is the God and Father of our Lord Jesus Christ that he feels compelled to view the violence of Phinehas negatively and the faith of Abraham in the God who brings life out of death positively. Moreover, as noted earlier, other scholars like Dunn and Wright have noted Paul's early embrace of Phinehas and implicitly acknowledged his later rejection of Phinehas (since Paul stopped persecuting the church) after meeting Christ. That hardly makes them, or the Paul they describe, Marcionite.

vine enemy love, divine inclusion and embrace.[74] This leads him ultimately to an ethic of dying rather than killing. It means that nonviolence and cruciform hospitality are at the heart of Paul's experience of God in Christ and thus at the heart of his gospel and at the center of his inhabitation of this God. The proper response to God in Christ for justification is not merely "simple trust" but also a concomitant rejection of the Phinehas approach to justification.[75]

Although James Dunn, for instance, recognizes both the importance of Phinehas for understanding Paul and the importance of Paul's conversion to Gentile inclusion, he does not (to my knowledge) specifically connect Paul's experience of the resurrected Jesus to his conversion out of violence per se. Yet this is a critical gap; for Paul, the ethic that grows out of the theological convictions discussed above is reinforced by his new soteriological convictions, because the two sets of convictions are of a piece. To know the God of nonviolent, reconciling enemy-love is also to know the God of inclusive, justifying grace, and vice versa.

Paul's abandonment of Phinehas-like zeal is not, however, to be confused with tepidity. Paul became single-mindedly passionate about the crucified and resurrected Messiah Jesus and about what God had done and was still doing in him, as Phil 3:7-14, for instance, indicates.[76] Paul's claim to "regard everything as loss because of the surpassing value of knowing Christ Jesus my Lord" (Phil 3:8) certainly suggests a new kind of zeal, an alternative to the persecuting zeal he mentions just two verses earlier (Phil 3:6). But it would be insufficient simply to say that Paul has replaced one form of zeal with another. The radically different content of his new desire cannot be minimized, as if his personality type has just found a new focus.[77] His new desire is to "know Christ and the power of his resurrection and the sharing of his sufferings by becoming like him in his death" (Phil 3:10). That is, he desires to share in the violence inflicted on Christ (in part by suffering on behalf of Christ's body, the church) rather than to inflict violence on Christ by persecuting the church, which is Christ's body.

---

74. I am of course echoing Miroslav Volf, *Exclusion and Embrace.*

75. The quotation defining faith is from Dunn, *Theology*, p. 378. In discussing justification Dunn acknowledges Paul's (pre-Christian) imitation of Phinehas's approach to righteousness (pp. 368-71, 376), but he does not make the connection between Paul and nonviolence that Paul's new understanding of faith seems clearly to entail.

76. Paul even appears willing to be considered a bit out of his mind (2 Cor 5:13).

77. That is, rather than seeing Paul's personality as essential violent, as Gager does, seeing his personality as essentially zealous.

To avoid confusion, then, we do well to speak, not of Paul's zeal, but of his passion for Christ or his passionate pursuit of conformity to Christ (Phil 3:10-11). Or, to use the language we have suggested throughout this book, his passion is for holiness, for Godlikeness, for theosis — understood as cruciformity now that precedes glorification later. In that relentless pursuit, Paul seeks to become fully Christlike — fully human and fully divine, as we argued in chapter one with respect to another text in Philippians, 2:6-11.[78] Returning to Romans and to Abraham, we may say that embracing Abraham-like faith also represents a truly human way — indeed, the most truly human way — to receive and experience life with God.[79]

Thus the appropriate response to God in Christ includes the rejection of the Phinehas approach to justification and the embrace of Abraham and of Abraham's faith. It means that only such faith (understood robustly, as in chapter two) results in justification and therefore life, and that the resurrection of Christ is the basis of justification (Rom 4:25). To be justified is not only to share in Christ's life-giving death, but also to share in his life-giving life.[80]

4. The Resurrection Provides an Alternative Means of Responding to Evil: Christ Within and Without

The theme of dying and rising with Christ is well known and widely discussed.[81] Some have wrongly connected it only with baptism; others have rightly linked it not only to baptism but also to post-baptismal daily life. But one dimension of this reality that is often overlooked is the significance of Christ's resurrection for the ongoing, indwelling presence of believers in

---

78. By "fully human and fully divine," I of course do not mean to assert Paul's being the incarnate eternal Son of God, but rather the embodiment of cruciform theosis, which is the true, essential mark of both humanity and divinity.

79. In this regard it is quite interesting that Paul seems to call on his audience in Romans to share both the faith of Abraham (4:16) and the faith of Jesus (3:26, reading *pistis Christou* as subjective genitive). Paul apparently sees them as having essentially the same approach to God.

80. On the significance of the resurrection for justification, with special reference to Romans, see J. R. Daniel Kirk, *Unlocking Romans: Resurrection and the Justification of God* (Grand Rapids: Eerdmans, 2008).

81. The classic work is Robert C. Tannehill, *Dying and Rising with Christ: A Study in Pauline Theology* (Berlin: Töpelmann, 1966).

Christ and of Christ in believers, both individually and corporately. While it is true that Paul speaks more often of us in Christ, rather than the other way around (Christ in us), both ways of speaking are central to Paul's experience and theology, and both testify to the importance of Christ as a living person and presence. The language of Christ in us and of us in Christ may be called the language of "mutual indwelling" or "reciprocal residence."[82] The resurrected Christ is both an internal, enlivening power and an external, life-giving and life-shaping reality. Paul also describes the reciprocal residence of Christ and believers as the reciprocal residence of believers and the Spirit: the Spirit within and in the Spirit.[83]

The Spirit given to believers is both the Spirit of the Father and the Spirit of the Son, as we stressed in chapter three. Because the Spirit who dwells in believers and in whom believers dwell is the Spirit of the One (God the Father) who raised Jesus from the dead, believers have God's resurrection power available to them (Rom 8:10-11).[84] This is the power of new life, of transformation, of theosis. At the same time, because the Spirit given to them is the Spirit of the crucified Jesus, the Son (Gal 4:6; cf. Gal 2:20), resurrection power takes the form of the cross; it is *cruciform* resurrection power. Just as the resurrection validates, vindicates, and completes the cross, so also the resurrection empowers us to embody that cross. *The living Christ of the resurrection is the loyal and loving Christ of the cross; the living one who dwells within us and within whom we dwell is the faithful and loving one who gave himself in obedience to God and in love for us.* This is the essential claim of Gal 2:20 and the heart of Paul's cruciform spirituality: "It is no longer I who

---

82. See my *Reading Paul*, pp. 126-30. As noted in chapter two n. 149, the technical theological term for this kind of reciprocal residence, or mutual interpenetration, perichoresis, is associated both with the relationship among the persons of the Trinity and also with the relationship between Christians and God in the process of theosis. See especially Elena Vishnevskaya, "Divinization as Perichoretic Embrace in Maximus the Confessor," in *Partakers of the Divine Nature: The History and Development of Deification in the Christian Traditions,* ed. Michael J. Christensen and Jeffery A. Wittung (Grand Rapids: Baker, 2007), pp. 132-45. Vishnevskaya writes that, according to Maximus, "in keeping with this Trinitarian ineffability [i.e., perichoretic union and love] . . . God, in the greatest act of self-donation, interpenetrates into human existence and, at the same time, opens himself up for human participation, that is, the Trinitarian Godhead creates conditions for mutual indwelling in divinization" (p. 143).

83. E.g., the Spirit within: Rom 8:11; 1 Cor 3:16; 6:19; 2 Cor 1:22; in the Spirit: Rom 14:17; 1 Cor 12:13; Phil 2:1; 3:3.

84. See also Wright, *Resurrection,* p. 301.

live, but it is Christ who lives in me. And the life I now live in the flesh I live by the faithfulness of the Son of God, who loved me by giving himself for me" (my translation).[85]

From the very day of his "conversion" or call, it seems, Paul understood what had happened to him as a revelation of the Son *in* him (Gal 1:16). It is absolutely crucial for our understanding of Paul to see the connection between (1) the *living Lord* who resides in and among believers, (2) the *suffering Messiah* who gave himself on the cross in non-retaliatory love, and (3) the *teaching Jesus* who spoke the words of non-retaliation echoed in texts like Romans 12 and 1 Corinthians 4. These three are in fact one nonviolent Lord, whose cross displayed the nonviolent power of God and whose Spirit continues the presence of that nonviolent divine power within and around his church.[86] The continuity and connection among these three must also be stressed. To live in *this* Christ, to walk in *this* Spirit, is to inhabit the God of life-in-death and power-in-weakness. It yields the style of life Paul depicts at the end of Romans 12:

> 14Bless those who persecute you; bless and do not curse them. 15Rejoice with those who rejoice, weep with those who weep. 16Live in harmony with one another; do not be haughty, but associate with the lowly; do not claim to be wiser than you are. 17Do not repay anyone evil for evil, but take thought for what is noble in the sight of all. 18If it is possible, so far as it depends on you, live peaceably with all. 19Beloved, never avenge yourselves, but leave room for the wrath of God; for it is written, "Vengeance is mine, I will repay, says the Lord." 20No, "if your enemies are hungry, feed them; if they are thirsty, give them something to drink; for by doing this you will heap burning coals on their heads." 21Do not be overcome by evil, but overcome evil with good. (Rom 12:14-21)

As Gordon Zerbe has noted in a very helpful essay, this passage and similar texts are primarily (though not exclusively) intended to show the church

---

85. This paragraph is adopted, with only minor additions, from my *Reading Paul,* p. 129. On Gal 2:20, see also chapter two above.

86. I do not mean to suggest that non-retaliation and nonviolence are synonymous but that a rejection of either would, on the whole, include a rejection of the other. Similarly, responses to one's own adversaries and responses to perceived adversaries of God and the community may not necessarily be identical, but to the extent that non-retaliation and/or nonviolence is either rejected or allowed, the fundamental ethical character of permissible responses to these different kinds of adversaries will be the same.

how to deal with outsiders, especially persecutors.[87] But it would not be inaccurate to call the offenders, generically, "enemies" or "adversaries." Zerbe speaks of a "field of proper responses to injury or persecution"[88] consisting of both "passive" and "active" behaviors that constitutes Paul's "ethic of nonretaliation and peace."[89] Passive responses include, for example, not repaying evil for evil, not taking vengeance, not cursing, and not litigating, while active responses include, among others, responding with kind deeds, blessing, conciliating, loving, and forgiving.[90]

Zerbe rightly notes that Romans 12 does not offer a specific Christological grounding in the teaching or example of Jesus; he does not think that Paul knew the words of Romans 12 as dominical sayings but may have simply inherited the sentiments from Judaism.[91] Nevertheless, Zerbe also rightly argues, the larger context of Romans and of Paul's letters more generally suggests both an apocalyptic and a Christological grounding for Paul's ethic of non-retaliation and peace.[92]

It is necessary, however, to nuance Zerbe's generally excellent analysis. It is highly unlikely, given Paul's affinities for Phinehas and his own violent activity, that he would have imported this kind of nonviolent ethic from his own "pre-Christian Jewish ethical heritage" as Zerbe suggests,[93] even though it certainly would have been found in some forms of Second Temple Judaism.[94] Rather, Paul needed a conversion from violence via a divine vindication of nonviolence — the resurrection — to conclude that nonviolence is the way of God and therefore also of the covenant people. It is likely, therefore, that the postconversion Paul *did* know the texts on nonviolence and non-retaliation as the teachings of Jesus (or at least as consonant with his teaching) and that he saw them as being in perfect continuity with the crucified and resurrected Lord, whose death he narrated as suffering, self-giving love, and whose life, he

---

87. Gordon Zerbe, "Paul's Ethic of Nonretaliation and Peace," in *The Love of Enemy and Nonretaliation in the New Testament,* ed. Willard M. Swartley (Louisville: Westminster/John Knox, 1992), pp. 177-222. The essay summarizes part of Zerbe's monograph, *Non-Retaliation in Early Jewish and New Testament Texts: Ethical Themes in Social Contexts,* JSPSS 13 (Sheffield: JSOT, 1993).

88. Zerbe, "Paul's Ethic," p. 179.

89. Zerbe, "Paul's Ethic," p. 180.

90. Zerbe, "Paul's Ethic," pp. 179-80.

91. Zerbe, "Paul's Ethic," p. 202.

92. Zerbe, "Paul's Ethic," p. 203.

93. Zerbe, "Paul's Ethic," p. 202.

94. This is one of the primary contentions of Zerbe's monograph.

claimed, animates the church. It is not, therefore, simply that "Christ is the prototype and exemplar in suffering"[95] — though he is that — but also that the Christ who was the incarnation of the nonviolent, reconciling love of God re-incarnates that life as the resurrected Lord in those individuals and communities he indwells and who dwell in him.[96] That is, perichoresis (mutual indwelling) effecting theosis is the true Pauline version of *imitatio Christi*.

Paul's allegedly violent language toward others has sometimes been offered as an argument for a violent apostle.[97] It is true, for example, that Paul threatens to come to the Corinthians with a stick (1 Cor 4:21) and that he wishes the Galatian circumcisers would self-mutilate (Gal 5:12). But in the former case he is obviously speaking metaphorically, and in the second hyperbolically. Practitioners of ancient rhetoric often resorted to such strategies. It is of course true that words can harm and in that sense do violence to others, but this is a far cry from the violent activity of the pre-conversion Paul. To equate the two is to overestimate the significance of the former and to underestimate the significance of the latter.

5. The Resurrection Provides a Guarantee That God Will Deal Finally with Evil

Finally, we come to our fifth and final theme: the resurrection and God's final defeat of evil. Paul turns to this explicitly and quite fully in two places, Romans 8, which deals with human and cosmic suffering prior to the final liberation and redemption (8:18-25), and 1 Corinthians 15, which deals with Sin and Death as enemy cosmic powers that God will ultimately defeat (15:24-28, 54-57).

The corollary of this theocentric apocalyptic answer to the reality of suffering and evil is twofold in Paul. First, it seems clear that just as God in Christ

95. Zerbe, "Paul's Ethic," p. 203.

96. It is also insufficient, therefore, to describe Christian existence fundamentally as "the mimesis of the crucified Christ," as Hamerton-Kelly does, offering mimetic theory as a better framework for understanding co-crucifixion with Christ in faith and baptism than "'mysticism' or 'corporate personality'" (*Sacred Violence*, pp. 68-70; quote from p. 69). Similar claims about mimesis appear throughout Hamerton-Kelly's description of Christian existence (e.g., pp. 85, 168, 174). As I have argued elsewhere, imitation (or mimesis) simply does not catch the dynamic character of mutual indwelling; see my *Cruciformity* (e.g., the summary on pp. 48-49).

97. See, e.g., Gager, "Violent Acts and Violent Language," pp. 17-19.

has suffered with and for us, so also believers need to be willing to suffer not only for the gospel but also with the rest of the creation that still moans and groans (Rom 8:18-25). Although Paul does not explicitly say that in Romans 8, the logic of his spirituality — that the same Christ who displayed suffering love for others indwells the church — demands such a conclusion. Moreover, Paul depicts the Spirit as participating with us in this cosmic groan (8:26).

Second, it seems equally clear that violent retribution is inappropriate for those who believe that the resurrection of Christ is the assurance that evil will be defeated. It is with this confidence, and only with this confidence, that Paul and we can affirm that it really is true that "[v]engeance is mine, I will repay, says the Lord" (Rom 12:19, alluding to Deut 32:35; Prov 20:22). This promise undergirds the exhortations to follow, or inhabit, Jesus on the path of nonviolence that surround this text and that we have just noted (Rom 12:14-21).[98]

Opposition to the argument here will largely come from those who see the full effects of the resurrection of Jesus in the future; they would likely accuse the position presented in this chapter of ignoring or collapsing eschatology and positing the present experience of resurrection, rather than future resurrection, as the time when violence will end.[99] It should be noted carefully, therefore, that the argument of this chapter affirms the eschatological resurrection as the theological and chronological framework within which all violence will cease. The Pauline summons to nonviolence grounded in the cross and resurrection does not deny the future, final cessation of violence as our eschatological hope. Rather, it is those who live between the past and the future — in the overlap of the ages — who can live without violence because they trust in God's *future* victory/resurrection guaranteed by God's *past* victory/resurrection.

Paul's Language of God's Wrath

This theme leads also to what is perhaps the most significant problem with the thesis that Paul is a true believer in nonviolence. It is a theological problem that is considered in most recent discussions of theology and vio-

98. On this, see also Zerbe, "Paul's Ethic," pp. 194-202.
99. See, e.g., Hans Boersma, *Violence, Hospitality, and the Cross* (Grand Rapids: Baker, 2004).

lence/nonviolence: leaving vengeance to God by deferring it to the divine eschatological judgment ultimately appears to make Paul — and, more importantly, God — violent. To be sure, Paul is not reticent to speak of God's eschatological wrath, judgment, and destruction of enemies. But is it right, with Gager, to call Paul's God "a violent actor"?[100]

Part of this debate at first appears to be only semantic. What one person labels divine *justice* or *wrath*, appropriate to the character of God as God, another calls divine *violence*, suggesting (at least) its inappropriateness to God. Moreover, both in the case of discussing Paul specifically and in the case of making a more general theological argument for nonviolence, allowing God to destroy enemies, whether literally or metaphorically, seems to render God either schizophrenic or hypocritical, since a key component of most theologies of nonviolence is imitation of God and/or Christ.

There are several ways to address this problem.[101] Some would argue that there is a "fundamental theological tension" between divine grace and divine justice.[102] Others — most eloquently Miroslav Volf — would stress that because God is different from humans, God has certain reserved powers, including the right to judgment and vengeance, even using violence.[103] However, even Volf qualifies this claim, suggesting that the eschatological violence of God depicted, for instance, in Revelation, "is the *symbolic portrayal of the final exclusion of everything that refuses to be redeemed by God's suffering love*."[104] Volf continues, "For the sake of the peace of God's good creation, we can and must affirm *this* divine anger and *this* divine violence" even while hoping that God's enemies will end their opposition to God and be saved.[105] Willard Swartley, by way of contrast, affirms divine judgment but calls the attribution of violence — a human evil — to God a "category fallacy," a "misnomer."[106]

100. See Gager, "Violent Acts and Violent Language," pp. 17-18.

101. For a helpful overview of recent discussion, with emphasis on writers of pacifist or near-pacifist persuasion, see Swartley, *Covenant of Peace*, pp. 383-98.

102. Zerbe, "Paul's Ethic," p. 201.

103. See Volf, *Exclusion and Embrace*, pp. 275-306, especially pp. 295-306. Volf argues that the human (Christian) practice of nonviolence requires belief in God's vengeance and violence, and that a "nonindignant God would be an accomplice to injustice, deception, and violence" (p. 297).

104. Volf, *Exclusion and Embrace*, p. 299.

105. Volf, *Exclusion and Embrace*, p. 299.

106. Swartley, *Covenant of Peace*, pp. 394-95. See also pp. 395-98, where Swartley argues that humans are not called to imitate divine wrath, with which Volf largely agrees.

This issue is both terribly difficult and terribly important. Paul may be able to help us, however, in a significant way. The fundamental character of his own spirituality, or experience of God, is a narrative spirituality of the cross, or cruciformity. The essential narrative character of this spirituality, especially as it manifests itself as love for others, derives from the story of Christ narrated in Phil 2:6-8 and echoed throughout the Pauline corpus. This narrative, the subject of chapter one, was summarized as follows:

although [x] not [y] but [z]

meaning

although [status] not [selfishness] but [selflessness], or

although [possessing rights] not [acting on those rights] but [forgoing those rights in action for the good of others][107]

In chapter one we argued that the narrative identity of Christ revealed in the narrative structure of Phil 2:6-8 is ultimately revelatory of the narrative identity of God. Christ, "the form of God," reveals God as one whose own identity can be narratively depicted as "although [x] not [y] but [z]." In Phil 2:6-8, "Christ's divinity, and thus divinity itself, is being narratively defined as kenotic and cruciform in character."[108] For both Christ and God, and for us, the fullest and truest exercise of "[x]" — our status and its inherent rights — is to exhibit the pattern "not [y] but [z]." In other words, to practice "not [y] but [z]" is not a contradiction of divinity or humanity, but an expression of it.

The "although [x] not [y] but [z]" pattern is implied throughout Romans and especially in 5:6-8, which, as we have seen, is at the heart of Paul's commitment to nonviolence. Paul says that God's love expressed in Christ's death was an abnormality when considered from a human perspective: people do not willingly die for evil people and enemies. Paul also implies, in the context of Romans as a whole, that although God has the right and the motivation to judge rebellious, sinful humans, whose deeds make them worthy of death (Rom 1:32; 6:16, 21, 23), God has chosen *at this time* to forgo that right and to act in Christ for humanity's salvation. This is what Paul means by grace. It is that act of grace, of "although [x] not [y] but [z]," that guarantees our salvation in the future (Rom 5:7-11) and our experience of divine love in the present, even in the midst of suffering (Rom 5:1-6; 8:28-39).

107. See chapter one above and also my *Cruciformity,* especially pp. 88-92, 164-69.
108. See chapter one, p. 25.

This is not to say, however, that God is now prevented from judging humanity at some future date. As God, God preserves the right to judge and to punish injustice; that is the divine status and right symbolized by "[x]" in the "although [x] not [y] but [z]" pattern when it is applied to God. Thus, although the narrative of "not [y] but [z]" does in fact *express* the divine identity, it does not *exhaust* it. God still maintains the right to judge and even to condemn and destroy all divine enemies, and in Paul's view God will exercise that right — indeed responsibility — at the time of the general resurrection (1 Corinthians 15).[109]

The resurrection of Christ, therefore, demonstrates both that in Christ's death God has freely expressed the abnormality of grace — which is paradoxically also essential to the divine character — and that God will exercise, as needed, the prerogative of eschatological judgment. This reality frees Paul — and us — from the need to practice violence now and from the fear that somehow evil and evil people may ultimately prevail.

The strength of Paul's conviction and the effect on his concrete practices is clear in his letter to the Philippians. There he affirms, first of all, the existence of "enemies of the cross" as well as "opponents" of Paul and the Philippians and, secondly, their final "destruction" (Phil 1:28; 3:18-19) — clearly implying "destruction" at the hands of God, not Paul or other humans. Paul courageously carries on, despite the presence of enemies, without even mentioning the possibility of zealous, purifying violence — which would almost certainly have been his pre-Damascus response. Neither violence nor fear is part of the economy of God revealed in the resurrection of the crucified Messiah that guarantees the salvation and resurrection of believers (Phil 3:20-21).

Paul's Christologically Grounded Practice of Nonviolence Today

Paul is frequently portrayed as the paradigm of Christian conversion, both in Christian spirituality and in Western art. He is touted as the one-time persecutor turned proclaimer, which is of course true. Seldom, however, is his turn from violence *qua* violence (as opposed to his turn from persecuting the early church to promoting the faith) seen as a constitutive part of his

---

109. Once again, as Volf reminds us, this is essentially God's final dealing with everything that does not wish to be included in God's grace.

conversion and new life, or as paradigmatic for, and therefore constitutive of, Christian conversion and new life more generally. If the conversion of Paul, grounded in the resurrection of Christ, is paradigmatic, it is paradigmatic in multiple ways, not least of which is his conversion from violence to nonviolence. Put differently, forsaking violence and embracing nonviolence is an essential part of Paul's theosis and of Christian theosis more generally.

Some may argue against a need for conversion away from violence as an essential component of Christian conversion and theosis because not all human beings are violent, and few are violent like Paul was. Although these claims may be true, it is nonetheless equally true that all human beings have the capacity for violence — as Karl Barth put it, we are all like caged wolves that may escape at any moment.[110] Moreover, Paul's embrace of nonviolence is not inherently dependent on his previous practice of violence; that previous practice only serves to make the embrace of nonviolence more dramatic. The Pauline call to nonviolence springs, not from Paul's conversion, but from the gospel of God's reconciling love in Christ. In other words, one does not have to identify with Paul's conversion narrative or turn from a previous practice of violence to embrace nonviolence and thereby to commit in advance, by God's grace, to foregoing violence in the future.

The necessity of seeing nonviolence as constitutive of Christian conversion and existence is all the more pronounced as we see an increase in sacred violence — or at least in versions of it peculiar to the twenty-first century. Especially in times of international turmoil, the first temptation Christians face, in Miroslav Volf's memorable words, is to "believe in the Crucified, but . . . to march with the Rider [i.e., Christ on the white horse, Rev 19:11-17]."[111]

The next logical temptation — to baptize violence in the name of God and/or Christ — is a perpetual one, but it manifests itself according to the times in which it is located. It seems particularly to be the case at the mo-

---

110. Karl Barth, *Church Dogmatics* III/4, trans. A. T. Mackay, *et al.* (Edinburgh: Clark, 1961), p. 413.

111. Volf, *Exclusion and Embrace,* p. 276. (In reality, the saints of Christ in the Book of Revelation do not take up arms with Christ, who in fact does not fight a literal battle. The victory over enemies in Revelation is by the gospel or Word of God, the death of Christ the Lamb, and the faithful witness of both Christ and his followers.) Sacred violence is not, of course, limited to the realm of international affairs. A case can be made, for example, that religiously based arguments for unrestricted abortion turn it into a form of sacred violence. See Michael J. Gorman and Ann Loar Brooks, *Holy Abortion: A Theological Critique of the Religious Coalition for Reproductive Choice* (Eugene: Wipf and Stock, 2003).

ment that Phinehas-like sacred violence has reemerged, not only in the zeal for vengeance and purity among so-called suicide bombers, but also in more subtle ways.

Sentiments like "It is the calling of our time to rid the world of evil" and "Let's go kill some terrorists" are remarkably similar to the underlying worldview of a Phinehas or a pre-conversion Paul in at least three ways. First, there is a similar goal of community purification, whether relatively local, as in the case of Paul, or global, as in some contemporary figures. Second, the violent means proposed to achieve the (allegedly) good end is believed to have divine approval and thus to be a form of sacred violence. And third, the proponents of purity by violence believe not only that they have a divine mandate/call, a solemn duty, but also that their place before God and in history — their justification, we might say — will be determined by their success in the sacred violence demanded of them by their historical circumstances.

That world leaders who call themselves practicing Christians (or Muslims or Jews) seem to espouse such views and that many others who follow such leaders seem prepared to carry out their allegedly sacred violence without question should concern us deeply. More specifically, as an alternative to this kind of thinking and acting, the church of Jesus Christ must make nonviolence a more central dimension of its life and teaching and a central corollary of its creedal affirmation that God raised the crucified Jesus from the dead, thereby ending the case for violence as the *modus operandi* of God and of God's people in the world.

Those who are in Christ today, with Paul, identify with the life-giving and reconciling cross of Christ, validated by God in the resurrection, not as an expression of a violent personality or a conviction that violence can be sacred and salutary, but in the paradoxical belief that in Christ and his cross God was nonviolently reconciling the world to himself and giving to us the ongoing task of nonviolent reconciliation of people to God and to one another. In that Spirit, we may need to be prepared to absorb violence, but not to inflict it. Such is one central aspect of the calling of our time to those justified, sanctified, and divinized in Christ.[112]

---

112. As this book went to press, I learned of the dissertation plans of David Wheeler-Reed working with L. Ann Jervis at Wycliffe College in the University of Toronto. Wheeler-Reed's work on a Pauline theology of nonviolence is also grounded in the argument that Paul was converted from violence to nonviolence, or what peace studies would call a radical change from threat power to integrative power.

Inhabiting the Cruciform God

Theosis as Paul's Narrative Soteriology

Paul's soteriology is, in very significant ways, a project of redefinition and reconstruction. In a spirit of both continuity and discontinuity, owing to the benevolent invasion and self-revelation of the God of Israel in the crucified and resurrected Messiah Jesus, Paul redefines and reconstructs God and the divine attributes, justification and faith, holiness and zeal. Indeed, he reconfigures salvation itself. As the introduction to this book argued, a theological project — and a spiritual reality — of that magnitude requires us either to invent or to borrow theological language that can express this reality as fully and appropriately as possible. It is, after all (as Paul might say), a new creation.

The basic claim of this book has been that Paul's soteriology is best described as theosis, or transformation into the image of the kenotic, cruciform God revealed in the faithful and loving cross of Christ, and that Spirit-enabled theosis is the substance of both justification and holiness. Justification is participatory and transformative, accomplished by co-crucifixion with Christ and embodied as holiness. Theosis is effected by the mutual inhabitation of those who are justified and the triune God who justifies them. Relating the thesis of this book to the more generally known and accepted notion of cruciformity in Paul, we have said that cruciformity is really theoformity, or theosis. For the sake of clarity and precision, we may wish to use the phrase *cruciform theosis* as shorthand for Paul's distinctive version of theosis.

We may now summarize the book's principal claims in more detail.

Paul's Narrative Soteriology: Inhabiting the Cruciform God

Throughout this book we have been arguing for a single Pauline soteriology of participation in the life of the triune cruciform God known in the cross of Christ, and we have called this theosis. We offered this definition of theosis in the introduction and repeated it in chapter three:

> Theosis is transformative participation in the kenotic, cruciform character of God through Spirit-enabled conformity to the incarnate, crucified, and resurrected/glorified Christ.

As noted above, this definition may be summarized in the words "cruciform theosis," for it is the crucified Christ as the self-revelation of God, and thus the *telos* of human existence in this world, that gives Paul's narrative soteriology its primary shape and substance.[1] Or, to stress the dynamic character of this salvation, we may borrow the title of this book: "inhabiting the cruciform God." We explored Paul's perspective on this reality in four chapters.

Chapter One: Kenosis and Theosis

Chapter one, which focused on Phil 2:6-11, established the foundation of Paul's soteriology. Phil 2:6-11 narrates the counterintuitive, kenotic, cruciform character of "the form of God" revealed in the incarnation and cross, and thus the character of God as God. Phil 2:6 should be translated not only "*Although* Christ was in the form of God, he did what he did," but also "*Because* he was in the form of God. . . ." His incarnation and crucifixion manifested a narrative pattern of "although [x] not [y] but [z]," or "although [status] not [selfishness] but [selflessness]." This pattern is theophanic, revelatory of the divine identity.

   The first chapter also argued that the incarnation and cross manifest (Phil 2:6-8), and the exaltation recognizes (Phil 2:9-11), Christ's true humanity, in contrast to Adam, as well as his true divinity. Therefore, to be truly human is to be Christlike, which is to be Godlike, which is to be kenotic and

---

1. As we will see below, the final goal of humanity is conformity to the resurrected and glorified Christ, but that goal is anticipated in the present by cruciform existence, following the narrative pattern of Christ himself (e.g., Rom 8:17; Phil 3:10-11).

cruciform. Cruciformity — conformity to the incarnate and crucified Christ — is really theoformity. The process of transformation into the image of the God revealed in Christ, through participation in the Spirit, may therefore be called theosis. It is counterintuitive, countercultural, and counter-imperial. A community that lives "in Christ" (Phil 2:1-5) will be shaped like the story of Christ narrated in Phil 2:6-8 as it experiences the present activity of Father, Son, and Spirit forming individuals and communities into the eternal, unchanging image of the eternal Son of God manifested in that story.

Chapter Two: Justification by Co-Crucifixion and Theosis

Chapter two, which focused especially on Gal 2:15-21 and Rom 6:1–7:6, with support from Rom 5:1-11; 2 Cor 5:14-21; and Phil 2:5-11, explored justification in Paul, arguing that justification is a rich, and potentially costly, experience of participating in Christ's resurrection life (which remains, paradoxically, cruciform) that is effected by co-crucifixion with him. We described this as justification by co-crucifixion, which can be abbreviated with the acronym JCC. The chapter argued specifically against the existence of two soteriological models in Paul (juridical and participationist) and for one, justification by co-crucifixion, understood also as theosis — becoming like God/Christ. In the introduction to the book, this chapter was called the book's "soul."

We saw that justification is first of all a relational and covenantal reality, synonymous with reconciliation, and that inherent within the very notion of reconciliation/justification are both participation and transformation. Paul's soteriology is one of participatory justification by means of participatory faith — participation in the faithfulness of Christ manifested in his death. Because Christ's death was the quintessential covenantal and human experience of fidelity to God and love for others (the "vertical" and "horizontal" dimensions of the covenant), participation in his death (co-crucifixion) fulfills the just, essential vertical and horizontal requirement of the Law. We therefore defined justification as follows:

> Justification is the establishment or restoration of right covenantal relations — *fidelity* to God and *love* for neighbor — by means of God's grace in Christ's death and our Spirit-enabled co-crucifixion with him. Justification therefore means co-resurrection with Christ to new life

within the people of God and the certain *hope* of acquittal/vindication, and thus resurrection to eternal life, on the day of judgment.

Justification by co-crucifixion means that a theological rift between justification and sanctification is *impossible* because the Spirit of Christ effects both initial and ongoing co-crucifixion with Christ among believers, which is a symbiosis of faith and love. This symbiosis of faith and love is not an addendum to justification (such as "sanctification" or "Christian ethics") but is constitutive of justification itself — being conformed to the image of the Son and becoming the righteousness of God, the embodiment of God's covenant fidelity and love. Thus justification itself is theosis — incorporation into the life and image of the faithful and loving Christ, in whom believers live and who lives in believers. The justified become a community of cruciform generosity and justice. Justification, we said, is an exegesis of the crucifixion, and precisely as an exegesis of the crucifixion, which is where God is revealed in the Son as kenotic and cruciform, justification is theosis.

The chapter stressed three additional points about justification by co-crucifixion: (1) it is not in any sense a self-generated experience ("salvation by works"); (2) although it is a personal (deeply self-involving) experience, it is not a private affair but a public and corporate reality; and (3) it is an experience of both death and resurrection, each of which must be emphasized. With respect to the second of these three points, we argued that justification is a communal theosis that is synonymous with the communal kenosis discussed in chapter one.

Chapter Three: Holiness and Theosis

In chapter three we explored Paul's Trinitarian, participatory, cruciform holiness, or — once again — theosis. We saw that Paul's understanding of holiness is grounded in his unique conviction that the crucified Messiah Jesus, the Son of God, is the revelation of the *holiness* of God the Father and in the corollary conviction that the justified — those co-crucified with Christ — are called to be holy through ongoing "co-crucifixion" with Christ by the power of the *Holy* Spirit, the Spirit of both the Father and the Son. Paul reconstructed the Jewish tradition of holiness into a counterintuitive divine attribute/activity and a countercultural human imperative that is inherently communal: "You shall be cruciform, for I am cruciform."

This cruciform holiness means, in sum, becoming like Christ by the power of the Holy Spirit of the Father and the Son, and thus also becoming like God — for God, as we have seen, is Christlike. Because Christ's death is the quintessential covenantal and human deed, it is also the quintessential holy deed. We become holy like God by participatory conformity to Christ, who is the embodiment of divine holiness. Holiness, or sanctification, therefore, is not an addition to justification but its actualization, or embodiment.

Chapter Four: Theosis and Nonviolence

In the last chapter, we addressed the topic of sacred violence and nonviolence, arguing that nonviolence was a constitutive part of Paul's conversion and apostolic identity and that it remains constitutive of Christian conversion and theosis. The argument of the chapter was in response to John Gager's accusation that Paul retained and demonstrated a violent personality after his call/conversion. The chapter also considered the interpretations of sacred violence offered by René Girard and especially his interpreter for Paul, Robert Hamerton-Kelly. It suggested that a more fruitful explanation of Paul's pre-conversion violence could be found in the phenomenon of a "will to purity," drawing on the work of Henri Lévy and Miroslav Volf.

Paul's conversion from persecuting the church was a conversion away from Phinehas-like violent zeal, expressing his will to purity within the covenant community, and a conversion to the way of Abraham-like faith in the God who nonviolently brings life out of death. Since it was God's resurrection of the Son that rendered Christ's cross significant and, indeed, theophanic, Paul looks to what God did in the cross as the norm for life in Christ. That is, God loved us while we were enemies, responding to our own violence and other sins, not with the infliction of violence but with the absorption of violence on the cross. A life of nonviolence and reconciliation is therefore an integral part of Paul's vision of justification and of participatory holiness — theosis.

God's resurrection of Christ signified to Paul at least five great realities: (1) the resurrection reveals the cross as a divine act of inclusion and embrace; (2) the resurrection reveals the cross as God's nonviolent reconciliation in Christ; (3) the resurrection provides an alternative basis for justification and life with God; (4) the resurrection provides an alternative means of responding to evil, which is Christ within and without; and (5) the resurrection provides a guarantee that God will deal finally with evil.

The existential implications of the resurrection for Paul may be summarized as follows: the living Christ of the resurrection is the loyal and loving Christ of the cross; the living one who dwells within us and within whom we dwell is the faithful and loving one who gave himself in obedience to God and in love for us. That is, perichoresis (mutual indwelling) effecting theosis is the true meaning of what is often called *imitatio Christi,* and it is the heart of Paul's cruciform spirituality of theosis.

We noted also in this chapter that Paul's transformation is seldom recognized as his turning from violence *qua* violence (as opposed to his turning from persecution of the early church to promotion of its faith). The turn to nonviolence is therefore seldom seen as a constitutive part of his conversion and new life, or as paradigmatic for, and therefore constitutive of, Christian conversion and new life more generally. The chapter argues, therefore, as noted above, that forsaking violence and embracing both nonviolence and peacemaking constitute an essential part of Paul's theosis and of Christian theosis more generally.

Theosis: The Final Stage

We have obviously focused in this book on theosis as moral transformation, dying and rising to new life in conformity to the Son, the image of God. But that is not the end of the story. Theosis means eventual conformity to the glorified, heavenly Christ.

In the introduction to the book, we noted that Stephen Finlan identifies three stages in the process of theosis in Paul: (1) dying to sin (and, we should add, dying with Christ), (2) moral transformation, and (3) eschatological transformation.[2] Our focus has not been on the third and final dimension, the eschatological, but on the first two, particularly moral transformation. In this conclusion, however, a few words about the final outcome of theosis seem appropriate.

2. Stephen Finlan, "Can We Speak of *Theosis* in Paul?" in *Partakers of the Divine Nature: The History and Development of Deification in the Christian Traditions,* ed. Michael J. Christensen and Jeffery A. Wittung (Grand Rapids: Baker, 2007), pp. 68-80; here p. 73.

In *Cruciformity*,[3] I devoted a chapter to cruciform hope, showing the relationship between present conformity to Christ crucified and eschatological conformity to Christ resurrected and glorified. Suffering and other forms of cruciform existence, for Paul, are the prelude to glory. This sounds like stages in a process, and indeed, from one perspective, that is true. The story of Christ, as Paul (and, in fact, much of the New Testament) reminds us, unfolds in two major stages: humiliation and exaltation, death and resurrection, suffering and glory. To participate in that story, or, better, to participate in the One whose narrative identity is disclosed in that story, is to embody a similar two-stage pattern. Full and total participation in the glory of God still awaits us.

And yet a narrative approach to Pauline soteriology also suggests that there is a great deal of continuity in the process of theosis. Already believers experience the resurrection life and power of God as they are enabled by the Spirit to be conformed to the resurrected crucified Christ. Already they experience power and life in the midst of weakness and death. Already they know the cruciform God whom they will one day know even as they are fully known (1 Cor 13:12).

The final outcome of theosis — conformity to Christ's resurrection body — is still future, but it is the finale of a story that has already begun; it is not a new story. Commenting on the significance of reading *pistis Christou* as a reference to Jesus' faith(fulness) and thereby also an encouragement to suffering believers to remain faithful, Douglas Campbell eloquently states the significance of a narrative, participatory soteriology:

> Just as Jesus faithfully endured suffering to the point of death and then received a triumphant and glorious resurrection, so too Christians who maintain their loyalty to God and to Christ until the end receive a resurrection. Moreover, in so doing, God is not asking them to imitate Christ — perhaps an impossible task — so much as *to inhabit or to indwell him.* That is, any such endurance through duress is evidence that the Spirit of God is actively reshaping the Christian into the likeness of Christ, and that they are already part of the story, a story that will result in eschatological salvation! Consequently, such enduring fidelity is critical evidence that God is at work, incorporating the believer into the prototypical story

---

3. Michael J. Gorman, *Cruciformity: Paul's Narrative Spirituality of the Cross* (Grand Rapids: Eerdmans, 2001).

of Christ. In essence, to be part of this first sequence, despite its difficulties, is to be guaranteed being part of its second: this is no mere *imitatio Christi*.[4]

There are details of Campbell's account that we may wish to refine. As we have highlighted throughout this book, *pistis* is more than fidelity in suffering, and participation is corporate as well as individual. But Campbell's perception of the narrative character of inhabiting Christ — and therefore, we would of course say, of inhabiting the cruciform God — is precisely what Paul would want us to see. *Kenosis, justification, holiness, cruciformity, theosis — these are all of a piece because they all refer to the single soteriological reality of inhabiting the cruciform God revealed in Christ by the power of the Spirit, from the first moment of faith to the eschatological goal of complete glory.*

Paul on Theosis, via Bonhoeffer

A reviewer of *Cruciformity,* my first book on Paul, suggested that it was something of an extended commentary on Dietrich Bonhoeffer's classic *The Cost of Discipleship,* or just *Discipleship* (the original German title being *Nachfolge*).[5] That reviewer was, in an important way, quite right. Although *Cruciformity* refers to Bonhoeffer explicitly on only three pages,[6] the spirit of Bonhoeffer, and specifically the spirit of his interpretation of Paul, faith, and the church, permeates the volume. Until I was actually writing the conclusion to the present book, however, I did not realize that Bonhoeffer may also have been behind it as well.

Many people are very familiar with Bonhoeffer's memorable discussions of cheap and costly grace, to which we referred in chapter two while introducing the topic of justification and the problem of cheap justification. Along with the equally memorable line, "When Christ calls a man, he bids him come and die," Bonhoeffer's words about cheap and costly grace appear

---

4. Douglas A. Campbell, *The Quest for Paul's Gospel: A Suggested Strategy* (London/New York: Clark, 2005), p. 93; emphasis added.

5. There are various editions of Bonhoeffer's book. In the discussion below, all quotations except the first are from Dietrich Bonhoeffer, *Discipleship,* Dietrich Bonhoeffer Works, vol. 4, trans. Barbara Green and Reinhard Krauss (Minneapolis: Augsburg Fortress, 2001). Page numbers from that edition are noted in parentheses.

6. Gorman, *Cruciformity,* pp. 145, 385-86.

early in *Discipleship*.[7] Fewer people are as aware of the ending of Bonhoeffer's book. The last chapter is called "The Image of Christ." It is essentially a Pauline argument for the story of salvation as a narrative of recapitulation and theosis, though Bonhoeffer does not explicitly use those terms or name, for example, Irenaeus or Athanasius. But he does quote the Fathers' exchange formula ("he became what we were . . .") at least twice, and he does quote Paul.

Bonhoeffer makes it clear in the last chapter of *Discipleship* that the destiny of those who follow Christ is to "become like Christ," referring to Rom 8:29 (p. 281). Created in the image of God, by our sin we began to live as human beings "without being truly human" (p. 282) and now need to "become [again] the image of God" (p. 283). Relying on Rom 12:2 and 2 Cor 3:18, Bonhoeffer says that we need a complete "reshaping, a 'metamorphosis'" (p. 283), which is made possible by the revelation of the image of God in the life and death of Christ (p. 283). "[T]his is God in human form, this is the human being who is the new image of God" (p. 284). Christ "became like human beings, so that we would be like him" (p. 285). And ultimately that means sharing in his heavenly glory (pp. 284-85).

This transformation is not a matter of human effort:

> To be conformed to the image of Christ is not an ideal of realizing some kind of similarity with Christ which we are asked to attain. It is not we who change ourselves into the image of God. Rather, it is the very image of God, the form of Christ, which seeks to take shape within us (Gal. 4.19). It is Christ's own form which seeks to manifest itself in us. Christ does not cease working in us until he has changed us into Christ's own image. Our goal is to be shaped into the entire *form* of the incarnate, the crucified, and the transfigured one.[8] (pp. 284-85)

We will one day share Christ's heavenly image, says Bonhoeffer again, quoting 1 Cor 15:49 (p. 286). However,

> whoever, according to God's promise, seeks to participate in the radiance and glory of Jesus must first be conformed to the image of the obedient,

---

7. In chapters one ("Costly Grace") and four ("Discipleship and the Cross") of 32 chapters. The memorable quotation is actually from the older English translation; *Discipleship* renders it "Whenever Christ calls us, his call leads us to death" (p. 87).

8. The similarity to the words of Campbell at n. 4 above should be noticed.

suffering servant of God on the cross. Whoever seeks to bear the transfigured image of Jesus must first have borne the image of the crucified one, defiled in the world. No one is able to recover the lost image of God unless they come to participate in the image of the incarnate and crucified Jesus Christ. (p. 284)

In the present, then, the Christian life is "a crucified life (Gal. 2.19)"; Christians must be "conformed to his death (Phil. 3.10; Rom 6.4f)" because on earth "[t]he image of God is the image of Jesus Christ on the cross" (p. 285). Although the highest form of conformity to Christ crucified is martyrdom, the entire Christian life, "from baptism all the way to martyrdom," is a sharing in Christ's suffering and death (p. 286). In this way "Christ himself attains visible form within his community," and "the new creation of the image of God through the crucified one" comes into existence (p. 286). This happens as we contemplate the image of God, Christ crucified, and are transformed into his image in community, Bonhoeffer says, quoting 2 Cor 3:18 (p. 286). "It is indeed the holy Trinity who dwells within Christians, who permeates and changes them into the very image of the triune God" (p. 287). This is our destiny: "Only because he was as we are can we be as he was. Only because we *already* are made like him can we be 'like Christ'" (p. 287).[9]

In other words, Bonhoeffer, the great proponent of costly, obedient discipleship, recognizes at the end of the day that discipleship is not about imitation or even obedience to an external call or norm. It is about transformation, theosis.

Theosis: The Center of Paul's Theology

What we find in Bonhoeffer is the Eastern Christian tradition of theosis merged with a radical interpretation of discipleship expressed primarily in the language of Pauline participatory theology/spirituality. Despite the sentiments of Bonhoeffer, the Western theological tradition, including the

9. It is interesting to note how many of the Pauline texts to which Bonhoeffer refers are among those traditionally seen as foundational to a proper understanding of theosis. See, for example, the list of such texts in the introduction to this book. In view of Bonhoeffer's other writings — especially *Life Together* — and the example of his life, we should interpret this experience of contemplation and transformation, not as something private or internal, but as something that occurs in community and in witness to the world.

Western interpretation of Paul, has not generally seen the story of salvation in any of these terms — theosis, participation, or radical discipleship. But the thesis of this book has been not only that Bonhoeffer's perspective is viable, but that it is indeed Pauline. Or, to put it more appropriately for the conclusion to a book about Paul, Paul's primary concern, and his fundamental soteriological model, is cruciform theosis.

We may now therefore arrive at the conclusion to which this book has been implicitly but ineluctably driving: that *theosis is the center of Paul's theology.* For reasons I have articulated elsewhere, I am less than completely comfortable with the notion of a center to Paul's theology[10] and might prefer language such as "focus," "central concern," or, as in the last paragraph, "primary concern." Better yet — since neither cruciformity nor theosis is merely an idea, conviction, or doctrine — is to speak of an "integrative narrative experience."[11] But the question of a theological center is how the scholarly discussion has been framed, so we must, at least on some level, work within the parameters of that question. Given those parameters, we may propose theosis, rather than, say, justification or reconciliation or even participation, as the center of Paul's theology. Justification and its Pauline synonym reconciliation are, as we have seen, a large part of theosis. And theosis is certainly a soteriology of participation. But "justification" and "reconciliation" are terms that are a bit too narrow to indicate the heartbeat of Pauline soteriology, while "participation" is inevitably a bit vague. Theosis is a better choice. It is, of course, *cruciform* theosis.[12]

Theosis: The Present Life and Calling

There may be some readers of this book who fear that the use of the term "theosis" to describe Paul's soteriology may result in the same problem that concerns them about certain interpretations of justification: that it promotes a self-centered, even isolated spiritual quest that is devoid of ethical content. This is an understandable, yet totally misguided, fear.

10. See *Cruciformity,* pp. 369-72.

11. *Cruciformity,* p. 371.

12. In proposing theosis as the center of Pauline theology and experience, I am not retracting the proposal made in *Cruciformity* (pp. 369-72) but merely refining it in light of the argument that cruciformity is really theoformity, or theosis. The phrase "cruciform theosis" seeks to express that truth succinctly.

The nature of theosis as we have seen it in Paul's letters is thoroughly communal as well as personal (without being private), and it is thoroughly horizontal ("ethical") as well as vertical ("spiritual").[13] *For the justified to become, in Christ, the justice of God in the world could not be otherwise.* Theosis, in other words, is a theopolitical reality as the church embodies, or actualizes, its justification in the world, bearing the image of the one true, holy, cruciform God among an array of other alleged deities and their communities. By the power of the Spirit, the church lives a countercultural life of fidelity and love, generosity and justice, purity and promise-keeping, nonviolence and peacemaking. It is, in other words, a Spirit-infused, living exegesis of the cross; or better, a living exegesis of the Crucified, who is the image of God. The church inhabits this triune, cruciform God, who in turn inhabits the church. Thus the church's life story embodies and thereby proclaims the narrative identity and gracious saving power of the triune God whom Paul encountered and preached: the source of justification, holiness, and peace — theosis.

To describe Paul's soteriology as theosis, and to posit it as the focus — or even the center — of his theology, does not therefore "over-spiritualize" salvation and thereby de-politicize it. Such a conclusion, which constructs a dichotomy where Paul sees only a unity, would be possible only if one were to ignore the argument of this book from chapter one to the conclusion. Furthermore, the use of the term theosis does not remove salvation from the larger narrative and divine project to which the Scriptures of Israel and the Pauline letters bear witness. Rather, salvation in Paul is the fulfillment of Israel's story, the calling of a new people composed of both Gentiles and Jews, being made children of Abraham as they are formed into the image of the Jewish Messiah (Gal 3:29; 6:16). Salvation in Paul is the remedy for humanity's predicament, the creation of a new humanity being remade into the likeness of Christ the last Adam (1 Cor 15:45-49). And human salvation in Paul is one dimension — the one that Paul stresses — of the cosmic drama of liberation (Rom 8:18-25), reconciliation (Col 1:19-20), and victory over all

13. On this, see also Richard B. Hays, "Christ Died for the Ungodly: Narrative Soteriology in Paul?" *HBT* 26 (2004): 48-69, in which Hays stresses the ecclesial and ethical character of Paul's participatory narrative soteriology (pp. 62-63). It is important to recall (see chapter two, p. 48 above) that using the terms "horizontal" and "vertical" is a heuristic device to designate two inseparable aspects of one reality. This point is made strongly also by Haddon Willmer in "'Vertical' and 'Horizontal' in Paul's Theology of Reconciliation in the Letter to the Romans," *Transformation* 24 (2007): 151-60, especially pp. 151-52.

evil powers (1 Cor 15:24-26, 54-57), which includes the universal acclamation of Jesus as Lord (Phil 2:9-11) and the completion of the process of theosis (Rom 8:29-30) before culminating finally in that mysterious reality when God will be "all in all" (1 Cor 15:28). In the meantime, by the power of the Spirit of Father and Son, the new people, the new humanity bears witness in word and deed to that glorious future by participating *now* in the life and mission of the triune cruciform God.[14]

14. For an interpretation of Paul's understanding of pastoral ministry that coheres very well with the vision of theosis presented in this book, see James W. Thompson, *Pastoral Ministry According to Paul: A Biblical Vision* (Grand Rapids: Baker Academic, 2006). For a view of the ministry of reconciliation containing many echoes of the themes of this book, see Miroslav Volf, "The Social Meaning of Reconciliation," *Int* 54 (2002): 158-72. Volf, however, unnecessarily subordinates justice to reconciliation when the two may be seen (in Paul) as essentially synonymous.

Anderson, Gary. Review of Michael J. Gorman, *Reading Paul, First Things* 184 (June/July 2008): 52-53.

Aune, David E., ed. *Rereading Paul Together: Protestant and Catholic Perspectives on Justification.* Grand Rapids: Baker Academic, 2006.

————. "Recent Readings of Paul Relating to Justification by Faith." In *Rereading Paul Together,* edited by David E. Aune, pp. 188-245. Grand Rapids: Baker Academic, 2006.

Barth, Karl. *Church Dogmatics,* III/4. Translated by A. T. Mackay, et al. Edinburgh: Clark, 1961.

————. *The Epistle to the Philippians.* Translated by James W. Leith. Richmond: John Knox, 1962.

Barton, Stephen C. "Dislocating and Relocating Holiness: A New Testament Study." In *Holiness Past and Present,* edited by Stephen C. Barton, pp. 193-213. London: Clark, 2003.

————, ed. *Holiness Past and Present.* London: Clark, 2003.

Bassler, Jouette M. *Navigating Paul: An Introduction to Key Theological Concepts.* Louisville: Westminster John Knox, 2007.

————, ed. *Pauline Theology,* vol. 1: *Thessalonians, Philippians, Galatians, Philemon.* Minneapolis: Fortress, 1991.

Bauckham, Richard. *God Crucified: Monotheism and Christology in the New Testament.* Grand Rapids: Eerdmans, 1998.

————. "The Worship of Jesus in Philippians 2:9-11." In *Where Christology Began,* edited by Ralph P. Martin and Brian J. Dodd, pp. 128-39. Louisville: Westminster John Knox, 1998.

Biddle, Mark E. *Missing the Mark: Sin and Its Consequences in Biblical Theology.* Nashville: Abingdon, 2005.

Bird, Michael F. *The Saving Righteousness of God: Studies in Paul, Justification, and the New Perspective.* Carlisle, UK: Paternoster, 2007.

Bischoff, Paul. "Participation: Ecclesial Praxis with a Crucified God for the World." *JCTR* 8 (2003): 19-36.

Blass, F., and A. Debrunner. *A Greek Grammar of the New Testament and Other Early Christian Literature.* Translated and revised by R. W. Funk. Chicago: University of Chicago Press, 1961.

Bloomquist, L. Gregory. *The Function of Suffering in Philippians.* JSNTSup 78. Sheffield: JSOT Press, 1993.

Blount, Brian K. *Then the Whisper Put on Flesh: New Testament Ethics in an African American Context.* Nashville: Abingdon, 2001.

Bockmuehl, Markus. *The Epistle to the Philippians.* BNTC. Peabody: Hendrickson, 1998.

Boersma, Hans. *Violence, Hospitality, and the Cross.* Grand Rapids: Baker, 2004.

Bonhoeffer, Dietrich. *Discipleship.* Dietrich Bonhoeffer Works, vol. 4. Translated by Barbara Green and Reinhard Krauss. Minneapolis: Augsburg Fortress, 2001.

Braaten, Carl E., and Robert W. Jenson, eds. *Union with Christ: The New Finnish Interpretation of Luther.* Grand Rapids: Eerdmans, 1998.

Brondos, David A. *Paul on the Cross: Reconstructing the Apostle's Story of Redemption.* Minneapolis: Fortress, 2006.

Brower, Kent E. and Andy Johnson, eds. *Holiness and Ecclesiology in the New Testament.* Grand Rapids: Eerdmans, 2007.

Brueggemann, Walter. *Theology of the Old Testament: Testimony, Dispute, Advocacy.* Minneapolis: Fortress, 1997.

Bryant, Robert A. *The Risen Crucified Christ in Galatia.* SBLDS 185. Atlanta: Society of Biblical Literature, 2001.

Byrne, Brendan. *Romans.* Sacra Pagina. Collegeville: Liturgical, 1996.

Campbell, Douglas A. *The Deliverance of God: An Apocalyptic Rereading of Justification in Paul.* Grand Rapids: Eerdmans, 2009.

———. *The Quest for Paul's Gospel: A Suggested Strategy.* London/New York: Clark, 2005.

Carson, Donald, Peter T. O'Brien, and Mark A. Seifrid, eds. *Justification and Variegated Nomism,* vol. 1: *The Complexities of Second Temple Judaism.* Grand Rapids: Baker, 2001.

———, eds. *Justification and Variegated Nomism,* vol. 2: *The Paradoxes of Paul.* Grand Rapids: Baker, 2004.

Chester, Stephen J. *Conversion in Corinth: Perspectives on Conversion in Paul's Theology and the Corinthian Church.* London: Clark, 2003.

———. "When the Old Was New: Reformation Perspectives on Galatians 2:16." *ExpTim* 119 (2007-8): 320-29.

Christensen, Michael J., and Jeffery A. Wittung, eds. *Partakers of the Divine Nature: The History and Development of Deification in the Christian Traditions.* Grand Rapids: Baker Academic, 2007.

Ciampa, Roy E., and Brian S. Rosner. "The Structure and Argument of 1 Corinthians: A Biblical/Jewish Approach." *NTS* 52 (2006): 205-18.

Crossan, John Dominic, and Jonathan Reed. *In Search of Paul: How Jesus's Apostle Opposed Rome's Empire with God's Kingdom.* San Francisco: HarperSanFrancisco, 2004.

Cummins, S. A. "Divine Life and Corporate Christology: God, Messiah Jesus, and the Covenant Community in Paul." In *The Messiah in the Old and New Testaments,* edited by Stanley E. Porter, pp. 190-209. Grand Rapids: Eerdmans, 2007.

Cyril of Alexandria. *Commentary on John.*

de Boer, Martinus C. "Paul's Use and Interpretation of a Justification Tradition in Galatians 2.15-21." *JSNT* 28 (2005): 189-216.

DeMaris, Richard E. "Can We Reread Paul Together Any Longer? Joseph A. Fitzmyer's View of Pauline Justification in Context." In *Rereading Paul Together,* edited by David E. Aune, pp. 95-197. Grand Rapids: Baker Academic, 2006.

Donaldson, Terence L. *Paul and the Gentiles: Remapping the Apostle's Convictional World.* Minneapolis: Fortress, 1997.

Dunn, James D. G. "Christ, Adam, and Preexistence." In *Where Christology Began,* edited by Ralph P. Martin and Brian J. Dodd, pp. 74-83. Louisville: Westminster John Knox, 1998.

———. "Did Paul Have a Covenant Theology? Reflections on Romans 9:4 and 11:27." In *Celebrating Romans: Template for Pauline Theology; Essays in Honor of Robert Jewett,* edited by Sheila E. McGinn, pp. 3-19. Grand Rapids: Eerdmans, 2004.

———. "Once More, *PISTIS CHRISTOU.*" In *Pauline Theology,* vol. 4: *Looking Back, Pressing On,* edited by E. Elizabeth Johnson and David B. Hay, pp. 66-81. Atlanta: Scholars, 1997.

———. "Paul and Justification by Faith." In *The Road from Damascus,* edited by Richard Longenecker, pp. 85-101. Grand Rapids: Eerdmans, 1997.

———, ed. *Paul and the Mosaic Law.* Grand Rapids: Eerdmans, 1996.

———. *The Theology of Paul the Apostle.* Grand Rapids: Eerdmans, 1998.

Edwards, Mark J. *Galatians, Ephesians, Philippians.* Ancient Christian Commentary on Scripture: New Testament VIII. Downers Grove, Ill.: InterVarsity, 1999.

Ehrman, Bart. *The New Testament: A Historical Introduction to the Early Christian Writings,* 3d ed. New York: Oxford University Press, 2004.

Fackre, Gabriel. "Affirmations and Admonitions: Lutheran and Reformed." In *The Gospel of Justification in Christ,* edited by Wayne C. Stumme, pp. 1-26. Grand Rapids: Eerdmans, 2006.

Fee, Gordon D. *God's Empowering Presence: The Holy Spirit in the Letters of Paul*. Peabody, Mass.: Hendrickson, 1994.

Finlan, Stephen. "Can We Speak of *Theosis* in Paul?" In *Partakers of the Divine Nature: The History and Development of Deification in the Christian Traditions*, edited by Michael J. Christensen and Jeffery A. Wittung, pp. 68-80. Grand Rapids: Baker Academic, 2007.

————, and Vladimir Kharlamov, eds. *Theosis: Deification in Christian Theology*. Eugene: Pickwick, 2006.

Fitzmyer, Joseph A. "Justification by Faith in Pauline Thought: A Catholic Perspective." In *Rereading Paul Together: Protestant and Catholic Perspectives on Justification*, edited by David E. Aune, pp. 77-94. Grand Rapids: Baker Academic, 2006.

Foster, Paul. "The First Contribution to the *pistis Christou* Debate: A Study of Ephesians 3.12." *JSNT* 85 (2002): 75-96.

Fowl, Stephen E. "Christology and Ethics in Philippians 2:5-11." In *Where Christology Began: Essays on Philippians 2*, edited by Ralph P. Martin and Brian J. Dodd, pp. 140-53. Louisville: Westminster John Knox, 1998.

————. *Philippians*. THNTC. Grand Rapids: Eerdmans, 2005.

Fredriksen, Paula. "Judaism, the Circumcision of Gentiles, and Apocalyptic Hope: Another Look at Galatians 1 and 2." *JTS* n.s. 42 (1991): 532-64.

————. "Paul and Augustine: Conversion Narratives, Orthodox Tradition, and the Retrospective Self." *JTS* n.s. 37 (1986): 3-34.

Frick, Peter. "The Means and Mode of Salvation: A Hermeneutical Proposal for Clarifying Pauline Soteriology." *HBT* 29 (2007): 203-22.

Furnish, Victor Paul. *II Corinthians*. AB 32A. Garden City: Doubleday, 1984.

Gager, John G., with E. Leigh Gibson. "Violent Acts and Violent Language in the Apostle Paul." In *Violence in the New Testament*, edited by Shelly Matthews and E. Leigh Gibson, pp. 13-21. New York: Clark, 2005.

Gasque, W. Ward, and Ralph P. Martin. *Apostolic History and the Gospel: Biblical and Historical Essays Presented to F. F. Bruce on His 60th Birthday*. Grand Rapids: Eerdmans, 1970.

Gathercole, Simon. "The Doctrine of Justification in Paul and Beyond: Some Proposals." In *Justification in Perspective: Historical Developments and Contemporary Challenges*, edited by Bruce L. McCormack, pp. 219-41. Grand Rapids: Baker Academic, 2006.

————. "Justified by Faith, Justified by His Blood: The Evidence of Romans 3:21–4:5." In *Justification and Variegated Nomism*, vol. 2: *The Paradoxes of Paul*, edited by Donald Carson, Peter T. O'Brien, and Mark A. Seifrid, pp. 147-84. Grand Rapids: Baker, 2004.

Giddens, Anthony. *Modernity and Self-Identity: Self and Society in the Late Modern Age*. Stanford: Stanford University Press, 1991.

Gorman, Michael J. *Apostle of the Crucified Lord: A Theological Introduction to Paul and His Letters.* Grand Rapids: Eerdmans, 2004.

————. *Cruciformity: Paul's Narrative Spirituality of the Cross.* Grand Rapids: Eerdmans, 2001.

————. *Reading Paul.* Eugene: Cascade, 2008.

————. "Romans 13:8-14." *Int* 62 (2008): 170-72.

————. "'You Shall Be Cruciform, for I Am Cruciform': Paul's Trinitarian Reconstruction of Holiness." In *Holiness and Ecclesiology in the New Testament,* edited by Kent E. Brower and Andy Johnson, pp. 148-66. Grand Rapids: Eerdmans, 2007.

————, and Ann Loar Brooks. *Holy Abortion: A Theological Critique of the Religious Coalition for Reproductive Choice.* Eugene: Wipf and Stock, 2003.

Grieb, A. Katherine. "The One Who Called You: Vocation and Leadership in the Pauline Literature." *Int* 59 (2005): 154-65.

————. "'So That in Him We Might Become the Righteousness of God' (2 Cor 5:21): Some Theological Reflections on the Church Becoming Justice." *Ex Auditu* 22 (2006): 58-80.

Gunton, Colin. *Act and Being: Towards a Theology of the Divine Attributes.* Grand Rapids: Eerdmans, 2002.

Hamerton-Kelly, Robert G. *Sacred Violence: Paul's Hermeneutic of the Cross.* Minneapolis: Fortress, 1992.

Harink, Douglas. *Paul among the Postliberals: Pauline Theology beyond Christendom and Modernity.* Grand Rapids: Brazos, 2003.

Harrington, Hannah K. *Holiness: Rabbinic Judaism and the Greco-Roman World.* London/New York: Routledge, 2001.

Harrisville, Roy A. *Fracture: The Cross as Irreconcilable in the Language and Thought of the Biblical Writers.* Grand Rapids: Eerdmans 2006.

Hastings, A., ed. *The Oxford Companion to Christian Thought.* Oxford: Oxford University Press, 2000.

Hauerwas, Stanley. *Sanctify Them in the Truth: Holiness Exemplified.* Nashville: Abingdon, 1998.

————, and William J. Willimon. *The Truth about God: The Ten Commandments in Christian Life.* Nashville: Abingdon, 1999.

Hawthorne, Gerald F. "In the Form of God." In *Where Christology Began: Essays on Philippians 2,* edited by Ralph P. Martin and Brian J. Dodd, pp. 96-110. Louisville: Westminster John Knox, 1998.

————. *Philippians.* WBC. Waco: Word, 1983.

Hay, David M. "Paul's Understanding of Faith as Participation." In *Paul and His Theology,* Pauline Studies vol. 3, edited by Stanley E. Porter, pp. 45-76. Leiden/Boston: Brill, 2006.

————, ed. *Pauline Theology,* vol. 2, *1 & 2 Corinthians.* Minneapolis: Augsburg/Fortress, 1992.

Hays, Richard B. "Christ Died for the Ungodly: Narrative Soteriology in Paul?" *HBT* 26 (2004) 48-69.

————. *The Conversion of the Imagination: Paul as Interpreter of Israel's Scripture.* Grand Rapids: Eerdmans, 2005.

————. "Crucified with Christ: A Synthesis of the Theology of 1 and 2 Thessalonians, Philemon, Philippians, and Galatians." In *Pauline Theology,* vol. 1: *Thessalonians, Philippians, Galatians, Philemon,* edited by Jouette M. Bassler, pp. 227-46. Minneapolis: Fortress, 1991.

————. *The Faith of Jesus Christ: The Narrative Substructure of Gal 3:1–4:11.* 2d ed. Grand Rapids: Eerdmans, 2002.

————. "Justification." In *ABD,* edited by David Noel Freedman, 3:1129-33. New York: Doubleday, 1992.

————. *The Moral Vision of the New Testament: A Contemporary Introduction to New Testament Ethics.* San Francisco: HarperCollins, 1996.

————. "*PISTIS CHRISTOU* and Pauline Theology: What Is at Stake?" In *Pauline Theology,* vol. 4: *Looking Back, Pressing On,* edited by E. Elizabeth Johnson and David B. Hay, pp. 35-60. Atlanta: Scholars, 1997.

————. "The Role of Scripture in Paul's Ethics." In *The Conversion of the Imagination: Paul as Interpreter of Israel's Scripture,* pp. 143-62. Grand Rapids: Eerdmans, 2005.

Heen, Erik M. "Phil 2:6-11 and Resistance to Local Timocratic Rule: *Isa theō* and the Cult of the Emperor in the East." In *Paul and the Roman Imperial Order,* edited by Richard A. Horsley, pp. 125-53. Harrisburg: Trinity, 2004.

Hellerman, Joseph H. *Reconstructing Honor in Roman Philippi: Carmen Christi as Cursus Pudorum.* SNTSMS 132. Cambridge: Cambridge University Press, 2005.

Hooker, Morna D. *From Adam to Christ: Essays on Paul.* New York/Cambridge: Cambridge University Press, 1990.

Hoover, Roy W. "The Harpagmos Enigma: A Philological Solution." *HTR* 64 (1971): 95-119.

Horsley, Richard A., ed. *Paul and Empire: Religion and Power in Roman Imperial Society.* Harrisburg: Trinity, 1997.

————. *Paul and Politics: Ekklesia, Israel, Imperium, Interpretation: Essays in Honor of Krister Stendahl.* Harrisburg: Trinity, 2000.

Hultgren, Arland. "Paul's Pre-Christian Persecution of the Church." *JBL* 95 (1976): 97-112.

Hunsinger, George. "*Fides Christo Formata:* Luther, Barth, and the Joint Declaration." In *The Gospel of Justification in Christ,* edited by Wayne C. Stumme, pp. 69-84. Grand Rapids: Eerdmans, 2006.

Hurst, L. D. "Christ, Adam, and Preexistence Revisited." In *Where Christology Began:*

Essays on Philippians 2, edited by Ralph P. Martin and Brian J. Dodd, pp. 84-95. Louisville: Westminster John Knox, 1998.

Husbands, Mark A., and Daniel J. Treier, eds. *Justification: What's at Stake in the Current Debate*. Downers Grove: InterVarsity, 2004.

Irenaeus, *Against Heresies*.

Jervis, L. Ann. "Becoming like God through Christ: Romans." In *Patterns of Discipleship in the New Testament*, edited by Richard N. Longenecker, pp. 143-62. Grand Rapids: Eerdmans, 1996.

Johnson, Andy. "The Sanctification of the Imagination in 1 Thessalonians." In *Holiness and Ecclesiology in the New Testament*, edited by Kent E. Brower and Andy Johnson, pp. 275-92. Grand Rapids: Eerdmans, 2007.

Johnson, E. Elizabeth, and David B. Hay, eds. *Pauline Theology*, vol. 4: *Looking Back, Pressing On*. Atlanta: Scholars, 1997.

Johnson, Luke Timothy. *Reading Romans: A Literary and Theological Commentary*. New York: Crossroad, 1997.

————. *Religious Experience in Earliest Christianity: A Missing Dimension in New Testament Study*. Minneapolis: Fortress, 1998.

Kärkkäinen, Veli-Matti. *One with God: Salvation as Deification and Justification*. Collegeville: Liturgical, 2005.

Käsemann, Ernst. *Perspectives on Paul*. Translated by Margaret Kohl. Philadelphia: Fortress, 1971; repr. Mifflintown, Pa.: Sigler, 1996.

————. "The Saving Significance of the Death of Jesus in Paul." In *Perspectives on Paul*, translated by Margaret Kohl, pp. 32-59. Philadelphia: Fortress, 1971; repr. Mifflintown, Pa.: Sigler, 1996.

Keck, Leander. *Romans*. ANTC. Nashville: Abingdon, 2005.

Keesmaat, Sylvia C. "Crucified Lord or Conquering Saviour: Whose Story of Salvation?" *HBT* 26 (2004): 69-93.

Kimbrough, S. T., Jr., ed. *Orthodox and Wesleyan Spirituality*. Crestwood, N.Y.: St. Vladimir's Seminary Press, 2002.

Kirk, J. R. Daniel. *Unlocking Romans: Resurrection and the Justification of God*. Grand Rapids: Eerdmans, 2008.

Kreitzer, Larry J. "'When He at Last Is First!': Philippians 2:9-11 and the Exaltation of the Lord." In *Where Christology Began: Essays on Philippians 2*, edited by Ralph P. Martin and Brian J. Dodd, pp. 111-27. Louisville: Westminster John Knox, 1998.

Litwa, M. David. "2 Corinthians 3:18 and Its Implications for *Theosis*." *JTI* 2 (2008): 117-34.

Loader, William. *The Septuagint, Sexuality and the New Testament*. Grand Rapids: Eerdmans, 2004.

Longenecker, Bruce W., "Defining the Faithful Character of the Covenant Community: Galatians 2.15-21 and Beyond: A Response to Jan Lambrecht." In *Paul and the Mosaic Law,* edited by James D. G. Dunn, pp. 75-98. Grand Rapids: Eerd-mans, 1996.

———. ed., *Narrative Dynamics in Paul: A Critical Assessment.* Louisville: Westminster John Knox, 2002.

Longenecker, Richard N. "A Realized Hope, a New Commitment, and a Developed Proclamation: Paul and Jesus." In *The Road from Damascus: The Impact of Paul's Conversion on His Life, Thought, and Ministry,* edited by Richard N. Longenecker, pp. 18-42. Grand Rapids: Eerdmans, 1997.

———, ed. *The Road from Damascus: The Impact of Paul's Conversion on His Life, Thought, and Ministry.* Grand Rapids: Eerdmans, 1997.

———, ed. *Patterns of Discipleship in the New Testament.* Grand Rapids: Eerdmans, 1996.

Mannermaa, Tuomo. *Christ Present in Faith: Luther's View of Justification.* Minneapolis: Fortress, 2005 (orig. 1989).

Marcus, Joel. "The New Testament and Idolatry." *Int* 60 (2006): 152-64.

Marshall, Bruce D. "Justification as Declaration and Deification." *IJST* 4 (2002): 3-28.

Martin, Ralph P. *A Hymn of Christ: Philippians 2:5-11 in Recent Interpretation and in the Setting of Early Christian Worship.* Downers Grove: InterVarsity, 1997; orig. *Carmen Christi,* 1967.

———, and Brian J. Dodd, eds. *Where Christology Began: Essays on Philippians 2.* Louisville: Westminster John Knox, 1998.

Martinson, Paul Varo. "Learning Its Meaning amidst the Religions." In *The Gospel of Justification in Christ,* edited by Wayne C. Stumme, pp. 141-59. Grand Rapids: Eerdmans, 2006.

Martyn, J. Louis. "Apocalyptic Antinomies." In *Theological Issues in the Letters of Paul,* pp. 111-23. Edinburgh: Clark; Nashville: Abingdon, 1997.

———. "Epistemology at the Turn of the Ages." In *Theological Issues in the Letters of Paul,* pp. 89-110. Edinburgh: Clark; Nashville: Abingdon, 1997.

———. *Galatians: A New Translation with Introduction and Commentary.* AB 33A. New York: Doubleday, 1997.

———. *Theological Issues in the Letters of Paul.* Edinburgh: Clark; Nashville: Abingdon, 1997.

Matera, Frank J. *Galatians.* Sacra Pagina. Collegeville, Minn.: Liturgical, 1992.

———. *II Corinthians.* New Testament Library. Louisville: Westminster John Knox, 2003.

Matthews, Shelly, and E. Leigh Gibson, eds. *Violence in the New Testament.* New York: Clark, 2005.

Mauser, Ulrich W. "One God and Trinitarian Language in the Letters of Paul." *HBT* 20 (1998): 99-108.

McCormack, Bruce L., ed. *Justification in Perspective: Historical Developments and Contemporary Challenges.* Grand Rapids: Baker Academic, 2006.

————. "*Justitia Aliena*: Karl Barth in Conversation with the Evangelical Doctrine of Imputed Righteousness." In *Justification in Perspective: Historical Developments and Contemporary Challenges*, edited by Bruce L. McCormack, pp. 167-96. Grand Rapids: Baker Academic, 2006.

————. "What's at Stake in Current Debates over Justification: The Crisis of Protestantism in the West." In *Justification: What's at Stake in the Current Debates*, edited by Mark A. Husbands and Daniel J. Treier, pp. 81-117. Downers Grove: InterVarsity, 2004.

McGinn, Sheila E., ed. *Celebrating Romans: Template for Pauline Theology; Essays in Honor of Robert Jewett*. Grand Rapids: Eerdmans, 2004.

McGuckin, J. A. "Deification." In *The Oxford Companion to Christian Thought*, edited by A. Hastings, p. 156. Oxford: Oxford University Press, 2000.

Minear, Paul S. "The Holy and the Sacred." *Theology Today* 47 (1990-91): 5-12.

Moule, C. F. D. "Further Reflexions on Philippians 2:5-11." In *Apostolic History and the Gospel: Biblical and Historical Essays Presented to F. F. Bruce on His 60th Birthday*, edited by W. Ward Gasque and Ralph P. Martin, pp. 264-76. Grand Rapids: Eerdmans, 1970.

————. "The Manhood of Jesus in the New Testament." In *Christ, Faith and History: Cambridge Studies in Christology*, edited by W. Sykes and J. P. Clayton, pp. 95-110. Cambridge: Cambridge University Press, 1972.

Nellas, Panayiotis. *Deification in Christ: Orthodox Perspectives on the Nature of the Human Person*. Translated by Norman Russell. Crestwood, N.Y.: St. Vladimir's Seminary Press, 1997.

Oakes, Peter. *Philippians: From People to Letter*. SNTSMS 110. Cambridge: Cambridge University Press, 2001.

Payton, James R., Jr. *Light from the Christian East: An Introduction to the Orthodox Tradition*. Downers Grove: InterVarsity, 2007.

Placher, William C. *Narratives of a Vulnerable God: Christ, Theology, and Scripture*. Louisville: Westminster John Knox, 1994.

Porter, Stanley, ed. *The Messiah in the Old and New Testaments*. Grand Rapids: Eerdmans, 2007.

————, ed. *Paul and His Theology*. Pauline Studies, vol. 3. Leiden/Boston: Brill, 2006.

Powell, Samuel M., and Michael E. Lodahl, ed. *Embodied Holiness: Toward a Corporate Theology of Spiritual Growth*. Downers Grove: InterVarsity, 1999.

Powers, Daniel G. *Salvation through Participation: An Examination of the Notion of the Believers' Corporate Unity with Christ in Early Christian Soteriology*. Contributions to Biblical Exegesis and Theology. Leuven: Peeters, 2001.

Reumann, John. "Justification and Justice in the New Testament." *HBT* 21 (1999): 26-45.

Roetzel, Calvin. *Paul: The Man and the Myth*. Minneapolis: Fortress, 1999.

Rusch, William G. "How the Eastern Fathers Understood What the Western Church

Meant by Justification." In *Justification by Faith: Lutherans and Catholics in Dialogue VII*, edited by H. George Anderson, T. Austin Murphy, and Joseph A. Burgess, pp. 131-42. Minneapolis: Augsburg, 1985.

Sanders, E. P. *Paul and Palestinian Judaism: A Comparison of Patterns of Religion.* Philadelphia: Fortress, 1977.

Savage, Timothy B. *Power through Weakness: Paul's Understanding of the Christian Ministry in 2 Corinthians.* SNTSMS 86. Cambridge: Cambridge University Press, 1996.

Schauf, Scott. "Galatians 2.20 in Context." *NTS* 52 (2006): 86-101.

Schönherr, Hartmut. "Concepts of Salvation in Christianity." *Africa Theological Journal* 12 (1983): 159-65.

Schreiner, Thomas R. *Romans.* Grand Rapids: Baker, 1998.

Segal, Alan. *Paul the Convert: The Apostolate and Apostasy of Saul the Pharisee.* New Haven: Yale University Press, 1990.

Seifrid, Mark A. "Paul's Use of Righteousness Language against Its Hellenistic Background." In *Justification and Variegated Nomism*, vol. 2: *The Paradoxes of Paul*, edited by Donald Carson, Peter T. O'Brien, and Mark A. Seifrid, pp. 39-74. Grand Rapids: Baker, 2004.

———. "Unrighteous by Faith: Apostolic Proclamation in Romans 1:18–3:20." In *Justification and Variegated Nomism*, vol. 2: *The Paradoxes of Paul*, edited by Donald Carson, Peter T. O'Brien, and Mark A. Seifrid, pp. 105-45. Grand Rapids: Baker, 2004.

Silva, Moisés. *Philippians.* 2d ed. BECNT. Grand Rapids: Baker, 2005.

Stanton, Graham N., and Guy G. Stroumsa, eds. *Tolerance and Intolerance in Early Judaism and Christianity.* Cambridge: Cambridge University Press, 1998.

Stubbs, David L. "The Shape of Soteriology and the *Pistis Christou* [Faith of Christ] Debate." *SJT* 61 (2008): 137-57.

Stuhlmacher, Peter. *Revisiting Paul's Doctrine of Justification.* Downers Grove: InterVarsity, 2001.

Stumme, Wayne C., ed. *The Gospel of Justification in Christ: Where Does the Church Stand Today?* Grand Rapids: Eerdmans, 2006.

Swartley, Willard M. *Covenant of Peace: The Missing Peace in New Testament Theology and Ethics.* Grand Rapids: Eerdmans, 2006.

———, ed. *The Love of Enemy and Nonretaliation in the New Testament.* Louisville: Westminster/John Knox, 1992.

———, ed. *Violence Renounced: René Girard, Biblical Studies, and Peacemaking.* Telford, Pa.: Pandora, 2000.

Sykes, S. W., and J. P. Clayton, eds. *Christ, Faith and History: Cambridge Studies in Christology.* Cambridge: Cambridge University Press, 1972.

Talbert, Charles H. *Romans.* Smith & Helwys Bible Commentary. Macon, Ga.: Smith & Helwys, 2002.

Tamez, Elsa. "Justification as Good News for Women: A Re-reading of Romans 1–8." Translated by Sheila E. McGinn. In *Celebrating Romans: Template for Pauline Theology; Essays in Honor of Robert Jewett*, edited by Sheila E. McGinn, pp. 177-89. Grand Rapids: Eerdmans, 2004.

Tannehill, Robert C. *Dying and Rising with Christ: A Study in Pauline Theology.* Berlin: Alfred Töpelmann, 1966.

———. "Participation in Christ: A Central Theme in Pauline Soteriology." In *The Shape of the Gospel: New Testament Essays*, pp. 223-37. Eugene: Cascade, 2007.

———. *The Shape of the Gospel: New Testament Essays.* Eugene: Cascade, 2007.

Taylor, Justin. "Why Did Paul Persecute the Church?" In *Tolerance and Intolerance in Early Judaism and Christianity*, edited by Graham N. Stanton and Guy G. Stroumsa, pp. 99-120. Cambridge: Cambridge University Press, 1998.

Thompson, James W. *Pastoral Ministry according to Paul: A Biblical Vision.* Grand Rapids: Baker Academic, 2006.

Thurston, Bonnie B., and Judith M. Ryan, *Philippians and Philemon.* Sacra Pagina. Collegeville: Liturgical, 2003.

Vallès, Jaume Botey, *El Dios de Bush* [*Bush's God*]. Cuadernos Cristianisme i Justícia 126. Barcelona: Centre d'Estudia Cristianisme i Justícia, 2004.

Vincent, M. R. *A Critical and Exegetical Commentary on the Epistles to the Philippians and Philemon.* ICC. New York: C. Scribner's Sons, 1897.

Vishnevskaya, Elena. "Divinization as Perichoretic Embrace in Maximus the Confessor." In *Partakers of the Divine Nature: The History and Development of Deification in the Christian Traditions*, edited by Michael J. Christensen and Jeffery A. Wittung, pp. 132-45. Grand Rapids: Baker Academic, 2007.

Volf, Miroslav. *Exclusion and Embrace: A Theological Exploration of Identity, Otherness, and Reconciliation.* Nashville: Abingdon, 1996.

———. "The Social Meaning of Reconciliation." *Int* 54 (2002): 158-72.

Watson, Francis. *Paul and the Hermeneutics of Faith.* London/New York: Clark, 2004.

———. *Paul, Judaism, and the Gentiles: Beyond the New Perspective.* Rev. ed. Grand Rapids: Eerdmans, 2007.

———. "The Triune Divine Identity: Reflection on Pauline God Language, in Disagreement with J. D. G. Dunn." *JSNT* 80 (2000): 99-124.

Webster, John. *Holiness.* Grand Rapids: Eerdmans, 2003.

Weima, Jeffrey A. D " 'How You Must Walk to Please God': Holiness and Discipleship in 1 Thessalonians." In *Patterns of Discipleship in the New Testament*, edited by Richard N. Longenecker, pp. 98-119. Grand Rapids: Eerdmans, 1996.

Willmer, Haddon. " 'Vertical' and 'Horizontal' in Paul's Theology of Reconciliation in the Letter to the Romans." *Transformation* 24 (2007): 151-60.

Witherington, Ben, III. *Friendship and Finances in Philippi: The Letter of Paul to the Philippians.* Valley Forge: Trinity, 1994.

Wright, N. T. *The Climax of the Covenant.* Minneapolis: Fortress, 1993.

————. *Justification in Pauline Perspective*. Downers Grove: InterVarsity, 2009.

————. "New Perspectives on Paul." In *Justification in Perspective: Historical Developments and Contemporary Challenges*, edited by Bruce L. McCormack, pp. 243-64. Grand Rapids: Baker Academic, 2006.

————. "On Becoming the Righteousness of God: 2 Corinthians 5:21." In *Pauline Theology*, vol. II: *1 & 2 Corinthians*, edited by David M. Hay, pp. 200-208. Minneapolis: Augsburg/Fortress, 1992.

————. *Paul: In Fresh Perspective*. Edinburgh: Clark; Minneapolis: Fortress, 2005.

————. "Paul's Gospel and Caesar's Empire." In *Paul and Politics: Ekklesia, Israel, Imperium, Interpretation: Essays in Honor of Krister Stendahl*, edited by Richard A. Horsley, pp. 160-83. Harrisburg: Trinity, 2000.

————. *The Resurrection of the Son of God*. Christian Origins and the Question of God, vol. 3. Minneapolis: Fortress, 2003.

————. *What Saint Paul Really Said: Was Paul of Tarsus the Real Founder of Christianity?* Grand Rapids: Eerdmans, 1997.

Yinger, Kent L. *Paul, Judaism, and Judgment according to Deeds*. SNTSMS 105. Cambridge: Cambridge University Press, 1999.

Yoder, John Howard. *He Came Preaching Peace*. Eugene: Wipf and Stock, 1998.

————. *The Politics of Jesus: Behold the Man! Our Victorious Lamb*. 2d ed. Grand Rapids: Eerdmans, 1994 (orig. 1972).

Zerbe, Gordon. *Non-Retaliation in Early Jewish and New Testament Texts: Ethical Themes in Social Contexts*, JSPSS 13. Sheffield.: JSOT Press, 1993.

————. "Paul's Ethic of Nonretaliation and Peace." In *The Love of Enemy and Nonretaliation in the New Testament*, edited by Willard M. Swartley, pp. 177-222. Louisville: Westminster/John Knox, 1992.

Ziesler, John. *Pauline Christianity*. The Oxford Bible Series, rev. ed. New York/Oxford: Oxford University Press, 1990.